CONTENTS

INTRODUCTION	4
Chapter One: The Silent Monsters	8
Chapter Two: The Monsters Of The 1930's	28
Chapter Three: The Monsters Of The 1940's	84
Chapter Four: The Monsters Of The 1950's	130
FILMOGRAPHY	156
FILM INDEX	160

INTRODUCTION

Imagi-Movie Marathon

By Frustrated J Ackerman

WHY FRUSTRATED? *Because, gentle reader, I'm having to reconstruct 2 days lost work. I love this weird processor but in the pre-computer days when I used an electronic typewriter at least I had hard copy I couldn't lose. In some inexplicable fashion, a couple thousand words I had composed, decomposed, and I spent several fruitless hours trying to find the Lost Ackermanuscript. On the way to my 50th birthday a quarter of a century ago I had a stack of heart attacks, laid at the door of too many deadlines and too much frustration. Here I am at 76, leaving town in 24 hours and having to get this to the publisher before I leave. As Shockspeare would have said: "Yoicks!"*

Where is an eidetic memory when I need it? I'll never be able to write this introduction a second time the way it was the first. For one thing, there's going to be a paucity of dates. I like to give as much information as possible about a film and that includes the time of its release but aside from indelible dates in my memory like those of ONE GLORIOUS DAY (the first fantastic film I ever saw, 1922 at the age 5-1/2) and milestone imagi-movies like THE PHANTOM OF THE OPERA, METROPOLIS, THE LOST WORLD, HIGH TREASON, FRANKENSTEIN, DRACULA, KING KONG et al, I haven't the time to check out when EEGAH, THE KILLER SHREWS, TEENAGE MONSTER, ROBOT MONSTER, THE MONSTER FROM THE OCEAN FLOOR, etc., were first spawned, together with any of their significant players. Sorry about that but what can I do?

Enough prologue and on with the show!

DR. JEKYLL AND MR. HYDE was one of the earliest horror stories tackled for the shiver screen. It was already being filmed as early as 1908 and it is a virtually forgotten fact that Carl Laemmle Sr. was responsible for a 2-reel silent version in 1913. Matinee idol John Barrymore ("The Great Profile") starred in the most famous silent version in the 1920's and of course Fredric March will be forever remembered for the award-winning Rouben Mamoulian version of the early 1930's. On the subject of March, I'll record that he followed his dual role with the role of Prince Sirki, Death incarnate, in DEATH TAKES A HOLIDAY.

When I was growing up my parents and grandparents would occasionally refer to a film that piqued my curiosity, one with a somnambulist (what was that?) and strange distorted surrealistic architecture. Something with a name like "The Carbonate of Dr. Cola-Gory." Readers more knowledgable than I may be familiar with the correct name. It starred Conrad Veidt, who would later in his career appear in THE HANDS OF ORLAC (one of the most disappointing fantasy films I ever saw; dull dull dull; in the same dustbin, alas, with ATLANTIDE - even if it did have the False Maria, Brigitte Helm herself, in the simultaneously filmed English, French and German versions. Early in the 1930's Conrad Veidt and Peter Lorre would play parts in Curt Siodmak's F.P. I DOESN'T ANSWER, done in English, German and French). Late in the 1920's he would star in his masterpiece (with PHANTOM'S Mary Philbin) as Gwynplaine, the man with the mutilated mouth (a permanent smile carved on it as a child by Gypsies), THE MAN WHO LAUGHS.

The first filmization of Mary Shelley's immortal monster, FRANKENSTEIN, was the Edison version of 1910, scarcely scary today, mainly of historical interest. I believe it first surfaced some years ago in France; I saw a print one evening in London in the home of master animator Ray Harryhausen. Before that one Alois Detlaf showed me his private print in my own home, the first time I an a number of local fans had ever seen it. I've been told by my friend who gave the owner a ride to his hotel that the owner of the print rode with a pistol on top of the film can, so zealously did he guard it!

LIFE WITHOUT SOUL was the second filming of the Frankenstein Legend, 1915, and (I'm just fortunate enough to remember these dates off hand) the fine Italian hand of an Italian producer was seen in 1920 in THE MONSTER OF FRANKENSTEIN. Frank-ly, that's the one title that makes sense to me. I never could understand why the original novel was called *Frankenstein*. Today, after 175 years, the title immediately conjures up a vision of the Monster, but in 1818? It was just a name. The creator might just as well have been Henry SMYTHE or Victor BORGE or....ACKERMAN! ("There are some things Man was meant to leave alone.") 1931, of course, was the real birth of FRANKENSTEIN.

monster (grunts and groans, in that case), Dracula, and even the voice of THE INVISIBLE MAN, although it is difficult to imagine anyone better in the part than Claude Rains, he of the superbly gravelly voice. However, Chaney as KING KONG? "Don't step on it, it may be Lon Chaney!"--- guess at 60 feet tall he would have been a little too big to step on.

Have I spoken of Paul Wegener, the Lon Chaney of Germany, yet? No, I don't think so. Let me scroll back through what I have written so far. I think I'm about at the midway point of where I was before, before I lost everything I'd written. Hefty Paul Wegener with his imposing Slavic features was the definitive Golem, playing the role of the Man of Clay, the Man of Slay, three times, two roles surviving, one (THE GOLEM AND THE DANCER) lost. Wegener also made an indelible impression on me in THE STRANGE CASE OF CAPTAIN RAMPER. Why is it I'm the only American I've ever met who ever saw it? Isn't there anyone my age (76) who saw it when they were 11 years old and is still an imagi-movie fan? I don't know if there is still a print of it in Germany, its country of origin, but it has never surfaced in America. An interesting story of an Arctic explorer who becomes lost and in order to survive reverts to beastlike existence. His brain goes dormant and by the time he is discovered and rescued he has become so animal-like that he is regarded as sort of a Missing Link and, brought back to civilization, is exhibited in a cage in a circus. A scientist reawakens his brain but it only causes him to sicken at the state of civilization (and this was 60 years ago, folks!) and he returns to the Arctic. (Surprised some enterprising filmmaker didn't have him meet up with Frankenstein's monster there). A forgotten fact: RAMPER included in the cast the appearance of Max Schreck of NOSFERATU fame. In America in the mid 1920's Wegener portrayed the alchemical seeker of the secret of life in the filmization of W. Somerset Maugham's novel inspired by the career of "The Great Beast," Aleister Crowley, THE MAGICIAN.

Hollywood seems to have a penchant for making a monkey of itself so while I'm at it I might as well mention THE WIZARD with Gustav von Seyffertitz, THE APE with Boris Karloff, THE APE MAN with Bela Lugosi, THE APE WOMAN (Italian), WHITE PONGO, NABONGA, MURDERS IN THE RUE MORGUE (Lugosi), CAPTIVE WILD WOMAN (introducing Acquanetta) and its sequel JUNGLE CAPTIVE (this time with Viki Lane as the ape-woman), JUNGLE MYSTERY (serial) and of course the inevitable RETURN OF THE APE MAN. There could easily be a whole genre of "Return Of--" films.

I'm going to have to speed this up - I'm running out of time.

The felictious teaming of Karloff and Lugosi resulted in some memorable imagi-movies, including THE INVISIBLE RAY, BLACK FRIDAY, THE BLACK CAT, THE RAVEN, and SON OF FRANKENSTEIN.

<u>Karloff</u> on his own delighted us as THE WALKING DEAD, THE MAN WHO LIVED AGAIN, THE MAN THEY COULD NOT HANG, THE MAN WITH NINE LIVES, THE MUMMY, THE GHOUL, (THE MASK OF) FU MANCHU - 159 films in all till Prince Sirki rang down the curtain on his career on 2 February 1969, the Sunday that will live in sorrow.

<u>Bela Lugosi</u> did not fare as well as Boris but we remember him well for his bravura performance as Ygor in SON OF FRANKENSTEIN, his vampiric impersonation in MARK OF THE VAMPIRE, his famous "hypnotized scene" in BLACK FRIDAY, his commanding WHITE ZOMBIE, his welcome RETURN OF THE VAMPIRE, the leader of the Manimals in Charles Laughton's ISLAND OF LOST SOULS, his "last hurrah" as Dracula in ABBOTT AND COSTELLO MEET FRANKENSTEIN.

<u>Lon Chaney, Jr.</u> He really didn't want to capitalize on his father's reputation, [referring to be known as Creighton Chaney, but the fates would have it otherwise and we remember him as the doomed Larry Talbot, lycanthrope - the way he walked was "t"orny," said Gypsy Maria Ouspenskaya, for even a man who was pure in heart and said his prayers at night could become a wolf when the wolfbane bloomed and the moon was full and bright (unquote scriptor Curt Siodmak). He was Count Alucard and the Mummy and the Frankenstein monster, inheriting the mantles of Karloff and Lugosi, but never quite as successfully. Nevertheless, he left quite a body of films which his fans remember warmly - and outside our genre he proved his acting ability with his Academy Award for the portrayal of the dim-witted Lenny in OF MICE AND MEN.

"Thanks for the bullet - it was the only way." Do you remember those dying words of <u>Henry Hull</u> in THE WEREWOLF OF LONDON?

"The Lord High Minister of All That is Sinister" was the way Hollywood heralded the arrival of <u>Peter Lorre</u> as he was cast in MAD LOVE, a remake of "The Hands Of Orlac," with Karl (THE MUMMY) Freund directing and Colin (FRANKENSTEIN) Clive costarring. Lorre was a welcomed addition to the hall of horror stars, giving us THE FACE BEHIND THE MASK, THE STRANGER ON THE THIRD FLOOR and THE BEAST WITH FIVE FINGERS, among other memorable performances.

I was at the Christmas day opening. William Castle ("Mr. Gimmick") would have been proud of the picture's publicists. An ambulance stood in front of the theater. Posters - now $80,000 collectors' items - and colorful sets of lobbycards lured the curious into the lobby, where white-starched nurses stood in attendance! As I recall, the day scenes in the film were in a sunlit amber, the night scenes were in blue, the eerie scenes in green and the climaxing fire sequence in red (And as I remember THE LOST WORLD from the time I was 8, it too had similar monochromatic coloring of day and night sequences and went red when the volcano erupted and the forest was on fire and Marcel Delgado's 49 dinosaurs were animatedly fleeing from the flames all over the screen via the stop-motion magic of Willis O'Brien). At one point in the picture a woman patron sitting on an aisle screamed, jumped up from her seat and ran up the aisle. I stayed to see the film a second time and so, apparently, did she, as she shrieked at the same moment in the movie and ran out of the auditorium. You don't think, do you? Is it possible? Hmm....

I believe in a recent poll of experts THE BRIDE OF FRANKENSTEIN has been acclaimed as more popular than the original. I had the privilege, one summer afternoon in 1935, of seeing the preview at the studio - including scenes snipped from the print when later released, losing, as I recall, some of the histrionics of Dwight Frye. Years later when Elsa Lanchester was a guest of honor at the Count Dracula Society, in lieu of a speech ("I really don't know what I can say to you") she gave us a shriek heard 'round the world.' It proved so popular that she gave the assemblage an encore.

Only once before Ray Bradbury's FAHRENHEIT 451 was there a film totally devoid of wordage: THE TERROR, 1928, where Conrad Nagel spoke the name of the producer, director, stars, et al. THE TERROR was one of the many popular Old Dark House mysterioso movies of the 1920's, including THE CAT AND THE CANARY, STARK MAD, THE LAST WARNING (famed director Paul Leni), THE FINAL PERFORMANCE (Conrad Veidt and Mary Philbin), THE BAT and its sound remake THE BAT WHISPERS, etc. Just while the thought surfaces I'll skip ahead to 1933 and record that we can all quit searching for any info on THE HORROR because a reliable authority told me recently (I'd give him credit if I could remember who) that nothing exists but the lobbycards and onesheet, which were created in an attempt to get a backer to sponsor the movie.

One Saturday in 1927 after I finished my music lesson (piano), I dashed downtown on the streetcar to see.....LONDON AFTER MIDNIGHT! The legendary longlost Lon Chaney horror film known in England as THE HYPNOTIST and remade by the same director, Tod Browning, in 1935 with Bela Lugosi as Count Mora, his personal protegee Carroll Borland as luna, and the make-up being the first job of award-winning William Tuttle. Chaney essayed the dual role of the detective and the ghoulish vampire. I have the Beaver that he wore in the film and his jagged porcelain teeth. Not a year passes but what there is some rumor of its discovery. Several years ago a fan in Australia was said to have recognized a clip from it in a TV commercial, rushed around to the studio and they said, Why yes, they had the whole film. At that point I was assured I would have a videocassette of it within three weeks. Three years or more have passed and I am still waiting. Then someone back east told me on the telephone that a friend of his had seen it on late night TV and had made a copy. "Now don't be too excited," he said, "it's very grainy and murky, about fifth generation..." Listen, who wouldn't settle for a 25th generation with scratches and sprocket hole jumps? But all that call generated was one more false hope. There's one thing, though, that worries me about LONDON AFTER MIDNIGHT being found and viewed at long last by thousands of aficionados acquainted with its rreputation I'm convinced that Groucho Marx saw it and patterned his croucho walk after it, so it might look like Chaney was copying him and being funny! I hope not; but the danger exists.

On the subject of the Man of a Thousand Faces, only the titles THE HUNCHBACK OF NOTRE DAME and PHANTOM OF THE OPERA need to be mentioned, for surely any reader of this book is sufficiently familiar with them. A BLIND BARGAIN for some reason has plenty of stills and a poster available but is another of the muchly-to-be-desired lost Chaney films, especially as once again he plays a dual role, eccentric scientist and ape-man. (In MR. WU, not strictly one of our genre films, he plays a triple role as three generations of Chinese son, father and grandfather). In THE MONSTER he's nutso Dr. Ziska who believes he can bring life back to the dead, this pic played for farce. Speaking of farce, the non-Lon film SEVEN FOOTPRINTS TO SATAN went beyond farce into ludicrous and, legend has it, caused its author (A. Merritt, "The Lord of Fantasy") to weep when he saw it. Not knowing any better, not having read the book when I saw the picture in 1927, and being 10 years old, I expect I found it pretty funny. Perhaps 50 years later I caught up with it in the Cinematheque in Belgium and found it pretty hilarious if you forgot all about the book, which I had read in the meantime. Fortunately Chaney lived to let us hear his voice in the remake of THE UNHOLY THREE and I suspect, had he lived, there never would have been a Boris Karloff or Bela Lugosi as we know them, as Chaney would have become the "Man of a Thousand Voices," portraying the Frankenstein

"POWER! Power to send multitudes screaming in terror at the touch of my little invisible finger!" Ah, the grandiloquent gravel-throated voice of Claude Rains, THE MAN WHO RECLAIMED HIS HEAD, the father of the Wolfman, the ultra-cunning conniver of CRIME WITHOUT PASSION.

GEORGE ZUCCO, LIONEL ATWILL, DWIGHT FRYE, GALE SONDERGAARD, PETER CUSHING, CHRISTOPHER LEE, OLIVER REED, JACK PIERCE, VINCENT PRICE and the ubiquitous "Manny Moore," each deserving of special treatment. But I, alas, am all but out of time. Next time don't ask an old man to do a young man's job - invite experts like Ron Borst o Scott MacQueen or even that teenager Robert Bloch (in an alternate universe he could have written "Psycho" and become famous), someone with a clock and twenty-five hours on it or a week with eight days.

Just time to acknowledge the existence of outstanding imagi-movies like DR. CYCLOPS, MIGHTY JOE YOUNG, the early works of RAY HARRYHAUSEN, THE MAZE, THE CLAIRVOYANT, THE INCREDIBLE SHRINKING MAN, Sabu's THIEF OF BAGDAD with the vizier Veidt crying "Wind! Wind!" , I ACCUSE! with the "Broken Faces" of World War One rising from the graves and marching on a horrified humanity, the legendary Val Lewton works with CAT PEOPLE leading al the rest, Fay Wray smashing Lionel Atwill's mask-face in MYSTERY OF THE WAX MUSEUM, the "synthetic flesh" of DR. X! *Let me interrupt long enough to tell you an amusing anecdote about the latter. I had dreamed for 32 years of seeing once again this early two-tone Technicolor scienti-film. A movie director friend, David Bradley, who discovered Charlton Heston in his late teens and cast him in PEER GYNT, told me he had a print he would be glad to project for me. I was set to see it when Bradley had to cancel. Another time I had to put it off for another day. Finally the day arrived when it seemed we were both in accord - when Ib Melchior called me out of the blue to ask if I'd care to play Technician #3, "getting things squared away," in THE TIME TRAVELERS. Reluctantly I gave up on the long-delayed viewing of DR. X. I sat down in the make-up chair next to the star of THE TIME TRAVELERS...Who was also the star of DR. X!* Now back to some other worthwhile imagi-movies of the pre-1953 sound era that I need to acknowledge: HOUSE OF WAX, THE MOST DANGEROUS GAME, shot at the same time as KING KONG and utilizing some of the same sets; one of the most remade and ripped-off plots, including A GAME OF DEATH, BLOODLUST, the little known BLACK FOREST, and the most recent version featuring Scream Queen Brinke Stevens and utilizing actual dialog from the original, SLAVE GIRLS FROM BEYOND SPACE(!); BEAUTY AND THE BEAST (Jean Marais), DELUGE, DEAD OF NIGHT, THE PHANTOM EMPIRE with Bela Lugosi, FREAKS THE CREATURE FROM THE BLACK LAGOON..... and whatever else of consequence (now there's a sneaky copout if I ever saw one!) that led up to the cutoff date of this book, 1959 and CURSE OF THE DEMON. You'll probably get a letter of criticism from the Castle of Frankenstein editor saying, "Nyah! Nyah! Ackerman is slipping!" Never mind that Calvin Beck is dead, you'll probably hear from him anyway.

I'm in too much of a rush to figure out a clever conclusion for this so I'll just fast finish up with a tried and true quotation, a favorite of one and all of us:

"Oh, no, 'twas Beauty killed the Beast."

May your sense of wonder survive and thrive, world without end!

Forrest J Ackerman

CHAPTER ONE
THE SILENT MONSTERS

Above: A scene from THE CABINET OF DR. CALIGARI (1919) in which Dr. Caligari (Werner Krauss) guards his henchman Cesare (Conrad Veidt).
Opposite Page: Charles Ogle as the screen's first Frankenstein monster in Thomas Edison's FRANKENSTEIN (1910).

THE SILENT FRANKENSTEIN

1910 was a very significant year for the genre of monster movies. This was the year in which the very first movie monster and monster movie was born. The film was Thomas A. Edison's FRANKENSTEIN (1910), and silent screen actor Charles Ogle portrayed the monstrous creation of Dr. Frankenstein (who was played by Augustus Phillips). The film, directed by J. Searle Dawley, was more of a melodramatic tale about the sins of Dr. Frankenstein rather than a film about a monster. The film was also a combination of the Dr. Jekyll theme created by author Robert Louis Stevenson and the famous Mary Shelley novel *Frankenstein*. The screenplay, also written by Dawley, does not follow the Shelley story faithfully as it deals primarily with Dr. Frankenstein's belief and attempt to create life without evil. With hopes of achieving his ultimate goal, the scientist is soon sickened by the sight of the disgusting, terribly evil monster he has created. During the final reels of the film, Frankenstein engages in a struggle with the monster. The scientist is overpowered, but as the creature prepares to leave the room, he gazes into a mirror and horrified by the sight of his reflection, he fades away to oblivion.

While FRANKENSTEIN deals with moral issues rather than horror, the most important aspect of the film is the birth of filmdom's first movie monster. The creature is brought to life by a series of chemical reactions contained in a cauldron (Hollywood had not yet attempted to explain the creation or existence of monsters by scientific means, therefore supernatural elements, witchcraft and unexplained sorcery was still effective). The film did bring to light two questions of scientific interest: Can "science" create life, and Should man have the right to tamper with the supernatural?

Charles Ogle's 1910 monster was a hideous, hunchbacked monstrosity with claw-like hands and wild shaggy hair. Only the physical appearance of Lon Chaney's memorable Quasimodo in THE HUNCHBACK OF NOTRE DAME (1923) could come close to Ogle's horrific monstrosity.

FRANKENSTEIN (1910) and Charles Ogle's characterization of the Frankenstein Monster is legendary, and a significant part of movie history. The film opened the doors for many

movie monsters to follow despite its supernatural premise. More important was its contribution the genre as being the very first

of many screen adaptations of the Mary Shelley novel.

LIFE WITHOUT SOUL (1915) and THE MONSTER OF FRANKENSTEIN (1920) were two silent but milder versions of the Mary Shelley novel.

LIFE WITHOUT SOUL was the second screen adaptation of Shelley's famous novel. In this film, the monster (played by Percy Darrell Standing) is really not a monster, but rather a Brute Man created by the devoted scientist (William A. Cohill). The brute man is far from grotesque with little or no make-up but in this film he manages to strangle more people than in the 1910 version. He is a creature without a soul and because of his extremely low intellect, he finds it very easy to kill. Frankenstein suffers great torment when his creation murders his sister, his best friend and finally, his own wife. The scientist, pleading to God for forgiveness, fires a shot that kills his horrid creation once and for all. But even after the monster's death, the scientist must live with the guilt of his blasphemy.

LIFE WITHOUT SOUL was directed by Joseph W. Smiley in a story-book fashion written by Jesse

Above: The Golem (Paul Wegener) accepts a gift from a child in DER GOLEM (1920).
Opposite Page: Soldiers are no match for the Golem in DER GOLEM.

J. Goldburg. Apparently producer George DeCarlton felt that they should lessen the impact on the audience by playing the film's horrific premise off as a fairy-tale.

THE MONSTER OF FRANKENSTEIN was an Italian-version of the Shelley novel that centered mostly around the confrontation between the creator and his horrid creation. Very little is known about this silent import. In any event, Edison's FRANKENSTEIN is far superior to both LIFE WITHOUT SOUL and THE MONSTER OF FRANKENSTEIN and Ogle's rendition of the infamous monster, although totally removed from the 1931 Boris Karloff characterization, is perhaps the most influential predecessor to the "Frankenstein film" sub-genre.

THE CLAY MONSTER

The Golem or clay monster of the silent screen was actually a take-off on the Frankenstein Monster, but ironically, it was the Golem of legend and literature that actually inspired Mary Shelley to write her famous novel *Frankenstein*. According to Yiddish Mythology, the Golem was a monster sculpted from a glob of lifeless clay and given artificial life by supernatural means. In retrospect, the Golem was actually the first monster of legend and the basis for the creation of the Universal Frankenstein films.

DER GOLEM (1914) was the first screen version about the legendary clay monster. The monster was created and portrayed on screen by famous German actor, director and producer Paul Wegener - the driving force behind many of the Golem films. The tale, written and directed by Henrik Galeen, is rather basic and traditional by today's standards. The monster is discovered in a cave and brought to life by way of supernatural means, only to be used for corrupt purposes and to be wrongly destroyed after falling in love with the film's beautiful heroine.

Other silent versions about the Golem Monster were made, including DER GOLEM (1916) and THE GOLEM AND THE DANCING GIRL (1917). But it was DER GOLEM (1920), written by Paul Wegener and Henrik Galeen and directed by Galeen, that was perhaps the single most important Golem film ever made. The film was the most authentic as far as the legend goes, and the plot was much more complex and intelligent, considering the subject matter. By 1920, Galeen and Wegener had improved the Golem to its furthest potential, and the result was a film that would become one of the silent era's most influential horror movies. DER GOLEM was also the single most influential silent film made in reference to the genesis of the later Universal Frankenstein films, beginning with FRANKENSTEIN (1931) and concluding with GHOST OF FRANKENSTEIN (1941). The film actually set the pattern for many other monster movies to come post 1920. Film historians have actually pointed out direct parallels in plot and similarities in circumstances between DER GOLEM and SON OF FRANKENSTEIN (1939) and GHOST OF FRANKENSTEIN (1941). For example, a certain character from the Golem film was a direct inspiration for the creation of Bela Lugosi's Ygor character in both of these Frankenstein films as well as influencing the horrid and

corrupt relationship between Ygor and the Frankenstein monster. Furthermore, it is a common and well publicized fact that director James Whale studied many of the Golem films, thus many of the key laboratory scenes in FRANKENSTEIN (1931) and THE BRIDE OF FRANKENSTEIN (1935) were ideas and occurrences already established in the Golem films of Galeen and Wegener. Finally, the Golem films are commonly known as the Jewish Frankenstein series. It is once again interesting and ironic to point out that the mythological legend of the Golem inspired Mary Shelley while writing her novel *Frankenstein*, which in turn inspired Edison to make the film FRANKENSTEIN (1910), which in turn inspired Galeen and Wegener to make DER GOLEM (1914-1920), which eventually trickled down and influenced filmmaker James Whale in the making of his monumental Frankenstein epics for Universal. It is very interesting to always look back into movie history to discover which films were the most influential in a certain genre. Each version of DER GOLEM were very influential in their own way.

MEET DR. JEKYLL! MEET MR. HYDE!

It has been said that Robert Louis Stevenson's novel *The Strange Case of Dr. Jekyll and Mr. Hyde* has been adapted to the screen more than any other literary work, including Bram Stoker's *Dracula*. In fact, Stevenson's novel was adapted to the screen as early as 1897 and is considered to be the very first fantasy film in movie history. Many obscure versions of the infamous tale were made prior to 1910, including the 1908 version from Polyscope entitled DR. JEKYLL AND MR. HYDE. However the first movie version of the novel that film historians have placed any importance onto is the Danish production of DEN SKAEBN SUANGRE OPFINDELSE (DR. JEKYLL AND MR. HYDE) of 1910. In this version, Danish actor Alwin Neuss portrayed both Dr. Jekyll and Mr. Hyde in an attempt to keep the character in accordance to the details of the novel. THE DUALITY OF MAN (1910) was yet another version of the Stevenson Tale; this one from Great Britain.

It was not until 1912 before the screen produced the first legitimate version of the Stevenson novel. This version, directed by Lucius Henderson, was also entitled DR. JEKYLL AND MR. HYDE. The silent film starred actor James Cruze as the well mannered, very restrained Dr. Jekyll and the fanged, crazy-eyed Mr. Hyde. Cruze's Jekyll was portrayed as a young and handsome physician who stumbles across a strange chemical mixture which can divide a person's evil side from their good side. He son becomes mortified by the evil creature he unleashes from within himself. The actor's Hyde characterization was a monster indeed, sadistic, crazed and purely

evil, but during the film's final reel, the monstrous Hyde manages to swallow a large dose of poison to free his good side from the dual evil side.

Henderson's DR. JEKYLL AND MR. HYDE offers some great dissolve scenes in which Jekyll transforms into Hyde and the story-line, co-scripted by Henderson, is a worthy adaptation of the original novel. The film is extremely well done and superior to the 1908 Polyscope version.

More significant was the German-made DER JANUSKOPF (JANUS-FACED) of 1920. The film was directed by F.W. Murnau (1888-1931), one of Germany's greatest silent filmmakers. Murnau's version of the Jekyll-Hyde tale was a bootlegged, unauthorized adaptation of the Stevenson novel. The story was still in copyright during the film's production and to avoid paying royalties, Murnau altered the plot situations of the novel and changed the names of the characters. As a result, Dr. Jekyll became Dr. Warren, while Mr. Hyde became Mr. O'Connor. In the dual role was Germany's greatest horror star, Conrad Veidt (1893-1943). Veidt, who had just been featured in the silent horror classic THE CABINET OF DR. CALIGARI (1919), was Germany's leading horror film star at the time and was the logical choice for the dual role. The German version, unlike the standard adaptations, centered around the supernatural rather than science. In the film, the catalyst for Dr. Warren to transform into the evil Mr. O'Connor is a bust of Janus, a Roman god with two faces, hence the dual identities. Possessed by the statute, Mr. O'Connor goes on a murdering spree. The film also co-starred up and coming horror film legend Bela Lugosi as Dr. Warren's Butler.

Finally, the epitome of all the silent adaptations of the Stevenson story was Paramount's DR. JEKYLL AND MR. HYDE (1920) from producer Adolph Zukor. The film, directed by John S. Robertson from a screenplay by Clara

Beranger, was the most legitimate screen adaptation to that point. More important was the landmark performance by distinguished Hollywood actor John Barrymore in the dual role. Barrymore was magnificent as both Dr. Jekyll and Mr. Hyde, and his Hyde is perhaps the most horrid and surreal interpretation in screen history. For Hyde, the actor took on the shape of an arachnid with long talon-like fingers as sharp as a razors's edge. Barrymore's Hyde is indeed a true movie monster and the film, next to the 1932 Academy-Award-winning version, is unquestionably the screen's most definitive Dr. Jekyll and Mr. Hyde movie and a classic reproduction of the Stevenson novel. Finally, Barrymore's performance was hailed as nothing less than excellent.

CALIGARI'S WALKING DEAD!

The sub-genre of walking dead movies did not really catch on until the 1930's and 1940's. However, one silent film in particular remains responsible for launching a genre that just did not exist. The film is THE CABINET OF DR. CALIGARI (1919), directed by legendary filmmaker Robert Wiene (1881-1938). The film is considered by many film historians to be the first true masterpiece of the horror film because of its strong expressionistic cinematography and trance-like aura. The visuals are distorted to suggest the vision from a madman's point-of-view, and shadows are actually painted on the ground to create a dream-like illusion.

Wiene was the master of the expressionist-style in German cinema and THE CABINET OF DR. CALIGARI was a prime example of his controversial style. In fact, when the film was originally released, it was considered quite scandalous. Wiene also directed the silent horror film classic THE HANDS OF ORLAC (1924).

THE CABINET OF DR. CALIGARI is considered Germany's crowning cinematic achievement from the silent era. The film's focal character or monster was Cesare (played melodramatically and with great style by Conrad Veidt), a somnambulist who has the ability to predict the future. In the film, Cesare is hypnotized by the evil Dr. Caligari (played by Werner Krauss) and turned into a monstrous, murdering henchman. When not in use, Cesare slumbers within a coffin and awaits his next murderous mission. Both the monster and his master's downfall arrives during the climax when Cesare, who becomes smitten by the heroine's beauty, finds that he cannot

Opposite Page: Mr Hyde (John Barrymore) strangles one of his many enemies in the silent masterpiece DR. JEKYLL AND MR. HYDE (1920).
Above: Cesare (Conrad Veidt) is pursued by the villagers as he abducts the film's heroine in Robert Wiene's infamous horror film THE CABINET OF DR. CALIGARI (1919).

destroy her as ordered by Dr. Caligari. Instead, Cesare kidnaps the heroine and carries her throughout the village with the townspeople in hot pursuit. Cesare eventually dies of overexhaustion.

Today THE CABINET OF DR. CALIGARI is studied by young and inspiring future filmmakers because of its strong expressionistic style and its ongoing influence on the genre of horror film. It is also common knowledge that filmmaker James Whale was strongly influenced by Veidt's characterization of Cesare when he and Boris Karloff began creating the mannerisms of the monster in FRANKENSTEIN (1931).

MAD SCIENTISTS, MAGICIANS & WIZARDS!

The sub-genre of mad scientists and their

morbid creations is as old as the beginning of film history. The most notorious of the lot are the films about Dr. Jekyll and Dr. Frankenstein. But Jekyll and Frankenstein were not the monsters of their films. Rather, they were merely the victims of their own monstrous creations. In the case of Dr. Jekyll, Hyde was the monster, while with Dr. Frankenstein, his creation was the monster.

THE MAGICIAN (1926), directed by Rex Ingram, was one of the first films to feature the familiar mad scientist that we have come to know. Like the story of Frankenstein, the plot of THE MAGICIAN, which is based on the 1908 story by Somerset Maugham, deals with the creation of artificial life. In the film, a mad doctor (played by Paul Wegener) discovers that he can create life, but to do so, he must have a steady supply of fresh blood from a maiden's heart. Although the basis for the mad doctor's experiment is a bit far-fetched and totally unbelievable by today's standards, one cannot help admire the director's style in creating a mood of horror. Ingram's slow moving direction concentrates heavily on composition, mood and lighting, and never gives in to suspense or action until the film's dramatic climax staged within the lavish laboratory. It is at that moment of height that the mad scientist is revealed as the film's true monster because of his morbid experiments.

THE MISSING LINK (1926), directed by Charles F. Reisner from a screenplay by Darryl F. Zanuck, yes, D. Zanuck himself, was another of countless science fiction - horror films that tackled Darwin's theory of evolution. In the film, a young struggling poet jumps on an ocean liner to escape his creditors. Little does he know that the vessel is headed for Africa. The young man makes friends with a famous game hunter who is traveling to Africa to search for Darwin's missing link. After a series of misadventures with wild animals and a romance with a colonel's daughter, the young man confronts the ape creature (played by Sam Baker), but because of certain circumstances, the evidence that they hoped would link the evolutionary bridge between primates and man, is destroyed by gunfire.

THE MISSING LINK is an inferior piece of fantasy that consists mainly of uninteresting thrills and chases. Even the ape-creature does not live-up to its fearsome description. It is believed that had the film dealt with the discovery of the unknown and had the film not been such a farce, THE MISSING LINK could have been an interesting vintage monster movie, much like THE WIZARD (1927) and

Chaney's PHANTOM OF THE OPERA (1925).

Like THE MAGICIAN, THE WIZARD (1927), beautifully directed by Richard Rosson, was another film that centered around the excursions of yet another mad scientist. The film, based on the Gaston Leroux novel *Balaoo*, told the story of a very mad Dr. Coriolos (played by Gustav Von Seyffertitz). In the film, Coriolos uses an ape-like monster (played by George Kotsonaros) to murder those responsible for his son's death.

Kotsonaros's performance as the ape monster was quite convincing for that period in time; a performance that even Lon Chaney, Sr. would have relished. Kotsonaros' ape-monster is extremely gruesome. During the film's climax, the ape-monster turns on its master after one-to-many horrible beatings and crushes him to death. The ape-monster is then shot with a rifle and released from its misery.

THE WIZARD is a well-made classic science fiction - horror film that occasionally offers unintentional humor. The film was remade in 1942 as DR. RENAULT'S SECRET.

Finally, one must not overlook Rudolph Klein-Rogge's magnificent performance as the silent screen's maddest scientist, Rotwang in Fritz Lang's German masterpiece METROPOLIS (1927).

METROPOLIS is first a science fiction film and second a horror film. This point is very clear, however, let us explore the fact that the scientist Rotwang could very well have been intended to be the film's identifiable monster. It is very clear throughout the film that Rotwang is purely evil and corrupt. The scientist is also a bit on the sadistic, sexually depraved side as well, and for these reasons, he can be considered mad enough to be the film's monster. But it is the scientist's actions that speak clearly. In the film, Rotwang creates a beautiful robot named Ultima (played by silent star Brigitte Helm) to lure laborers to their own destruction. It is all part of a retched scheme concocted by the industrial leaders of the futuristic city to gain control. But their evil bidding is gleefully carried out by the horrid Rotwang. If you were to take away the futuristic setting, what would remain would be a beautifully mounted silent horror film. Is FRANKENSTEIN (1931) not a horror film that deals with the creation of life? METROPOLIS is also such a film, and in both films, both scientists use scientific means and electrical apparatus to create life. The only difference is that one creation is presented in the form of a monster, while the other (Ultima) is beautiful

Opposite Page: Rudolph Klein-Rogge as Rotwang, the silent screen's maddest scientist in Fritz Lang's METROPOLIS (1927).
Above: Count Orlock (Max Schreck) prowls for victims onboard a ship in NOSFERATU (1922).

THE LOST WORLD (1925) is considered by film historians to be a revolutionary film. It was the first major film to feature the special effects technique known as stop-motion photography, developed by Willis O'Brien, who would later proceed to work on KING KONG (1933).

All photos from THE LOST WORLD.

Above: An impressive lobby card for the film.
Left: A giant Tyranosaurous takes a bite out of a fellow dinosaur.
Opposite Page: The destruction of London by a Brontosarous.

and seductive, but unquestionably destructive. But the real monster in METROPOLIS is not the creation, but rather Rotwang as a result of his madness. For this reason, the film should at least be given some kind of mention in this chapter for being the vintage horror film of sorts that it has become to be known and for featuring Rotwang - perhaps the silent screen's greatest mad scientist! In addition to all of this, METROPOLIS is perhaps the single most influential film that inspired filmmaker James Whale during the production of both FRANKENSTEIN (1931) and THE BRIDE OF FRANKENSTEIN (1935). Make no mistake, METROPOLIS is perhaps the greatest and most influential genre film from the silent era.

A VAMPIRE NAMED ORLAC!

There have been literally countless screen adaptations of Bram Stoker's infamous novel *Dracula*. The first screen version of the novel was F.W. Murnau's NOSFERATU - A SYMPHONY OF TERROR (1922). As mentioned earlier in this chapter, Murnau had no regard for copyright laws when he made DER JANUSKOPF (1920), and in two years following the release of that film, little had changed by way of the filmmaker's regards for copyright laws and ownership rights. The filmmaker proceeded to film the unauthorized version of Stoker's *Dracula*, changing the names of the characters and switching the location of the story to avoid legal complications. With plagiarism laws not as strict and readily enforced during the 1920's, Murnau was able to get away with making DER JANUSKOPF and NOSFERATU without having to pay royalties to the copyright owners of the literary work from which his films were borrowed from, or better yet, based on.

For his version and to avoid any legal problems, Murnau changed the name of Count Dracula to Count Orlock. Count Orlock was truly one of the silent era's most gruesome monsters and perhaps the most hideous vampire ever to prowl the screen. The vampiric Orlock was played very effectively by Max Schreck, a German actor whose own name Schreck, when translated, meant evil. Count Orlock was a pale-faced, repugnant-smelling, rodent-like creature of the night with elongated fangs, rat-like ears and razor sharp finger nails. The vampire resembled some hellish demon rather than some being that was once a living man. It was believed that Orlock's grotesque physiognomy was actually a ploy to throw off the copyright owners, since, in the Stoker book, Dracula was portrayed as being a handsome, polished gentleman. Unlike the Dracula's of later films, Orlock was a stiff, slow-moving vampire who would lurk in the shadows and then stalk his unsuspecting victims. Orlock was a true monster that rose from the pits of Hell, only contemplating his next attack and his next drink of blood. The monster never took time out to seduce the young maidens.

The story-line of NOSFERATU is still very effective today and some of the film's scenes have never been equalled in effectiveness. The film begins with Jonathan Harker's (name changed to Waldemar Hutter) timeless voyage to Transylvania where he encounters the vampire, but most impressive are the terrifying scenes aboard the ship. One by one, Orlock, accompanied by hordes of rats, kills off the members of the crew. Brilliant even today was the vampire's destruction by sunlight, which would become a trademark in many of the later vampire films to come. Hutter's wife Ellen sacrifices her own life to save the thousands of others who have fallen ill from the demon's plague. She allows the monster to drink her blood, keeping him occupied until sunrise. Orlock perishes before the lethal rays of the sun, and the plague is lifted from Bremen (the films setting was altered from London to Bremen to coincide with the great plague of Bremen).

NOSFERATU is indeed a true classic horror film and Orlock is unquestionably that period's most memorable movie monster. The film is a perfect example of the silent German horror film that used its expressionistic style to create terror. One must truly admire the atmospheric camera of Fritz Arno Wagner, who photographed shadows of Orlock and used them incredibly effectively during the darkest moments of the film. A true masterpiece of horror.

GIANT MONSTERS!

One of the silent screen's greatest monsters were not even human. Instead, they were dinosaurs from the adventure thriller THE LOST WORLD (1925), based on Arthur Conan Doyle's original novel. The film featured giant prehistoric beasts engaged in fierce battles with each other to the death in a strange mysterious world completely lost to civilization. Moviegoers had never witnessed anything like this before, and for them, THE LOST WORLD provided a thrill of a lifetime. The dinosaurs of THE LOST WORLD were effectively

Lon Chaney, Sr. was considered the grandfather of the American monster movie. He created lasting images of horror and disfigurement on the screen.
Above: Lon Chaney as Quasimodo in the silent classic THE HUNCHBACK OF NOTRE DAME (1923).

created by special effects master Willis O'Brien, who would later go on to create the King of all Monsters, King Kong! But for 1927, these creatures were amazing oddities, capturing the minds and curiosities of moviegoers during the silent days of film with dramatic erupting volcanoes, a variety of stampeding monsters and, most of all, the destruction of London by a Brontosaurus.

THE LOST WORLD was a major contribution to the monster genre, and more important, to the science fiction film genre of the silent era. The showcase special effects of Willis O'Brien and the models of Marcel Delgado were incredible achievements for its time (O'Brien had previously worked on THE DINOSAUR AND THE MISSING LINK in 1917 for producer Herman Wobber and next on 10,000 B.C. also in 1917. Both films were sold to an released by Edison Film Company). THE LOST WORLD cost producers Watterson Rothacker and Earl Hudson an unprecedented one million dollars to produce. The film is undoubtedly an unusual and stunning cinematic achievement.

In Germany, Fritz Lang made SIEGFRIED (1924) an adventure epic with giant dragons. There was also a short length feature entitled THE GHOST OF SLUMBER MOUNTAIN (1919), a fantasy in which Willis O'Brien tested his skills in stop motion photography by creating a giant prehistoric monster, much like the ones he created in THE LOST WORLD.

THE MAN OF A THOUSAND FACES!

The genre of silent monster (horror) movies was mostly influenced and dominated by German productions, and it was not really until the late 1920's and early 1930's when America introduced itself as the leading manufacturer of monster movies. From this era emerged a talented actor and the major force behind many of the silent American horror and monster movies, Lon Chaney, known today as "The Man Of A Thousand Faces."

Chaney was born in 1883 in Colorado Springs, Colorado to deaf-mute parents. Between 1912 and 1918, Chaney appeared in over seventy-five moving pictures for the newly formed Universal Studios, or little Europa, as it was sometimes called. Chaney mostly performed in a variety of character roles during which he developed remarkable make-up skills that would later allow him to land major roles in monster movies.

The actor's big break came in 1919 when he starred as a cripple in the fantasy film directed by Tod Browning THE MIRACLE MAN. This was the first film in which the actor utilized his talent as a make-up artist to win him a role. Because of his make-up techniques, producers loved Chaney. He was easy to work with and he could cost-effectively take on the role of dual characters in a single film, costing them less than it would cost to hire an additional actor. For example, in A BLIND BARGAIN (1922), directed by Wallace Worsley for Samuel Goldwyn, the actor starred as both the sadistic Dr. Lamb and his mutant hunchback creation. The premise, based on the story by Barry Bain *The Octave of Claudius*, focuses on the theory of extending life by the transplantation of animal parts to replace human organs. Chaney's performance in A BLIND BARGAIN was perhaps his best role thus far and has been hailed as a worthy equal to John Barrymore's dual performance in DR. JEKYLL AND MR. HYDE (1920).

Chaney also starred in a series of gangster and adventure thrillers such as TREASURE ISLAND (1920) in dual roles as pirates; OUTSIDE THE LAW (1921) as both a gangster and a Chinese; and in OLIVER TWIST (1922) as Fagin. During the early 1920's, the actor was earning a mere $75 per week for his sensational dual performances. When Chaney initially requested a pay raise from $75 to $125 per week, Universal refused, only to be forced into paying the actor nearly $2500 per week after his magnificent performance as THE HUNCHBACK OF NOTRE DAME (1923). Chaney proved to the executives that he could actually create a character in a film that would generate big box office returns. One of the actor's finest performances was that of Quasimodo in Universal's THE HUNCHBACK OF NOTRE DAME. For the role Chaney endured much pain in the application of the monster make-up. This was usually the case for the actor, who, for Quasimodo, wore a forty pound rubber hump on his back to create the illusion of being an actual hunchback. The actor earned every bit of his $2500 a week salarUniversal's THE HUNCHBACK OF NOTRE DAME was the first legitimate version of the famous Victor Hugo novel *Notre Dame De Paris*, costing the studio an unprecedented $1,250,000. The film was hailed an instant masterpiece and Chaney's performance was described as brilliant. The massive waves of publicity resulted in the studio earning back its total investment at the box office as well as making Chaney a star. Even today, critics and film historians praise the actor for his Quasimodo

THE PHANTOM OF THE OPERA (1925) is undoubtedly the silent era's greatest horror and monster film.
Opposite Page: The Phantom (Lon Chaney) terrorizes Mary Philbin.
Above: A vintage poster from the film.
Right: The grand masque ball in which the Phantom makes his elaborate appearance to prove his existance.

characterization and his remarkable ability to communicate with the audience without the advent of sound.

Chaney's career began to soar and mold into roles associated with the genre of fantastic movies. He played everything from monsters to mad scientists. His next meaty role was as Doctor Ziska, a mad scientist who becomes determined to revive the dead in Irvin Thalberg's THE MONSTER (1925). The film was based on the play by Crane Wilbur.

After completing Tod Browning's THE UNHOLY THREE (1925), Chaney was hired by producer Carl Laemmle to star in a new project for Universal. The new monster movie was destined to be a masterpiece and a box office hit. The horror film was THE PHANTOM OF THE OPERA (1925), the studio's most lavish and costly production thus far.

THE PHANTOM OF THE OPERA was based on the famous novel by Gaston Leroux and was a showcase for Chaney's celebrated make-up craftsmanship. His monstrous make-up in THE PHANTOM OF THE OPERA is considered to be the silent era's most stunning and shocking The film is no doubt Chaney's supreme screen characterization. Audiences of that era could never fathom the actor ever surpassing his Quasimodo characterization, but he proved them wrong. His Phantom actually put the terror in horror films very effectively. With special make-up combined with special lighting and technical effects, Chaney was able to create the cinema's greatest horror.

The story is grand and timeless, but basically it tells how a living skeleton haunts the lower region of the Paris Opera House, residing in a Medieval torture chamber over which the opera house was constructed. The spirit of the Phantom has been coaching a beautiful singer named Christine Daae (Mary Philbin) to become the prima donna of the opera, but when his plans go awry, terrible and ghastly events occur at the opera house.

The film is indeed quite grand and Director Rupert Julian makes the best use of the lavish sets, rich and innovative Technicolor, and fabulous period costumes. The facsimile of the Paris Opera House was convincingly stunning, with reproduced stages, platforms, balconies, ornate chandeliers and elaborate subterranean passages. Julian teases the audience with brief and sudden scenes of Chaney's masked Phantom by way of shadows and shuddering voices. The director carefully and ever-so-slowly builds up the suspense until the climatic unmasking sequence, which remains the screen's greatest shock scene even to this day (producer Carl Laemmle was not pleased with Julian's final version of Leroux's novel and decided that new footage be added under the helm of action director Edward Sedgwick).

THE PHANTOM OF THE OPERA awarded Universal great riches considering the film cost the studio over one million dollars. THE PHANTOM OF THE OPERA was classified among the top ten films of 1925, thus Chaney was given his next role as a movie monster, this time as the pseudo vampire in LONDON AFTER MIDNIGHT (1927).

Based on the story *The Hypnotist* written by filmmaker Tod Browning, who also directed, LONDON AFTER MIDNIGHT features Chaney in another dual role. The actor portrays an inspector who stages vampire happenings in an old dark house to uncover the identity of a murderer as well as the lead vampire in the film.

LONDON AFTER MIDNIGHT is very effective up until the final moments of the climax when Chaney, as the vampire, reveals himself to be Inspector Burke! But he does get his man! In any event, Chaney's make-up as the rigid-toothed vampire was an incredible technical accomplishment for 1927 and many of the pseudo-supernatural events that occur during the film were quite effective. Browning's eye for atmospheric settings was tastefully effective in this eerie horror tale. LONDON AFTER MIDNIGHT was remade in 1935 with Bela Lugosi as the not so effective MARK OF THE VAMPIRE. As for Chaney, the actor went on to star in a number of other fantastic films in which the actor displayed his make-up talents. Some of these films included THE UNKNOWN (1927), MOCKERY (1927), LAUGH CLOWN, LAUGH (1928), WEST OF ZANZIBAR (1928), MR. WU (1928), WHERE EAST IS EAST (1929), THUNDER (1929) and the sound remake of his silent film of the same title THE UNHOLY THREE (1930).

Chaney was the first true great horror film star not long before Boris Karloff and Bela Lugosi found stardom in the 1930's. The actor will reign as the king of the horror and monster movies of the silent era because of his numerous and memorable screen characterizations, as well as his incredible and innovative make-up techniques. The actor will always be remembered for his characterizations of Quasimodo in THE HUNCHBACK OF NOTRE DAME (1923); Dr. Ziska in THE MONSTER (1925); Erik in THE PHANTOM OF

Top: a vintage poster for LONDON AFTER MIDNIGHT (1927).
Above & Right: Lon Chaney as the pseudo-vampire in LONDON AFTER MIDNIGHT.

THE OPERA (1925); and as the pseudo vampire spectre in LONDON AFTER MIDNIGHT (1927). Long live the King!

THE CAT, THE CANARY & THE GORILLA!

THE CAT AND THE CANARY (1927) from First National Pictures is perhaps the grandest of all the old dark house romps made during the silent era. The film was directed by Paul Leni and based on the successful John Willard Broadway play of 1922. The story of wealth and greed is cleverly combined with the old dark house theme. Most memorable are the scenes in which the monstrous cat monster (played by William Abbey) emerges from the shadows to strike at an unsuspecting victim. The preposterous plot fools the audience into thinking the cat monster is real when in the film's actuality, the monster is nothing more than a greedy heir who dons the hideous make-up and claws to scare one of his relatives out of her newly inherited millions.

Despite the pseudo horror, the trappings are superb. In fact the New York Times credited the film as being "the first time that a mystery melodrama has been lifted into the realms of art." The film utilized much of the shadows and imagery that the German filmmakers used to create moments of horror and atmosphere. THE CAT AND THE CANARY has been remade countless times throughout film history, but the silent version remains the most faithful to the Broadway play.

Another popular film that was also remade numerously throughout motion picture history was the silent classic THE GORILLA (1927), in which an eight foot tall ape (played by Walter Pidgeon) goes on a murdering spree. The film, like the Ralph Spence play it is based upon, builds up the comic relief with Keystone comic Charlie Murray in the lead role. The gorilla proved to be a viable Hollywood monster during the early 1930's and the theme was used unsparingly through the 1940's, 1950's and even in the 1960's.

Finally, MGM's THE THIRTEENTH CHAIR (1927) featured a houseful of sliding panels, creaking doors howling wind and threatening sofas operated from a secret switchboard. The film was directed by genre filmmaker Tod Browning and starred Lionel Barrymore as Dr. Leroy, who would go on a murdering spree at night and return home in time to cover his tracks. Bela Lugosi was billed sixth in the cast as Inspector Delzante, who cracks open the case and uncovers the murderer's identity (Lugosi's involvement with Browning would lead to his starring role in DRACULA (1931).

TALES OF MADNESS AND DISFIGUREMENT!

The silent era produced several tales of madness and disfigurement. The best of this sub-genre of horror films is undoubtedly Universal's THE PHANTOM OF THE OPERA (1925) with Lon Chaney's memorable characterization of a disfigured Erik. However, before THE PHANTOM OF THE OPERA was WAXWORKS (1924), directed by Paul Leni - the first of these tales. With expressionism a fashion statement among many of the German filmmakers, Leni's mind was able to run wild. The tale opens with a starving poet (played by William Dieterle, who would later become William, the director) being hired to create tales around model waxwork figures such as Ivan the Terrible (played by Conrad Veidt), Haroun Al Raschid (played by Emil Jannings) and Jack The Ripper (played by Werner Krauss), all of whom were monsters in their own right. Veidt, Jannings and Krauss were giants of fantastic cinema in Germany and are all in excellent form in WAXWORKS. Most prominent was Veidt's version of Ivan the Terrible, perhaps cinema's most disturbing characterizations.

Conrad Veidt returned to the screen to play Paul Orlac in THE HANDS OF ORLAC (1924), the first screen adaptation of Maurice Renard's popular novel directed by Robert Wiene. In the classic tale, Orlac is a concert pianist whose hands are crushed in a train crash. A mad surgeon replaces the damaged hands with the hands of a murderer. In time, the killer's hands take over the mind of Orlac and soon he finds himself committing murder. Like the remake it spawned, the murders committed in THE HANDS OF ORLAC prove to be nothing more than a horrid plot to drive the pianist mad, nevertheless Veidt was quite effective as the demented Orlac.

Finally, Universal's THE MAN WHO LAUGHS (1928), directed with such great style by Tod Browning, is another tale of madness and deformity. In a role originally intended for Lon Chaney, Sr., Conrad Veidt plays the fearsome Gwynplaine in this masterful screen adaptation of the Victor Hugo story. The film tells how Gwynplaine's face as a child is surgically disfigured by a band of outlaws as a vengeance against his father. The child grows up to become a beloved clown and to fall in love with a young blind girl (played by Mary Philbin). The young girl can only see the beauty of his soul and not the ugliness of his face.

Artistically, THE MAN WHO LAUGHS is perhaps the greatest of Universal's silent horrors, and it is quite odd that the studio never attempted a sound remake. Veidt's Gwynplaine is so strikingly horrid that his mere presence could make the skin crawl.

FAUST AND THE DEVIL AND MORE!

Films about the Devil had surfaced as early as 1896 in fantasy films by French filmmaker Georges Melies. However, it was not until 1913 with the release of A BARGAIN WITH THE DEVIL when the genre took off. The film was advertised as being "Better than Faust and Dr. Jekyll and Mr. Hyde" and was based on Alfred de Mussset's allegorical poem of mysticism and supernaturalism.

THE STUDENT OF PRAGUE (1926) was yet another famous supernatural film that emerged from the silent era. In it Conrad Veidt sells his soul to Satan (who is brilliantly played by Werner Krauss in a top hat and coat).

In 1926, F.W. Murnau and photographer Karl Freund produced FAUST, in which the silent cinema's most sinister devil is conjured up in the form of actor Emil Jannings. Jannings's Satan was a huge, horned creature. In an incredibly eerie and technically stunning scene orchestrated by Freund, Satan flies through the night and engulfs an entire village with the shadow of his cloak. The city is now under his horrid spell. This creative scene that has never been equalled in film history is perhaps the height of an era of German horror films that died with FAUST.

1927 marked the year of the final silent horror film - SEVEN FOOTPRINTS TO SATAN. The film was based on Abraham Merritt's classic fantasy tale of Devil worship and ended with all involved exposed as actors hired as a hoax.

ONE LAST LOOK BACK!

Looking back in time to the silent era of monster and horror movies, it is quite obvious that the German films such as THE CABINET OF DR. CALIGARI (1919), THE GOLEM (1920), NOSFERATU (1922), THE HANDS OF ORLAC (1924), METROPOLIS (1927), and FAUST (1926), to name only a few, were superior to American-made films in creating true horror. German filmmakers had created and perfected techniques that American filmmakers picked-up on and developed. F.W. Murnau, Robert Wiene and Fritz Lang were geniuses. They were unequalled in their fields. Actors Werner Krauss, Emil Jannings and, especially Conrad Veidt, possessed enormous amounts of talent. The screen would never again see the likes of these true horror stars, at least not in their current form, that is to say, how they appeared in films during the silent era.

While Lang and Veidt created lasting images of horror in silent German films, they also extended their talents to Hollywood during the late 1920's and on through the 1940's. Lang fled Germany and his wife (screenwriter Thea von Harbou, who had joined the Nazi party as an official screenwriter) when his films were banned in Germany because he refused to make films for the cause of the Third Reich. Veidt also extended his talents to Hollywood with the dark but lavish horror film THE MAN WHO LAUGHS (1928), an American-made film with strong German influenced expressionism. Veidt made eight films in all in Hollywood, including CASABLANCA (1942). The actor died in 1943 in Hollywood, while Lang, who returned to Germany during the 1950's to continue filmmaking, died in 1978. Two great legends who strongly influenced the genre of horror films and whose mark belongs among the silent films.

To say that the German films were superior to the American films is not to say that Hollywood did not produce quality, highly influential films. Hollywood film companies discovered that Germany could make such frightening horrors such as THE CABINET OF DR. CALIGARI (1919) and NOSFERATU (1922) and American filmmakers Tod Browning, Rupert Julian and Paul Leni found ways to improve the techniques that made these films so scary. THE PHANTOM OF THE OPERA (1925), LONDON AFTER MIDNIGHT (1927), THE CAT AND THE CANARY (1927) and THE MAN WHO LAUGHS (1928) are exceptional examples of quality, high-gloss American horror films. Much credit must go to the filmmakers of these great extravaganzas as well as to horror film legend Lon Chaney, who passed away in 1930.

The advent of sound led to the end of the great German and American silent horror films. The once thrilling terrors of the silent screen soon became thrilled no more and were lost in the wake of such great new sound horrors like DRACULA (1931) and FRANKENSTEIN (1931). Fortunately, recent interest in this lost art form has caused a resurfacing of these great classics. Who would have ever thought one would could watch Lon Chaney in PHANTOM OF THE OPERA (1925) on video, or Fritz Lang's METROPOLIS (1927)? Perhaps we can discover the horrors that once were once more!

Above: The film's hero battles with the cat monster in THE CAT AND THE CANARY (1927).
Left: A rare scene from F. W. Murnau's FAUST (1926).
Opposite Top: A lobby card from the genre's last silent horror film SEVEN FOOTPRINTS TO SATAN (1927).
Opposite Bottom: Universal's THE MAN WHO LAUGHS (1928) is considered an epic horror-romance. In this scene, Conrad Veidt plays Gwynplaine, a disfigured monster who falls in love with blind girl Mary Philbin.

27

CHAPTER TWO
THE MONSTERS OF THE 1930'S

Above: A scene from James Whale's horror masterpiece THE BRIDE OF FRANKENSTEIN (1935).
Opposite Top: A Re-release poster from Tod Browning's DRACULA (1931).
Opposite Bottom Right: Bela Lugosi as the infamous Count Dracula in Universal's first sound horror classic DRACULA (1931).

A NEW ERA!

The end of an era and an art form died in 1927 with the release of the last documented silent horror film, SEVEN FOOTPRINTS TO SATAN (1927). The advent of sound introduced new movie monsters played by new and talented actors. The silent stars like Conrad Veidt and Lon Chaney, Sr. had to decide weather they were going to survive in the new age of sound movies or simply fade away. Many of the silent movie stars did not survive and died with their art form, but others like actors Veidt and Chaney and filmmakers Fritz Lang and Tod Browning survived the revolutionizing of sound in films. Others, who were dormant during the silent era flourished with the coming of talking films. Actors such as Bela Blasko (Lugosi) and William (Boris Karloff) Pratt and filmmakers such as James Whale and Karl Freund found fame and stardom in the horror genre.

The first talking horror film was Warner Brother's THE TERROR (1928), directed by Roy DelRuth. As the first sound horror film, audiences could actually hear the howling wind, or the creaking of a door, and the very first scream! The novelty of sound allowed filmmakers to take horror to a new height. Novelties that we take for granted today. The film starred Conrad Nagel as a creepy, hooded

mad man who stalked the corridors of an old dark house. THE TERROR was remade as a comedy in 1934 as RETURN OF THE TERROR!

With the advent of sound becoming increasingly popular, Hollywood remade many of the silent era's famous horror films. THE BAT WHISPERS (1930) was Roland West's sound remake of the silent classic THE BAT (1926). THE GORILLA (1930) was a sound remake of the 1927 silent film of the same title. Director Rupert Julian remade THE CAT AND THE CANARY (1927) as THE CAT CREEPS (1930). Edison's FRANKENSTEIN (1910) and LIFE WITHOUT SOUL (1915) were remade as FRANKENSTEIN (1931) while F.W. Murnau's NOSFERATU (1922) became Tod Browning's DRACULA (1931). This chain reaction carried on through the early to mid 1930's during the cinema's first wave of sound horror classics.

I AM COUNT DRACULA!

With the advent of sound upon them and with three major horror masterpieces under their belt, Carl Laemmle and executives at Universal Pictures were greatly inspired to produce a Gothic horror masterpiece that would surpass all others, including Lon Chaney's THE HUNCHBACK OF NOTRE DAME (1923) and PHANTOM OF THE OPERA (1925) as well as Tod Browning's THE MAN WHO LAUGHS (1927). Producers wanted another spellbinding film adaptation of yet another famous literary work. They chose Bram Stoker's tale of romanticism and supernatural horror, *Dracula*.

Straight from the beginning, DRACULA (1931) was Universal's greatest masterpiece of horror to date. The film is elegantly directed by Tod Browning from an intelligent screenplay written by Garrett Fort. The Gothic tale of a vampire who survives centuries by drinking the blood of others was translated onto the screen as a grand epic that begins in Transylvania and concludes in England. The film that inspired hundreds of remakes, sequels and imitations remains intriguing today because of the wonderful photography of Karl Freund, the elegant and slow-paced direction of Tod Browning and the lavish Gothic sets. But most of all, the spellbinding characterization of Count Dracula by Hungarian actor Bela Lugosi (born 1882 in the country of Transylvania) still fascinates new generations of horror movie fans even today.

Lugosi was relatively an unknown actor when Universal produced DRACULA. Up until 1931, the actor had starred in numerous silent films and Broadway plays, including F.W. Murnau's DER JANUSKOPF (1920), THE LAST OF THE MOHICANS (1920), and Tod Browning's THE THIRTEENTH CHAIR (1929), to name only a few.

Lugosi's career in both German and American films consisted merely of uncredited roles and bit parts. In fact in an interview, Lugosi once commented that he had always considered his screen assignments as unrewarding, that is, until he made DRACULA. Lon Chaney, Sr. was originally the studio's first choice for the part of Dracula, however, the king of horror films passed away just before the cast could be selected. John Wray was the studio's next choice. Wray had just given an impressive performance in Universal's epic tale ALL QUIET ON THE WESTERN FRONT (1930). But producers wanted an actor whose name was familiar with audiences, therefore Universal considered actors Paul Muni, Ian Keith and even Conrad Veidt for the role. Lugosi was nearly passed over for the part, but eventually, the actor was chosen in September 1930 while playing in a road version of the Broadway play *Dracula*. Lugosi was the obvious choice because of his familiarity with the character and the novel and because of his handsome features and his native Transylvanian accent. The actor was paid a mere $500 a week for seven week's work in what was a gold-mine for Universal. Looking back on Lugosi's career in horror films, it becomes very clear that the actor was extremely well-suited in playing Dracula on film. This was both fortunate and unfortunate. With DRACULA, Lugosi had found super-stardom. However, the same film was the actor's downfall. At the age of forty-eight, the actor reached a grand climax to a thirty year career. True, the actor continued to star in films up through his death in 1959, however, the actor could very rarely escape the image he had created for himself in DRACULA. The same role that made him a superstar hindered his career. Bela Lugosi was and always will be considered Count Dracula.

Not since F.W. Murnau's NOSFERATU (1922), a pirated version of the Stoker novel, had the tale been adapted to the screen. Unlike the silent film's evil and repulsive Count Orlock, Lugosi's Count Dracula, no less evil, was a suave and polished aristocrat dressed in formal black and white. Lugosi's vampire was a venomous fiend who actually hid behind his own handsome disguise, but one man, Professor Van Helsing (masterfully enacted by Edward Van Sloan), Dracula's timeless arch-enemy, manages to flush-out the nobleman's horrid identity to the surface.

DRACULA is a landmark horror film and is considered, along with its counterpart FRANKENSTEIN (1931), to be one of the greatest monster movies from the vintage era. The film cost Universal a mere four-hundred-thousand dollars, but the returns have been perpetual.

DRACULA inspired a wealth of many other vampire movies during the 1930's and the decades that followed. VAMPYR (1931) was one such film.

VAMPYR (1931) was directed by Carl Theodor Dreyer and was based on the classic vampire novel *Carmilla* written by Sheridan Le Fanu. VAMPYR was carefully adapted to the screen by Christian Jul, who also produced the film and starred as its hero. The film, like the novel, is an undisputed masterpiece of the macabre and is perhaps the best vampire film ever crafted. VAMPYR is a slow moving, elegant tale of foreboding horror that captures the intimate fears within ourselves and explodes them onto the screen with great style and with a powerful uneasiness; a style that Alfred Hitchcock would focus on in many of his suspense-horror pictures of later years.

In the film, a traveler (Christian Jul) inadvertently stumbles into a town plagued by vampire killings. His first encounter is with an old man who gives Gray a package to be opened in the event he dies. After a series of bizarre events, Gray learns of the old man's death. The old man is survived by two daughters, the older of which is fading away from a horrible, unknown disease. Gray opens the package and finds a book, "Strange Tales of the Vampires." Next, he gives the surviving daughter a blood transfusion, during which he passes out and experiences a nightmare in which he is locked within a coffin. Suddenly, the face of an old withered woman (the film's central vampire) peers at him through the lid's transom. After awakening from the transfusion and confronting immeasurable fears within himself, Gray and a group of vampire-killers encounters the vampiress herself in a graveyard and drives an iron pole through her heart.

VAMPYR was unquestionably a mood piece rather than a commercial investment. Dreyer hired accomplished German cinematographer Rudolph Mate (Nominated for an Academy Award for his cinematography in FOREIGN CORRESPONDENT, THAT HAMILTON WOMAN, SAHARA and COVER GIRL) and together they created a film of atmosphere and subtlety. Because of its nontraditional sense, VAMPYR did poorly at the American box office. American distributors considered the film to be pale next to the more "dramatic" and "commercial" film DRACULA (when viewed today, however, DRACULA appears very passive and subtle compared to the Hammer and splatter horror films of the 1960's - 1990's). In any event, as a result of its limited distributorship in America, VAMPYR faded away for many years, out of sight and out of mind until a print surfaced during the 1960's. It was then that VAMPYR was rediscovered as the masterpiece of vintage horror that it truly is.

It is an amazing fact that Universal never featured actor Bela Lugosi in another vampire film during the 1930's. It was not until the late 1940's when the actor was given the role of the vampire king out of pity in ABBOTT AND COSTELLO MEET FRANKENSTEIN (1948). It is also an unfortunate fact that Lugosi was never respected by Universal executives after he refused to play the role of the Frankenstein monster in FRANKENSTEIN (1931) and after the disappointing box office returns of MURDERS IN THE RUE MORGUE (1932). Lugosi was not exactly that studio's favorite performer at the time because of a lot of animosity. The studio used the argument that the actor simply could not bring freshness and originality to a new character. The character of Count Dracula stuck to Lugosi like feathers on tar, and the poor actor simply could not shake that image off. All hopes of molding Lugosi into the new Lon Chaney at Universal collapsed when Boris Karloff landed the part of the Frankenstein monster. The result of which created a new horror star. Karloff received many of Universal's better parts, while poor Bela Lugosi ended up landing horrible roles in independent horror films for poverty row film companies like Monogram and PRC. During the golden years of Hollywood, major studios owned their stars, and Universal actually saw to it that Lugosi never achieve stardom in horror films after DRACULA. Universal was very unfair to Lugosi, and this showed in later years, but the actor did manage to land the part of the pseudo-Dracula character in the Tod Browning film MARK OF THE VAMPIRE (1935) from MGM (not Universal).

MARK OF THE VAMPIRE, originally entitled THE VAMPIRE OF PRAGUE, was a remake of Browning's silent horror mystery LONDON AFTER MIDNIGHT (1927) with Lon Chaney, Sr. For the remake, Browning divided Chaney's dual detective-vampire roles into two separate

Above: Vintage poster for FRANKENSTEIN (1931).
Opposite Page: Dr. Frankenstein (Colin Clive) and assistant Dwight Frye hard at work in the laboratory from James Whale's FRANKENSTEIN (1931).

parts: Professor Zelen (played by Lionel Barrymore) and the vampire Count Mora (played by Lugosi). However, the premise remained basically the same with actors (Lugosi and Carol Borland) impersonating vampires so that the inspector (Lionel Atwill) could trap a murderer. The script written by Guy Endore added incest between Count Mora and his daughter-lover Luna (Borland). Unfortunately, this idea was cut from the film. Incest, as we all know, was a device used in many of the literary works dealing with female vampirism.

MARK OF THE VAMPIRE offers an eerie atmosphere, good scripting and well paced direction that makes it worthy of being a hardy Gothic-style classic of the horror film. Browning very clearly follows the formula that made DRACULA a success, disguising the trappings with new sets and an entirely new cast. If anything, Browning improved on DRACULA with imaginative camera-work and special effects. Of special note, Lionel Atwill is brilliant as Inspector Neumann, but Lionel Barrymore tends to overact as Professor Zelen, an authority on vampires.

The successful release of MARK OF THE VAMPIRE encouraged Universal to produce a sequel to DRACULA (1931). Originally, Lugosi was scheduled to star in the sequel as Count Dracula as promised prior to the release of MURDERS IN THE RUE MORGUE (1932), but because Lugosi had fallen out with Universal, executives put the film on the shelf for four years and when producers decided to make the sequel, the actor was approached but unavailable due to obligations at another studio. Lugosi was unable to return to the role of Dracula, thus the script was redrafted and the title, which was originally DRACULA RETURNS, was changed to DRACULA'S DAUGHTER (1936).

DRACULA'S DAUGHTER starred beautiful actress Gloria Holden in the role of Countess Marya Zaleska - the ill-fated and illegitimate daughter of Count Dracula. Despite the lack of the infamous Count, the sequel remained consistent with the original, beginning with the climax of DRACULA in which the vampire's remains are cremated. Professor Van Helsing

(Edward Van Sloan) is in a heap of trouble with the authorities when he is found with the impaled corpse of Count Dracula. Van Helsing is taken for questioning, and the new film begins.

The premise of DRACULA'S DAUGHTER is quite simple. Basically, Countess Dracula, using the name of Marya Zaleska, desires a cure from her wretched condition. A condition that she has endured for five hundred years. She meets Dr. Garth (Otto Kruger), a scientist who does not believe in the existence of vampires. Dr. Garth believes that the countess suffers from mental anxieties and he sets out to cure her. However, matters become complicated when the vampire's servant, Sandor (Irving Pichel), believes that young Dr. Garth is a threat to the eternal life promised him by the Zaleska, so he proceeds to tempt her blood lusts with young and beautiful Nan Grey. As expected, the vampire becomes inflamed by temptation and Sandor's wish is fulfilled. Eventually with the aide of Professor Van Helsing's knowledge and after a series of bizarre events, Dr. Garth soon realizes that the countess's condition is real and not mental. During the final moments of the film, Countess Marya Zaleska is voluntarily impaled by a wooden arrow.

DRACULA'S DAUGHTER, stylishly directed by Lambert Hillyer, was based on Bram Stoker's novel *Dracula's Guest*. Unlike the Universal horror films that followed beginning with SON OF FRANKENSTEIN (1939), DRACULA'S DAUGHTER is a much more subtle film with restrained acting, strong atmosphere and fantastic Gothic sets. The film is technically superior to DRACULA. There is good dialogue and very credible performances by Gloria Holden and Irving Pichel. Edward Van Sloan is an old pro at playing the arch-enemy of the Draculas.

Many film historians believe that DRACULA'S DAUGHTER marked the end of an era in the history of Universal's horror films. I, too must agree. The film was the studio's final horror film under Carl Laemmle's reign. The horror films that followed lacked the grandeur and Gothic beauty of DRACULA (1931), FRANKENSTEIN (1931), THE MUMMY (1932), THE BRIDE OF FRANKENSTEIN (1935) and DRACULA'S DAUGHTER, to name only a few. These were incredibly stylish and quality horror masterpieces produced under the careful direction and control of legendary filmmakers James Whale, Tod Browning and Karl Freund. Between 1923 and 1936, Universal executives were mostly interested in producing masterpieces of Gothic horror first and then the profits would follow. DRACULA'S DAUGHTER was the end of that era. On March 14, 1936, J. Cheever Cowdin's Standard Capital Corporation and magnate Charles R. Rogers took over the harnesses of Carl Laemmle's Universal Pictures as a result of a poor financial business decision the Laemmles had made in 1935. The Laemmles resigned and DRACULA'S DAUGHTER marked the end of Universal's first wave of sound horror films. Rogers axed several similar projects of horror, including the upcoming Karloff/Lugosi vehicle THE ELECTRIC MAN, which was later made as MAN MADE MONSTER (1941) with Lionel Atwill and Lon Chaney, Jr.

AND GOD CREATED MAN!

Upon its release, DRACULA (1931) was instantly hailed a masterpiece but even the attractive box office returns could not help the studio out of its quickly declining state. Universal Pictures suffered a $2.5 million loss in 1931. The studio closed down for six weeks to regroup. During this time, Carl Laemmle and various executive producers decided to put together yet another masterpiece of horror. The film's purpose would be to save the studio from bankruptcy and to provide its newest and brightest star, Bela Lugosi, with the leading role in yet another great adaptation of a Gothic horror novel. Keep in mind that all this occurred while Lugosi was still on the good-side of Universal executives.

The task of creating the new story was assigned to writer Robert Florey. It was Florey who came up with the idea of adapting Mary Wolfestonecraft Shelley's novel *Frankenstein* to the screen. The story outline was just what Universal wanted, but not what Lugosi wanted. Lugosi learned that producers wanted him to play the role of the Frankenstein monster. The actor exploded with anger and argued that any

half wit extra could play the part (how wrong he was). Florey backed-up Lugosi's argument, agreeing that it would be a waste to misuse the actor's great talents and that a star like himself should receive the part of Dr. Frankenstein instead. They both fought a loosing battle. Lugosi's chance to super-stardom flew right out the window when the roles of both the Frankenstein monster went to British actor Boris Karloff and the role of the scientist went to Colin Clive. Furthermore, James Whale was given the task to direct the film that Robert Florey had hoped for. Finally, Florey's original story was redrafted by writer John L. Balderston. The film that came to be a masterpiece and perhaps the greatest monster movie ever made was released as FRANKENSTEIN (1931). But one cannot help wonder how the film would have turned out had Florey directed Lugosi as either the monster or his maker as he had originally scripted. One thing is certain, the film, as we know it today, is brilliant and is perhaps the single-most influential horror film of our time.

As previously mentioned, the role of the Frankenstein monster went to British-born actor Boris Karloff. Born Henry William Pratt on November 23, 1897 in London, England, Karloff was destined to play the Frankenstein monster from day one. He began his career in silent films in villainous roles. His first horror film was THE BELLS (1926) in which he played a carnival mesmerist who forces a confession out of murderer Lionel Barrymore. MGM's THE UNHOLY NIGHT (1929) with Lon Chaney, Sr. from director Lionel Barrymore (Karloff's friend) featured the actor as a Hindu servant. Karloff also starred in THE MAD GENIUS (1931) as an abusive father and numerous other films. But it was Karloff's performance as a gangster in Universal's GAFT (1931) that inadvertently led to his infamous part of the monster in FRANKENSTEIN. GAFT was directed by famed filmmaker James Whale (born 1896 in Dudley, England). Whale and Karloff became friends on the set of the film, and when the task of selecting the cast for FRANKENSTEIN became that of the director, he chose Karloff for his impressive size and gaunt features. In fact Whale once commented in an interview that he was always fascinated by Karloff's face. Whatever he meant by that certainly was enough to select the actor for this very key role. Today, as a result of his magnificent, sympathetic and powerful performance as the Frankenstein monster, Karloff became the premiere actor most associated with the horror film, and his image as the king of horror films still exists long after his death. Karloff's popularity reached heights beyond the stardom Lugosi had established from his role in DRACULA. Karloff's grand performance proved one thing to Lugosi; the role of the monster would take more talent than a half-wit extra could ever contribute. Without the genius of Karloff in the role, FRANKENSTEIN could have been nothing more than just another horror film. Looking back, it is amazing to think how the actor was paid a mere $500 to create the greatest movie monster ever. Furthermore, the actor was never invited to the film's premiere.

Karloff achieved super-stardom in the role of the monster, however he was not alone. Creating the character was not an easy task. Make-up artist Jack Pierce spent weeks with the actor creating and improving the physical appearance of the creature. In fact, at one point during the initial makeup session both Karloff and Pierce nearly threw in the towel and even considered recalling Bela Lugosi. But as history has it, both Karloff and Pierce were triumphant in creating the screen's greatest monster.

The plot is as famous today as it was in 1931. The story is the captivating tale of scientist Dr. Frankenstein (Colin Clive), who is fully obsessed with creating life from death. The film opens in an eerie cemetery immediately after a funeral where Dr. Frankenstein and his demented hunchback, grave-robbing assistant Fritz (played by Dwight Frye) exhume a fresh corpse. This cadaver houses the remaining human organs necessary to complete the experiment. With stolen body parts, Frankenstein is amazingly able to give life to an inanimate body. But the creation turns out to be an inarticulate, brute monster with the brain of a killer. There are several scenes in which the monster displays human emotions and there are moments of sheer horror. During the climax, the monster confronts his maker atop a burning windmill where he is supposedly destroyed in the flames.

The role of Henry Frankenstein, originally intended for Leslie Howard, went to actor Colin Clive, and the role of Frankenstein's dwarf and hunchback assistance went to Dwight Frye, who had just given a magnificent performance in DRACULA. Edward Van Sloan was cast in the role of Frankenstein's mentor and Mae Clarke played Elizabeth Frankenstein, the scientist's wife. The cast of FRANKENSTEIN was carefully

Above: Dr. Frankenstein (Colin Clive) and his new female creation (Elsa Lanchester) in THE BRIDE OF FRANKENSTEIN (1935).

picked by filmmaker James Whale, and the director's good casting call proved to be the film's major contributing attribute.

FRANKENSTEIN touched a new peak in horror and grossed over $1 million during its first domestic release and an additional $13 million in the short years that followed. The film cost Universal a mere $250,000, but due to the wonderful performances, magnificent Gothic sets, and the extremely fluid camera of James Whale, the film became an instant classic. But the key to the film's success was undoubtedly Karloff's very sympathetic performance as the Frankenstein monster.

FRANKENSTEIN, like Universal's DRACULA, inspired numerous remakes, sequels and spin-offs throughout movie history. Only one horror film can hold a candle to FRANKENSTEIN, and, guess what, that film is THE BRIDE OF FRANKENSTEIN (1935), the sequel to FRANKENSTEIN.

THE BRIDE OF FRANKENSTEIN proved that a second film in a series could be better than the original. In fact, film historians, critics and movie fans consider the sequel to be THE greatest horror movie ever made. The reasons are simple. To begin with, THE BRIDE OF FRANKENSTEIN is actually a much closer adaptation to the Mary Shelley novel than its predecessor. In the novel, the underlying conflict between the monster and his creator developed when the doctor refused to build a mate in the same likeness. In the book, Dr. Frankenstein never completes the creation of a mate for the monster, but in the film, the mate or "The Bride" is brought to life in one of the cinema's most electrifying sequences that actually surpasses the creation scene in the original film in both suspense and technical effects.

In addition to its faithfulness to the Shelley novel, the sequel also develops subplots - as in the case of the evil Dr. Pretorious (played by Ernest Thesiger). Pretorious connivingly befriends the monster (once again played by

WARE
THEATRE - BEVERLY
3 DAYS
THUR. FRI. SAT.
STARTING JULY 18
I DEMAND A MATE!
WARNING!
BEWARE!
CARL LAEMMLE PRESENTS
KARLOFF
IN
"The BRIDE of FRANKENSTEIN"
COLIN CLIVE · VALERIE HOBSON · ELSA LANCHESTER · UNA O'CONNOR · ERNEST THESIGER · C.C. CLIVE
directed by
JAMES WHALE
produced by
CARL LAEMMLE, JR.
A UNIVERSAL PICTURE

Opposite Page: Publicity poster for THE BRIDE OF FRANKENSTEIN (1935).
Above Left: Vintage poster for SON OF FRANKENSTEIN (1939).
Above Right: Basil Rathbone, Bela Lugosi and Boris Karloff in SON OF FRANKENSTEIN (1939).

Karloff) and promises him a mate in the likeness of his monstrous self in return for his brute strength, which he uses to carry-out his evil bidding. Once the monster has killed for Pretorious, the mad scientist enlists the services of Dr. Frankenstein (once again played by Colin Clive) to create a mate for the monster he brought life to. Not too much to ask? That is, if you don't mind loosing your sanity during the horrid process. Frankenstein refuses, but Pretorious threatens the fine doctor with the death of his lovely wife with the hands of his creation. And so the film elaborately sets off on its course of horror, suspense and betrayal, and during the final quarter of the movie, the electrifying sequence in which the mate is given life to is upon us. "She's Alive! Alive!" rejoices Frankenstein.

The female monster stands upright in the laboratory, shorn of her bandages. Her Nefertiti-style hair, streaked with two dashes of white; her towering body covered with a long white gown.

"The Bride of Frankenstein!" proclaims Dr. Pretorious with a madden glow cast upon his face.

The bride (played remarkably well by British actress Elsa Lanchester) is repulsed by the monster's appearance and during the final moments of the film, Frankenstein and his wife escape the laboratory where the monster, a tear falling down his face, pulls a lever that causes an explosion as he emotionally proclaims, "We belong dead!" (referring to himself, his mate and the cursed Dr. Pretorious.

The film begins happy and quickly turns sinister, offering every imaginable emotion from the mind of director James Whale. The special effects of John P. Fulton are magnificent and the massive sets are incredible (especially the impressive seventy-foot laboratory tower). The photography of John Mescal (who also photographed Universal's THE BLACK CAT of 1934) is breathtaking. But we find ourselves consumed by the moving performances of the film's monsters (Karloff and Lanchester).

There is a scene in THE BRIDE OF FRANKENSTEIN that I find quite interesting. In the film, the monster develops a touching relationship with a blind man (played by O.P. Heggie). The time they spend together in the film releases some fascinating emotions on behalf of Karloff's monster. They find themselves needing each other's company to comfort their loneliness. The scene is quite moving and a perfect display of the type of talent Karloff was able to inject into the highly dimensional character of the monster that would later become a victim of Lon Chaney, Bela Lugosi and Glenn Strange's mechanized, one dimensional - style performances.

During its 1935 release, THE BRIDE OF FRANKENSTEIN smashed all box office records including the record set by the classic picture IMITATION OF LIFE (1934). THE BRIDE OF FRANKENSTEIN became the biggest money-making film of all time. The film is unequalled by none other and is considered to be director James Whale's finest film. For Whale, there could never be another horror films, for the filmmaker believed that he could never surpass a film so perfect and artistically beautiful.

By 1938, Karloff had become the biggest box office draw, and the role that originally earned him $500 would now earn him over $2500 per week. Naturally, Bela Lugosi, who had lost his thrown to Karloff as the undisputed King Of The Monster Movies, envied the actor's career and was kicking himself for turning down the role of the monster in FRANKENSTEIN (1931). During the early to mid 1930's. Lugosi was denied any roles as a romantic lead, and for a long fifteen month stretch, the actor was unemployed and forced to sell his house. By 1938, Universal was once again facing bankruptcy. The studio that depended on horror films for its financial stability had not produced one monster film between 1936 to 1938. Vice President Charles Rogers resigned and was replaced by Cliff Work, formerly from RKO Pictures. Under Work's supervision, the "new" Universal began shooting on their next and most significant project, a little horror epic entitled SON OF FRANKENSTEIN (1939).

When Cliff Work and Universal began production on SON OF FRANKENSTEIN, they had no idea that it would become the classic epic that it is. Studio executives simply hoped for a quick profit from material that was already a proven money-maker. Universal allotted a preliminary budget of $250,000, (the same amount it cost the studio to make THE BRIDE OF FRANKENSTEIN) however, the film's producer and director, Rowland V. Lee, was the studio's most powerful figure at the time, and he had other ideas of what the film should be. Lee railroaded the studio into doubling the budget to a whopping $500,000, which was twice the cost of FRANKENSTEIN. With his strong influence, Lee also managed to assemble a top rate cast for the project.

Boris Karloff returned to the role of the Frankenstein monster for the third consecutive time. The story, written by Willis Cooper, placed the story twenty-five years after the death of Henry Frankenstein - since actor Colin Clive had passed away prior to the making of this film. As a result of Clive's death, Cooper created the character of Wolf Von Frankenstein, the son of Henry. The role was originally intended for actor Peter Lorre, but the Lorre turned down the role in fear that his image as a horror film actor would grow larger. Bela Lugosi made a request to play the scientist, but he was turned down when producers made a fuss. Thus the role went to distinguished actor Basil Rathbone.

Rowland V. Lee, however, insisted that Cooper write in a part especially for Lugosi, thus Ygor, the hideous and demented shepherd - grave-robber was born. In the film, Ygor fiendishly uses the monster to kill those responsible for sentencing him to death, which he obviously escaped from without explanation. Ygor was Lugosi's greatest role since DRACULA (1931), and his first in over fifteen months thanks to the film's director. Lee also helped enlarge what was a minor role for Lugosi into a more significant part, as he felt the actor was greatly underestimated by the studio. Lugosi was paid $500 per week Needless to say, the actor was very happy to be working again.

Actress Josephine Hutchison played Frankenstein's wife, while distinguished horror actor Lionel Atwill was given the impressive supporting role of Police Inspector Krogh. Atwill was surprisingly quite satisfied receiving fourth billing under Lugosi; the actor almost always received top billing. But considering the circumstances surrounding the actor's sordid rape trial accusations, I imagine he was just happy to have work (Atwill was always a favorite at Universal).

Originally, Cooper's script also had elements of THE BRIDE OF FRANKENSTEIN in which the monster threatened to kill Wolf Von Frankenstein's wife and his son had the scientist not created him a mate. But producer and director Lee wanted originality as well as consistency, thus the character of Ygor was added for Lugosi and the plot changed from the monster wanting a mate to Ygor bringing the monster to Frankenstein and wanting to rejuvenate the creature to its full strength.

SON OF FRANKENSTEIN is a well mounted classic monster movie with all the ingredients that make such a film a classic: eerie atmospheric photography, handsome sets, great performances by the cast and well paced direction. SON OF FRANKENSTEIN was perhaps the best of the new Universal horror films from a technical point of view. The film also marked the end of an era of horror. For one, Karloff swore that he would never return to the role of the Frankenstein monster, and he remained faithful to his promise. Secondly, the studio never invested as much money and time on another monster film. From this point on, the Universal Frankenstein films of the 1940's would take on a totally new shape. Never again would the monster be portrayed as a sympathetic being. Instead, the Frankenstein monster would become a wanton engine of destruction. SON OF FRANKENSTEIN was the last of the classic Frankenstein movies but by no means the last Universal Frankenstein film!

THE HORROR STAR THAT NEVER BECAME KING!

When one thinks of actors who are most-associated with vintage monster movies, the names that usually come to mind are Boris Karloff, Bela Lugosi and the Chaney's. Actor Lionel Atwill, a favorite among fans of classic horror films, is almost always overlooked. Yet Atwill was one of the leading actors of the horror film during the 1930's and a major supporting star during the 1940's.

Born in Corydon, England in 1885, Atwill made his horror film debut in the First National classic, DR. X (1932). The film was a Technicolor masterpiece directed with great style by Michael Curtiz, who was undoubtedly one of the most talented and accomplished directors from the vintage era of cinema, with films like CASABLANCA (1942), YANKEE DOODLE DANDY (1942) and MILDRED PIERCE (1945) and four Academy Award nominations to his credit. As Dr. Xavier, Atwill delivered his most meaty dialogue as a scientist who heads a medical school. Somebody on the doctor's staff is guilty of committing six ghastly cannibalistic murders. The other cast members fear that Dr. X is responsible, but director Curtiz takes the audience through a series of shocking revelations that lead to the discovery of the monster's true identity.

Atwill's performance as Dr. X is quite good, and actress Fay Wray makes a good stereotypical heroine. Curtiz's direction stresses shadows and sharp angular images to create the film's shock and horror. His Gothic style in a more modern, post-Gothic setting works well and the laboratory scenes as well as the monster scenes are quite effective. DR. X is a classic monster movie from the old school of horrors and should not be missed by fans of vintage horror films. In fact, for those who are not familiar with the film, DR. X is now available on video cassette.

Amazingly, this incredible horror film never spawned a sequel, however THE RETURN OF DR. X (1939) was a misleading film that tricked moviegoers into believing it was a sequel to the original Lionel Atwill film. This was not the case. Instead of featuring Lionel Atwill, the film starred Humphrey Bogart as a Doctor X look-alike who actually turns out to be a vampire! The low budget Warner film was produced on the assumption that it would be able to capitalize on the "Dr. X" fame, but the project could not stay afloat with such big horror films as THE SON OF FRANKENSTEIN (1939) circulating in theaters. In any event, it was a film that legendary actor Humphrey Bogart despised making, but because of contractual obligations, he was forced into starring in a horror picture.

Director Michael Curtiz and Lionel Atwill teamed up again to star in yet another Technicolor, post-Gothic masterpiece of the horror film, MYSTERY OF THE WAX MUSEUM (1933). The film presents Atwill at his best in his famous screen characterization of Ivan Igor - a former sculptor and current curator of a wax museum. Fay Wray returned as the heroine, and together, both actors provide the right chemistry needed to create a fabulous horror film.

MYSTERY OF THE WAX MUSEUM was the first successful horror film to use a contemporary setting; and thus became known as the first modern horror film. This was a rarity since most of the successful horror films were set in a Gothic period. But Curtiz proved that horror could still exist amidst the skyscrapers of New York.

The character of Igor was an incredible

Above: Lionel Atwill in THE VAMPIRE BAT (1933).
Left: Lionel Atwill in a publicity shot from MYSTERY OF THE WAX MUSEUM (1933), the actor's greatest film.

triumph for Atwill; a characterization that even Lon Chaney, Sr. would have admired. According to the script, the museum curator (Atwill) had been terribly disfigured when his business was deliberately sabotaged for insurance money by greedy partners. Igor, now disfigured, crippled and confined to a wheel chair, becomes one of the most demented of all screen villains and monsters. In the film, the madman uses the bodies of his enemies and especially his saboteurs to create incredibly life-like waxwork figures.

THE MYSTERY OF THE WAX MUSEUM helped to re-establish the old Lon Chaney-style of disfigurement in the horror film that had long vanished with the era of silent films. The infamous unmasking sequence in which Mrs. Wray inadvertently knocks off the mask from Atwill's face as she struggles to free herself from his clutches is as shocking today as it was sixty years ago. This shock sequence that actually shows us the film's monster is one of the vintage cinema's most impressive horror moments and is equivalent in shock to

Chaney's memorable unmasking sequence in THE PHANTOM OF THE OPERA (1925).

THE MYSTERY OF THE WAX MUSEUM clearly defined Lionel Atwill as a leading star of the horror film. For his next film, THE VAMPIRE BAT (1933), the actor portrayed Dr. Otto Von Niemann, a truly mad scientist who fiendishly hypnotizes his butler (played by Robert Fraser) and then compels him to don a black cloak and roam the streets at midnight to seek fresh blood off of innocent victims for his morbid experiments.

THE VAMPIRE BAT offered Atwill the type of role he relished the most, that of a mad scientist with rich dialogue that focuses on his descent to madness. Even Dwight Frye (who starred in DRACULA and FRANKENSTEIN) is featured in a role tailored especially for his talents. Frye portrays Herman, a lunatic who raises pet vampire bats. The actor's role closely resembles his characterization of Renfield, the lunatic in DRACULA (1931). Naturally, Herman is considered the prime suspect responsible for committing the vampire killings, however, the truth comes out during the climax when the film's heroine (played again by Fay Wray) is saved from the demented scientist's clutches by actor Melvyn Douglas.

THE VAMPIRE BAT was Majestic's attempt to capitalize on the success of Universal's DRACULA (1931) by using the word "vampire" in its title. Despite the film's low budget, THE VAMPIRE BAT does offers some great and often melodramatic performances by the cast and slick and fast-paced direction by Frank Strayer. The film's most significant flaw, however, is a result of the dated, melodramatic performances by the cast members; thus THE VAMPIRE BAT holds-up poorly by today's standards.

MURDERS IN THE ZOO (1933) presented Atwill to the public amidst some rather grim subject matter. Unfortunately for Atwill, the film lacked the appealing Gothic style that most of the horror films of its time offered and because of this handicap, the film was not as well received by the masses as say DRACULA (1931) and FRANKENSTEIN (1931). This brings up the question, why DR. X and MYSTERY OF THE WAX MUSEUM, both set against contemporary backdrops, did better than MURDERS IN THE ZOO? This is not to say that MURDERS IN THE ZOO is a poorly-made film. On the contrary. The fast paced thriller directed by Edward Sutherland offers some rather innovative photography and some very credible performances, and much like Atwill's other horror vehicles, the film builds up suspense and momentum straight through to its shocking climax.

In MURDERS OF THE ZOO, Atwill plays a zoologist who fiendishly uses his wild animals to murder his unfaithful wife's (played by Kathleen Burke) lovers. Atwill's performance truly dominates the film as he delivers some very meaty dialogue. Atwill is truly a monster in this film in what is probably his most underrated performance.

Just for the record while we are on the subject of Lionel Atwill - the horror star that never made king, in addition to having played the leading roles of DR. X (1939), THE MYSTERY OF THE WAX MUSEUM (1932), THE VAMPIRE BAT (1933) and MURDERS IN THE ZOO (1933), Atwill also starred in supporting roles in SECRET OF THE BLUE ROOM (1933) involving a murder in an old castle; THE MAN WHO RECLAIMED HIS HEAD (1935) - a classic thriller with Claude Rains and Joan Bennett; Tod Browning's MARK OF THE VAMPIRE (1935) as Inspector Neumann; SON OF FRANKENSTEIN (1939) as Inspector Krogh (and one of the actor's best performances); THE GORILLA (1938) - a horror comedy with the Ritz Brothers; and THE HOUND OF THE BASKERVILLES (1938) - a famous Sherlock Holmes thriller with Basil Rathbone. In addition to these famous 1930's movies, the actor also starred in numerous horror films during the 1940's, all of which are covered in the following chapter.

Lionel Atwill was the horror film star that never became King! However, his popularity continues to grow from generation to generation, and he, in my opinion, has definitely contributed to the genre of vintage horror films equally as much as Boris Karloff, Bela Lugosi and Lon Chaney. Lionel Atwill is a legend in his own right and the epitome of the vintage monster movie star.

CLASSIC EDGAR ALLAN POE MONSTERS!

After completing filming on DRACULA (1931) and after being removed from the production of FRANKENSTEIN (1931), actor Bela Lugosi, who would always and forever be typecast as the mysterious Count Dracula throughout his entire career, went on to star in several tales of the macabre based on the famous literary works of Edgar Allan Poe. In these Universal films, he occasionally starred alongside Boris Karloff.

To clearly understand the events that occurred

during this period in film history, certain facts must be clarified. As we have already established in this chapter, Lugosi had achieved super-stardom in what was already a thirty year career. As the handsome and mysterious new star of Hollywood, the actor was enjoying the success of DRACULA (1931) and had just turned down the part of the monster in FRANKENSTEIN (1931), and we already know how that episode turned out. After loosing his chance to star in the greatest horror film of all time, Lugosi needed a new and original horror hit, and Universal agreed to feature the actor in MURDERS IN THE RUE MORGUE (1932), a new horror film adaptation of Edgar Allen Poe's story.

Universal executives gave the first project, MURDERS IN THE RUE MORGUE (1932), to Lugosi and writer and director Robert Florey as payment for having removed both men off the production of FRANKENSTEIN. It was the studio's way of saying sorry. Both Florey and Lugosi had total control, but ironically, Lugosi was billed under actor Sidney Fox.

MURDERS IN THE RUE MORGUE featured Lugosi, now in curls and slightly overgrown eyebrows, as Dr. Mirakle, a side show hypnotist who commands a gorilla (the film's monster enacted by Charles Gemora) to abduct the film's heroine (Arlene Francis) over the rooftops of Paris. In the film, Dr. Mirakle attempts to cross breed the heroine with the gorilla to prove his theory of evolution. The film proved to be a failure, lost in the wake of FRANKENSTEIN's

Opposite Top: Bela Lugosi as the fiendish Dr. Mirakle in MURDERS IN THE RUE MORGUE (1932).
Opposite Bottom: With the aide of Boris Karloff (Left), Bela Lugosi proceeds to torture an enemy in Universal's THE RAVEN (1936).
Above: A vintage poster from the film THE BLACK CAT (1935).

success, but, once again, this is not to say that the film was poorly made.

Florey's film quite obviously bares a resemblance to Robert Wiene's silent German masterpiece THE CABINET OF DR. CALIGARI (1919) despite the story's roots as a Poe film. Lugosi's performance as Dr. Mirakle, a scientist devoted to his experiments and who calmly murders to achieve his goals, is rather bizarre. In fact, the acting is a bit too much on the melodramatic side for its own good. On the positive side, the film offers the stunning photography of Karl Freund and the images of Lugosi walking through the streets of Paris at night stalking his victims in his carriage are cinematically beautiful for a film from this period. Freund's camera is extremely fluid for 1932, but not even the great cinematography and atmospheric scenes can overshadow the many flaws offered by this vehicle. It is a shame that the film did not receive the notoriety it deserved.

After MURDERS IN THE RUE MORGUE, Lugosi's career began to dwindle and the actor found himself working in low budget serials such as THE WHISPERING GHOST (1933) and THE RETURN OF CHANDU (1934). While Lugosi's career dropped, Boris Karloff's film career began to soar with films like THE MUMMY (1932), THE OLD DARK HOUSE (1932) and THE BRIDE OF FRANKENSTEIN (1935) to his remarkable credit. In 1934 Universal Pictures helped to save Lugosi's declining career by double-billing him with Karloff in another Edgar Allan Poe adaptation. Executives at Universal decided that they could double their income by featuring the names of both Karloff and Lugosi in a new horror picture.

THE BLACK CAT (1934) was cleverly directed by Edgar G. Ulmer (who once served as an art director for German filmmaker F. W. Murnau) and based on the famous short story by Edgar Allan Poe. The film starred Karloff as Avant Garde architect Hjalmar Poelzig - an

43

incarnation of pure evil. Lugosi was the good-spirited Yitus Verdegast. For Karloff, his role as Poelzig was perhaps one of his greatest screen characterizations (aside from the Frankenstein monster), offering the actor rich dialogue and plenty of footage. Lugosi also rose to the occasion in one of his finest screen performances since DRACULA (1931) and in a rare opportunity he portrays a somewhat benevolent but tortured character with sympathetic overtones.

The original script for THE BLACK CAT was written by Peter Ruric and combined both Poe's *The Fall Of The House Of Usher* and *The Black Cat*. However, Ulmer redrafted the story wherein part of the plot was based on *The Black Cat*, while the other part was based on the bizarre life of Aleister Crowley, whose Devil Worshipping activities circulated the tabloids around the time this film was made. THE BLACK CAT is considered a cult classic and a true vintage horror classic. John Mescall's photography provides a bizarre atmosphere that enhances the eeriness of this dynamic little horror classic.

Universal's THE RAVEN (1935), directed by Louis Friedlander from a screen adaptation written by Guy Endore, David Boehm and Jim Tully, was also based on the famous Edgar Allan Poe tale and once again featured the all-to-rare combined talents of Bela Lugosi and Boris Karloff. This time around the roles are reversed and the real villain in THE RAVEN is portrayed by Lugosi, who plays a demented plastic surgeon Richard Vollin. Karloff, on the other hand, plays Edmond Bateman, a fugitive murderer from San Quentin who conveniently arrives into Vollin's life demanding the surgeon give him a new face to hide his identity. In return, Vollin swindles Karloff into carrying-out his mad schemes of torture and murder. Even Karloff's character becomes a victim of Lugosi's madness by the end of this film.

THE RAVEN provided Lugosi with his sole screen opportunity to dominate Karloff. The actor delivered meaty dialogue in what is his best performance next to DRACULA. THE RAVEN is an exceptionally good horror film, and both Karloff and Lugosi are brilliant in their well cast roles. The subplot of how Karloff, once a murderous and lecherous character who is now willing to reform until Lugosi's coverts him back to his old ways for his own reasons, is surprisingly good. In fact, we find ourselves sympathizing with Karloff's murderer. The well written script deals with morality and dual personalities and asks the inevitable question, "who is the real monster?"

WHEN THE DEAD WALK!

Universal Pictures had just begun shooting on FRANKENSTEIN when Paramount announced that Boris Karloff would star in MURDER BY THE CLOCK (1931), a film about a murderer who is himself murdered twice and revived again only to be destroyed once more. Because of a contractual obligations with Universal, Karloff's role went to Irving Pichel.

MURDER BY THE CLOCK (1931), directed by Edward Sloman, beat FRANKENSTEIN (1931) to release, and because of its skillfully planned release date, the film created quite an impact on its audience. Moviegoers had not yet been thrilled by FRANKENSTEIN, therefore MURDER BY THE CLOCK was considered fresh material and its mood, suspense and shocks, That are relatively dated and tame by today's standards, were quite impressive for its time. Unfortunately, this tale of the walking dead immediately became lost in the wake of Universal's big budget horror films.

Bela Lugosi had just completed DRACULA (1931) and MURDERS IN THE RUE MORGUE (1932) for Universal when the Halperin Brothers approached the actor to star in their new independently produced horror film, WHITE ZOMBIE (1932) released by United Artists. Lugosi happily accepted the offer and Victor Halperin directed the film from a screenplay written by Garnett Weston. Lugosi reportedly contributed to the rewriting and filming of certain sequences. The film, considered overly melodramatic by today's standards, was a big success during its initial release primarily due to Bela Lugosi's Mephisto-like character and his restrained performance. Although his character's name was Murder Legendre, his mannerisms were once again much like his mysterious Count Dracula. As the evil sorcerer with penetrating eyes, Murder Legendre exhumes dead bodies to work his sugar cane mills in Haiti. He also manages to frighten and then bewitch a young girl (played by silent star Madge Bellamy) with the aide of his army of walking zombies.

Despite the weak premise, the dreamlike horror film was beautifully photographed by cinematographer Arthur Martinelli and director Halperin's use of lights and shadows are quite impressive for a film of its low budget standards. THE WHITE ZOMBIE is also the first recorded film about zombies. Both Val Lewton's

Above: A vintage poster for THE MUMMY (1932).
Right: Boris Karloff as the mummy in THE MUMMY (1932).

I WALKED WITH A ZOMBIE (1943) and THE SERPENT AND THE RAINBOW (1987) by Wes Craven are adaptations of the same subject matter.

Karl Freund's THE MUMMY (1932) is considered by film historians to be technically superior to both DRACULA (1931) and FRANKENSTEIN (1931). Freund, who was the brilliant cinematographer for both DRACULA (1931) and MURDERS IN THE RUE MORGUE (1932), directed the film for Universal and it is his direction, along with Charles Stumar's photography, that steals the show. Freund's camera is stylishly fluid, much more so than Universal's DRACULA and FRANKENSTEIN. In one of the cinema's most horrifying sequences, the mummy comes to life and moves ever so slowly under the careful and unhurried direction of Freund. This scene was most impressive, but the director's assignment of Boris Karloff as the compassionate and sympathetic mummy is what makes this film so hauntingly moving. As a reincarnated being for whom we feel

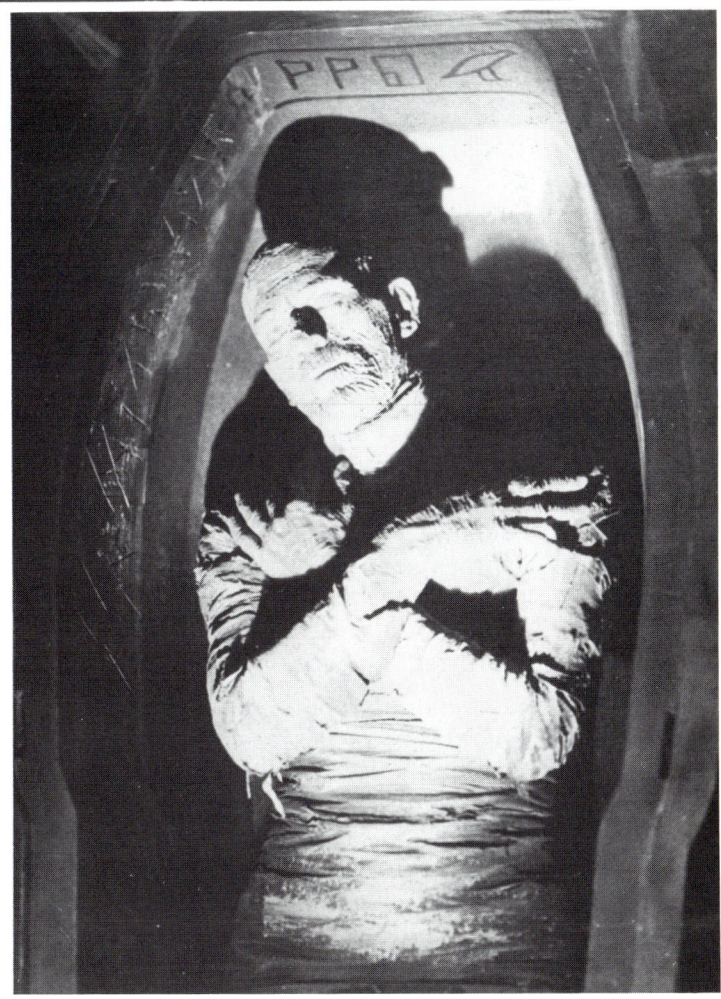

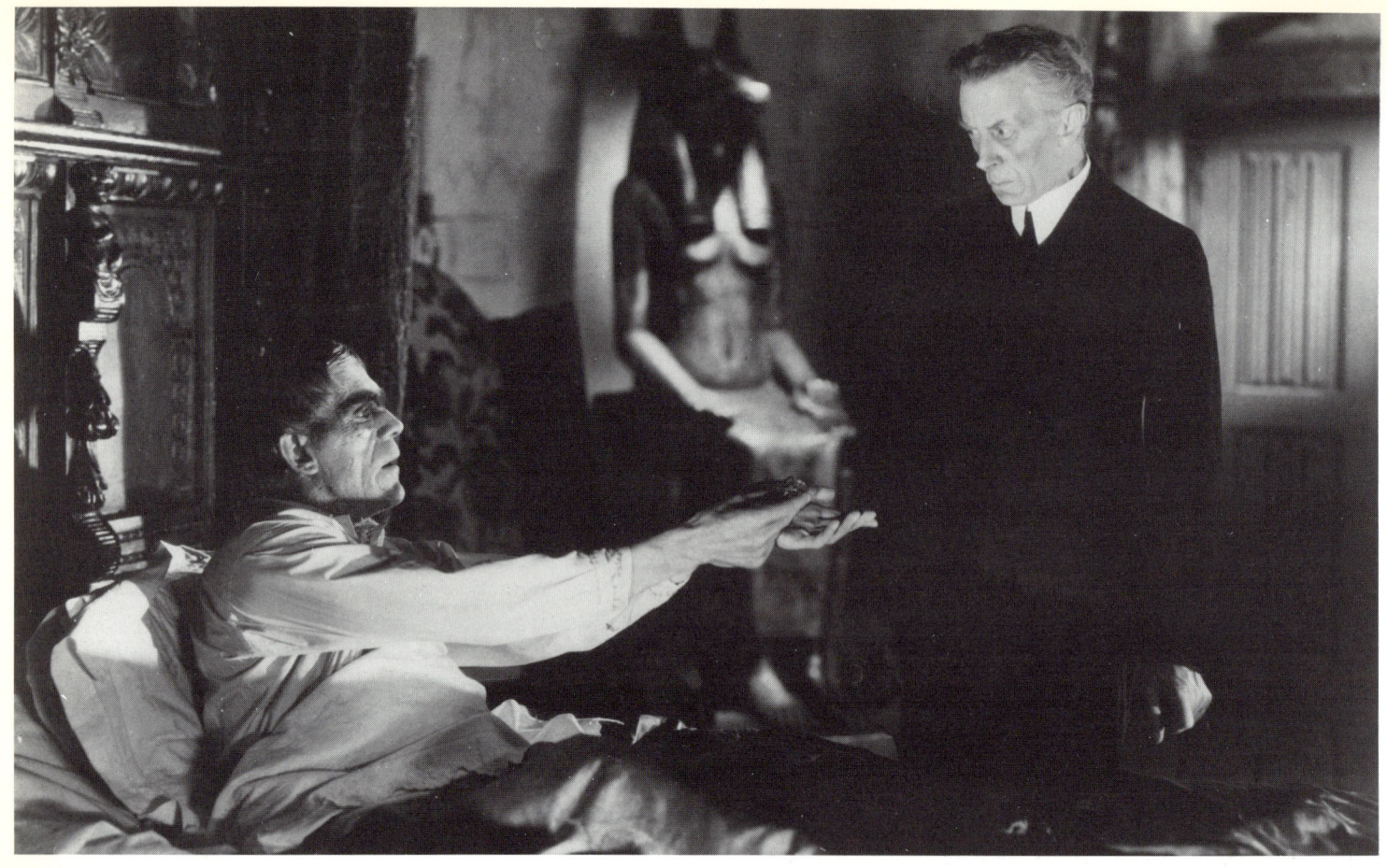

Above: Boris Karloff as the death-stricken Professor Moriant and his faithful butler (played by Ernest Thesiger) in THE GHOUL (1933).
Opposite: A reproduction of an original lobby card from THE WALKING DEAD (1936).

compassion for (unlike the monstrous Chaney, Jr. incarnations of the 1940's), Karloff's restrained mummy characterization is simply brilliant and I cannot help but note that the actor has taken his original Frankenstein monster to bigger and better heights of emotions. Karloff had the natural talent to bring more than life to a movie monster. Freund's decision to cast Edward Van Sloan as a Van Helsing-type authority on Egyptian occult and the supernatural provided a good balance between the forces of good and evil. David Manners is great as the film's hero and savant, while Zita Johann and Bramwell Fletcher are great in their offbeat supporting roles.

This timeless tale of poetic love and horror called THE MUMMY is a masterpiece. THE MUMMY is undoubtedly the definitive walking dead film of the 1930's.

THE GHOUL (1933) was a British-made Gothic horror tale that also starred Boris Karloff. In the film Karloff portrays Professor Moriant, a wealthy eccentric who dabbles in the Egyptian occult. The story, written by Rupert Downing, is slow and haunting and begins when Moriant requests from his faithful butler (played by Ernest Thesiger) that upon his death he be buried with a priceless Egyptian jewel that he believes will bring about his resurrection from the dead after which he will live life eternally. According to Moriant these occurrences would be carried out under the divine powers of the Egyptian God Anubis. As guessed, Moriant dies, and the burial scene that follows is very effective and grim. However, even more frightening is Moriant's resurrection sequence. The professor rises from his grave to seek revenge on those who have defied his tomb and stolen his precious gem. Moriant ultimately recovers the jewel but not until the viewer experiences some very moving moments, both technically and performance wise.

THE GHOUL was atmospherically directed by T. Hayes Hunter for the British-based film company Gaumont. Karloff's performance as the walking dead is closely patterned after his supernatural character in THE MUMMY. Once again, the actor delivers a compassionate and sympathetic monster characterization, one that we, the viewer, cannot help feel pity towards. Even the supporting cast, including Ernest Thesiger, is above par. THE GHOUL is much more of a horror film than THE MUMMY (1932) only because it actually applies horror elements such as shock and suggestive atmosphere to create the basic mood for this film about the supernatural. Most impressive, though, is the unhurried photography of Gunther Krampf, who actually makes good use of the elaborate sets. THE GHOUL never gives into creating a cheap thrill for the sake of commercial purposes. Looking back into film history and unaware of the film's origin, It is very easy for one to believe that the film is actually a product of vintage Hollywood horror.

THE GHOUL is undoubtedly a gem of a horror film from the vintage era and should be recognized as a classic that ranks alongside of DRACULA (1931) and THE BRIDE OF FRANKENSTEIN (1935). I would also go as far as to say that THE GHOUL was perhaps the single most influential film that shaped the premise and look of the Universal "mummy" films of the 1940's - seven years before THE MUMMY'S HAND (1940).

Boris Karloff had just completed filming on Universal's THE INVISIBLE RAY (1936) when he was loaned to Warner Brothers to star in another film in which he is brought back to life after death. The film was THE WALKING DEAD (1936), a classy, stylish little "B" movie competently directed by Michael Curtiz. In the film, Karloff portrays an innocent man who is executed for a murder he did not commit. His fresh corpse is revived by a mad scientist (played by Edmond Gwenn) in a series of remarkably good laboratory scenes straight out of FRANKENSTEIN (1931).

THE WALKING DEAD is actually far superior and more intelligent than its commercial title suggests, however the film remains one of Karloff's most underrated and lessor known horror movies. To say THE WALKING DEAD was produced for a mere $150,000, the film looks as glossy and as grand as the larger-budgeted horror epics from Universal. Most of the film's stylish gloss was unquestionably the result of a fine cast and the craftsmanship and talent of director Michael Curtiz, the genius behind DR. X (1932) and THE MYSTERY OF THE WAX MUSEUM (1933).

HIS MAJESTY KONG!

Looking back in film history, certain movies come to mind as being among the greatest films ever made: GONE WITH THE WIND (1939), WUTHERING HEIGHTS (1939), THE WIZARD OF OZ (1939), CITIZEN KANE (1941), CASABLANCA (1942), LAWRENCE OF ARABIA (1962), DOCTOR ZHIVAGO (1965) and STAR WARS (1977). But one film stands out as being the greatest movie ever made and that film is without a doubt a masterpiece in its own right. The film is KING KONG (1933) an epic film starring the world's greatest movie monster, Kong! To understand the impact that KING KONG continues to have over generations of moviegoers, we must start from the very beginning.

The year 1933 is a very significant year in the history of motion pictures, and particularly the history of vintage monster movies. It was the year KING KONG was released. The film was three years in the making by producers Merian C. Cooper and Ernest B. Schoedsack. In fact the film ended up costing more in time than the $430,000 it cost to make the film. $430,000 was a hefty sum in 1933.

The strange story about a sea expedition led by the fearless filmmaker Carl Denham (Robert Armstrong) to the mysterious, uncharted Skull Island located somewhere in the middle of the Pacific Ocean was originally created by Merian C. Cooper and Edgar Wallace and adapted to the screen by James Creelman and Ruth Rose. But it is the actual basis for the premise of KING KONG that is a timeless common denominator in most vintage horror films, that of " Beauty and The Beast!" It is from this basic concept that the entertaining and captivating film emerges.

Once on Skull Island, the crew (led by actors Armstrong, Bruce Cabot, Fay Wray and others) encounter a primitive colony of natives who (in the cinema's most memorable confrontation between monster and girl) sacrifice Fay Wray (in her greatest role) to their great god Kong! As we all know, King Kong is a fifty-foot tall gorilla who the natives respectfully worship and fear. During the course of this exciting adventure film, some of the crew members are killed off by a number of other prehistoric dinosaurs as they chase the giant gorilla down in an attempt to save the girl. They also manage to capture Kong alive and bring him back to New York where he escapes and causes havoc, finally finding his way to the Empire State Building. It is on top of the skyscraper where the king meets his demise when shot to his death by fighter planes in one of the screen's greatest and most memorable sequences. The story is timeless and well known by all, especially fans of vintage monster movies. Oddly enough, the tale still manages to entertain and fascinate even the newest generations of moviegoers with its remarkable state-of-the-art special effects thanks to the advent of video and modern television programming.

The true star of KING KONG is not Fay Wray, Armstrong or Cabot. The star of the film is indeed King Kong himself and the innovative special effects of stop-motion photographer Willis O'Brien and model-maker Marcel Delgado. Together, the two special effects artists created and gave life to the gorilla known as King Kong. With their revolutionary special effects techniques, they actually made a miniature twelve inch model of Kong appear to be fifty feet tall on film. In fact, in a published interview O'Brien's wife stated that Kong even had some of his creator's mannerisms. Perhaps this is the secret that makes Kong one of cinema's most popular monsters. Kong is frightening as hell while, because of his personality, the fifty-foot beast can be as likeable as Toto from THE WIZARD OF OZ (1939). He is both sympathetic and destructive. But most of all, he is King!

KING KONG was hailed as " The Greatest Film The World Would Ever See!" RKO Pictures produced the film under the direction of Ernest B. Schoedsack and Merian C. Cooper. The studio was very proud of the final production and very pleased by the box office receipts. To this day KING KONG continues to inspire so many sequels, remakes, spin-offs, and variations, none of which can hold a candle to the original.

The success of KING KONG prompted RKO Pictures to hastily produce a sequel that is not nearly as good nor was it nearly as successful as the original. SON OF KONG (1933) was quickly produced and ushered into release in a fraction of the time that it took to produce KING KONG. The sequel cost $250,000 to create, most of which went to the special effects of Willis O'Brien and Marcel Delgado. Actor Robert Armstrong reprised his Carl Denham character, and there were a few recycled scenes left over from the original film that were used-up in the sequel.

SON OF KONG is more of a lighthearted version of the original film, and its title character, Kong, Jr., was used more for fun rather than for horror and shock. Because of the

Above: A real scary moment from the old house thriller THE CAT AND THE CANARY (1939).
Bottom Right: Gloria Stuart is about to have a confrontation with Boris Karloff in James Whale's THE OLD DARK HOUSE (1932).

unfortunate lack of originality on behalf of the premise, the film quickly became lost in the wake of the original's success and popularity. Like THE BRIDE OF FRANKENSTEIN (1935), SON OF KONG could have been a fantastic, well-mounted sequel that could have easily surpassed its predecessor.

OLD DARK HOUSES AND CREEPY CATS!

Old House romps originated as early as the silent era of cinema with classic films like THE CAT AND THE CANARY (1927), THE GORILLA (1927) and the sound film THE TERROR (1928). THE CAT CREEPS (1930) was a sound remake of the 1927 film THE CAT AND THE CANARY. The sound remake follows the plot and trappings of the original film identically. In the film, Neil Hamilton portrays the creepy cat creature who turns out to be nothing more than an eccentric millionaire who tries to scare the film's heroine into giving up here inherited fortune. The entire film directed by Rupert Julian takes place in a creepy old house and the eerie trappings are enhanced by the powerful atmospheric photography of Hal Molar. THE CAT CREEPS is undoubtedly a genuine horror from the old school of horrors.

49

THE CAT CREEPS was remade in 1939 as THE CAT AND THE CANARY (again) by Paramount Pictures under the direction of Elliott Nugent. This film combined the old dark house premise with the comedic talents of actors Bob Hope and Paulette Goddard. In the role of the cat monster was Douglas Montgomery and on hand in solid supporting roles were George Zucco (as the lawyer) and Gale Sondergaard (as the housekeeper), two future movie villains of the 1940's. The setting was switched from upstate New York to the more atmospheric Louisiana swamp. The film was remade the following year as THE GHOST BREAKERS (see chapter three) and in 1978 as THE CAT AND THE CANARY with Carol Lynley.

While Bela Lugosi was filming the independent horror film WHITE ZOMBIE (1932), Boris Karloff was involved in yet another horror masterpiece as the horror heavy in the classic old house romp THE OLD DARK HOUSE (1932).

THE OLD DARK HOUSE is the definitive old house thriller directed by supreme filmmaker James Whale. The film was based on the novel *Benighted* by J. B. Priestley and adapted to the screen by screenwriters R.C. Sheriff and Ben W. Levy. The film depicts the precarious predicament of five travelers, all of whom are caught in a torrential thunderstorm and forced to spend the night at an old dark house inhabited by the most peculiar and mysterious Femm Family.

The film provides the exceptional British cast (intentionally selected and cast by James Whale) beautiful dialogue, and together with the splendid photography and superb sets the film has resulted into becoming a true masterpiece of satirical horror and the apex of old dark house films. As with the case of THE OLD DARK HOUSE, director Whale almost always used British actors for his horror films. In an interview he once said that the reason was very simple. He chose British talent for his horror films because it gave the film authenticity during a time when the horror film was in its infant stages. Whale was very clearly on target with his hypothesis about using British actors in horror films, since he is responsible for four of the greatest vintage monster movies ever made.

Naturally, Karloff plays the film's monster, Morgan, the brute butler for the Femm Family. Although Karloff was aware that he would be billed under actor Raymond Massey (a role that Lugosi would have refused), he was quite wise in accepting the role. The character of Morgan was a key role and with each appearance, the camera would zoom to a close-up of Karloff's face. His few appearances were really built up and given heavy attention to by director and friend James Whale. In fact, Karloff did no more than grunt in the film, but because of his many highlighted entrances and carefully planned close-ups, his performance in the highly successful film helped enhance his career to the status of super-stardom. The celebrated cast also included Raymond Massey, Melvyn Douglas, Charles Laughton, Ernest Thesiger, Gloria Stuart and Eva Moore.

THE GORILLA (1939) was a sound remake of the original silent film of the same title, both of which were based on the famous 1925 Broadway play by Ralph Spence and on the 1927 silent and 1931 sound films from First National about a gorilla who captures its victims around the midnight hour. Before Fox bought the rights to the film, Warner was preparing yet another remake in 1937 with Hugh Herbert and Peter Lorre, but Lugosi stepped-in and replaced Lorre.

The elaborate mystery-thriller was adapted to the screen for Twentieth Century Fox by Rian James and Sid Silvers and tailor-made to suit the mysterious aura of actor Bela Lugosi and the comedy team of the Ritz Brothers. The film could have been a handsome old house thriller second to THE OLD DARK HOUSE and THE CAT AND THE CANARY had only the film's director restrained the silly comedy antics of the Ritz Brothers. In fact, there was a moment prior to the shooting of this film wherein the Ritz Brothers were nearly dropped from the project because they refused to play in another "B" picture. Fox suspended the comics and slapped a $150,000 lawsuit that motivated the comedy team to return to Fox and begin shooting the film. Needless to say, after THE GORILLA, Fox dropped the comedy team from the payroll. Just as a note of record, Lugosi plays the role of a butler in THE GORILLA while the gorilla, created by make-up artists Jack Pierce and Perc Westmore at a price tag of $2,800, is enacted by stuntman Art Mills. The supporting cast included genre great Lionel Atwill as a zoologist.

THE INVISIBLE MONSTER!

After completing both FRANKENSTEIN (1931) and THE OLD DARK HOUSE (1932), acclaimed filmmaker James Whale chose another fantasy-horror tale from Universal's list of future, potential projects. Whale decided to adapt H.G. Wells' famous literary classic *The*

50

Invisible Man to the screen. Keep in mind that THE INVISIBLE MAN (1933), was made two years prior to his masterpiece THE BRIDE OF FRANKENSTEIN (1935) Whale, as a filmmaker, was very confident in himself, even when Universal executives feared the film may bomb based on their narrow-mindedness. Producers simply could not conceive how a monster you could not see be as frightening as the Frankenstein monster of Count Dracula. How narrow-minded they were back in the 1930's. Whale proved them wrong and although the film is not equivalent to his ultimate production THE BRIDE OF FRANKENSTEIN, THE INVISIBLE MAN is undoubtedly one of the most ingenious genre films from the golden era because of many contributing factors, the most obvious of which is the talent of its director.

James Whale created horror from the unseen, something no other filmmaker had accomplished in the past. The monster of THE INVISIBLE MAN was virtually unseen throughout ninety percent of the film. At the same time, the director enjoys poking fun at the genre with witty dialogue from certain cast members, a classic trademark of the director's cinematic style. Together with special effects technician John P. Fulton, Whale was able to create a new monster, one whose vocals were most important. The special effects of Fulton were impressive for its time and still hold up rather well when viewed today. However, there was more to the film's success than the talent of James Whale and the innovative effects of Fulton. There was the voice behind the unseen character.

Actor Claude Rains made his screen debut as the star of THE INVISIBLE MAN, a role originally intended for Boris Karloff. In the film, the actor portrays eccentric scientist Jack Griffin. Prior to starring in THE INVISIBLE MAN, Rains was one of the leading members of New York's Theater Guild and was chosen for the part by Whale mainly because of his strong presence and his distinct voice (the same reason why he won the part for the lead role in Universal's 1943 classic THE PHANTOM OF THE OPERA). Rains was a brilliant actor, and director Whale knew that he would be able to inject the type of emotions and characteristics into the role of the Invisible Man, who, for the most part, would go unseen throughout the majority of the film. Voice and presence were the key factors in bringing the character of Jack Griffin to life and Rains possessed these trademark qualities.

THE INVISIBLE MAN is the incredible story of Jack Griffin, a very dedicated scientist who experiments with a special serum from India that makes his body invisible. Unfortunately, the injection of this drug causes terrible side effects, one of which is madness. Eventually, the crazed scientist becomes bent on using his invisibility to create havoc, murder and mayhem as he attempts to rule the world.

As guessed by director James Whale, Rains was brilliant as the Invisible Man. The actor delivered every well written line better than he had anticipated. In fact, as a result of his performance in THE INVISIBLE MAN, Rain's career skyrocketed, eventually leading to his more notable performances in such vintage classic s as MR. SMITH GOES TO WASHINGTON (1939), CASABLANCA (1941), MR. SKEFFINGTON (1945), NOTORIOUS (1946) and, of more importance to horror genre fans, THE WOLFMAN (1941) and THE PHANTOM OF THE OPERA (1943).

As they still say in Hollywood, "all good monsters never die," as with the case of the Invisible Man. Universal's THE INVISIBLE MAN'S REVENGE (1939) was the first of many sequels and imitations that followed. In the sequel, actor Vincent Price plays Geoffrey Radcliffe, the new Invisible Man!

THE INVISIBLE MAN'S REVENGE was directed by Joe May from a screenplay written by May and Curt Siodmak. The sequel featured all of the mayhem and spectacular special effects of the original film, and although the second film is classified as a "B" movie rather than the Grade "A" film like the original, the sequel continues to hold up rather well with some good atmospheric photography and good dialogue. Actor Vincent Price, like Claude Rains, was chosen for the role because of his distinct voice, which, in the case of Price, would become his trademark in horror films.

THE INVISIBLE MAN and THE INVISIBLE MAN'S REVENGE introduced a new movie monster who would return in various forms during the 1940's and 1950's. But for now, THE INVISIBLE MAN'S REVENGE marked the infamous character's final appearance during the 1930's.

THE HUMAN MONSTERS!

Movies about people who transform into monsters or human monsters had not reached popularity until the successful release of THE WOLFMAN (1941), however, the 1930's offered a couple good films on what was then considered a new subject matter. ISLAND OF

Above: Mad doctor Moreau (Charles Laughton) fends off his monstrous "mansters" in ISLAND OF LOST SOULS (1932).
Left: Richard Arlen and Kathleen Burke are confronted by two of Moreau's monsters in ISLAND OF LOST SOULS.
Opposite Top: The werewolf (Henry Hull) struggles with Warner Oland in WEREWOLF OF LONDON (1935).
Opposite Bottom: Scientist turned werewolf Henry Hull in his laboratory seeking a cure to his condition in WEREWOLF OF LONDON.

53

LOST SOULS (1932) was the first of these films.

ISLAND OF LOST SOULS was more of a science fiction film with monsters rather than a straight-forward, atmospheric horror movie like DRACULA (1931) and THE MUMMY (1932). The film was based on the unusual H.G. Wells story *The Island of Dr. Moreau* and tells how a mad scientist named Dr. Moreau (played by Charles Laughton) produces a breed of creatures that are half man half beast. On occasion, the creatures were able to speak, but for the most part, they were used mostly for fright and occasionally to create sympathy and pity. Even actor Bela Lugosi was involved. The actor, who refused to wear loads of make-up and play "the idiotic monster" in FRANKENSTEIN (1931), has a small part in this film as an ape creature. The role even granted the actor dialogue, which constituted a reason why he should be buried under layers of make-up for this film. As the leader of Moreau's band of monstrosities, Lugosi delivers a touching performance

Actor Charles Laughton is well cast as the insensitive scientist Dr. Moreau, and it is he who steals the show in this film; something Lugosi despised, for he had his eyes on the lead role. The adaptation of H.G. Wells novel by Phillip Wylie and Waldemar Young is quite good and still frightening by today's standards, more so than the recent remake THE ISLAND OF DR. MOREAU (1978). ISLAND OF LOST SOULS was stylishly directed by Erle C. Kenton and photographed by famous cinematographer Karl Struss.

Universal was the first to bring the word "werewolf" to the attention of moviegoers. During the height of the first cycle of horror movies from Hollywood, Universal produced the first legitimate tale of lycanthropy, THE WEREWOLF OF LONDON (1935). The film was originally announced as THE WOLFMAN and was originally to star Boris Karloff (ironically, Karloff never played a werewolf in his entire career). Karloff was dropped from the project to begin production on THE BRIDE OF FRANKENSTEIN (1935). Even actor Bela Lugosi was turned down for the lead part of floriculturist Dr. Glendon. Thus the role went to actor Henry Hull, who was selected by the film's director Stuart Walker.

THE WEREWOLF OF LONDON is a very simple tale by today's standards. The film tells how Dr. Glendon is attacked by a werewolf in Tibet while studying a rare species of plant life. Actor Werner Oland (star of several Charlie Chan classics) was cleverly chosen to play the mysterious Dr. Yogami, an Oriental doctor who actually turns out to be the original werewolf that attacks Dr. Glendon during the beginning of the film (the role of Yogami was Lugosi's second choice after he had been turned down when he requested to play the role of Glendon, but the director chose Werner Oland instead of Bela. Poor Lugosi).

Hull, a newcomer to the genre, was actually quite good as Universal's new monster. The werewolf make-up by Jack Pierce and the transformation sequences were rather innovative for its time. The screenplay by Robert Harris intelligently combines the European folklore with the already-familiar Jekyll and Hyde theme. Because of the similarities between the laboratory scenes in this film with that of the Stevenson novel, we see Dr. Glendon as a Dr. Jekyll-Mr.. Hyde persona rather than the Wolfman that we have learned to expect from the later Chaney films. This was clever scripting on Harris's behalf because it gave the supernatural occurrences a scientific explanation that audiences were already familiar with and could relate to. Audiences of 1935 were just not ready to accept a man that could transform into a beast due to a curse or spell and even Universal was not prepared to bank their investment on that concept. Instead, Harris developed a scientific approach to the curse known as lycanthropy, which is all relative by today's standard, depending on which film you have just seen. Unfortunately, THE WEREWOLF OF LONDON became lost in the wake of the enormous success and publicity created by THE BRIDE OF FRANKENSTEIN (1935). Universal did not touch the subject matter again until 1941.

MAD MEN AREN'T ALWAYS SCIENTISTS!

The 1930's had its share of madmen and not all of them were scientists like Dr. Frankenstein, Dr. Moreau and Dr. Jekyll. In CHANDU THE MAGICIAN (1932), Bela Lugosi portrayed Roxor, a real devil of a madman who attempts to rule the world with the help of his flashy apparatus (all created by special effects and camera photography). The film serial, directed by William Cameron Menzies and Marcel Yarnell was Fox's version of MGM's flashy film THE MASK OF FU MANCHU (1932).

THE MASK OF FU MANCHU was Samuel Goldwyn's elaborate thriller in which Boris Karloff portrayed the Oriental genius as another madman bent on conquering the world. The film was lavishly illuminated with all the gloss

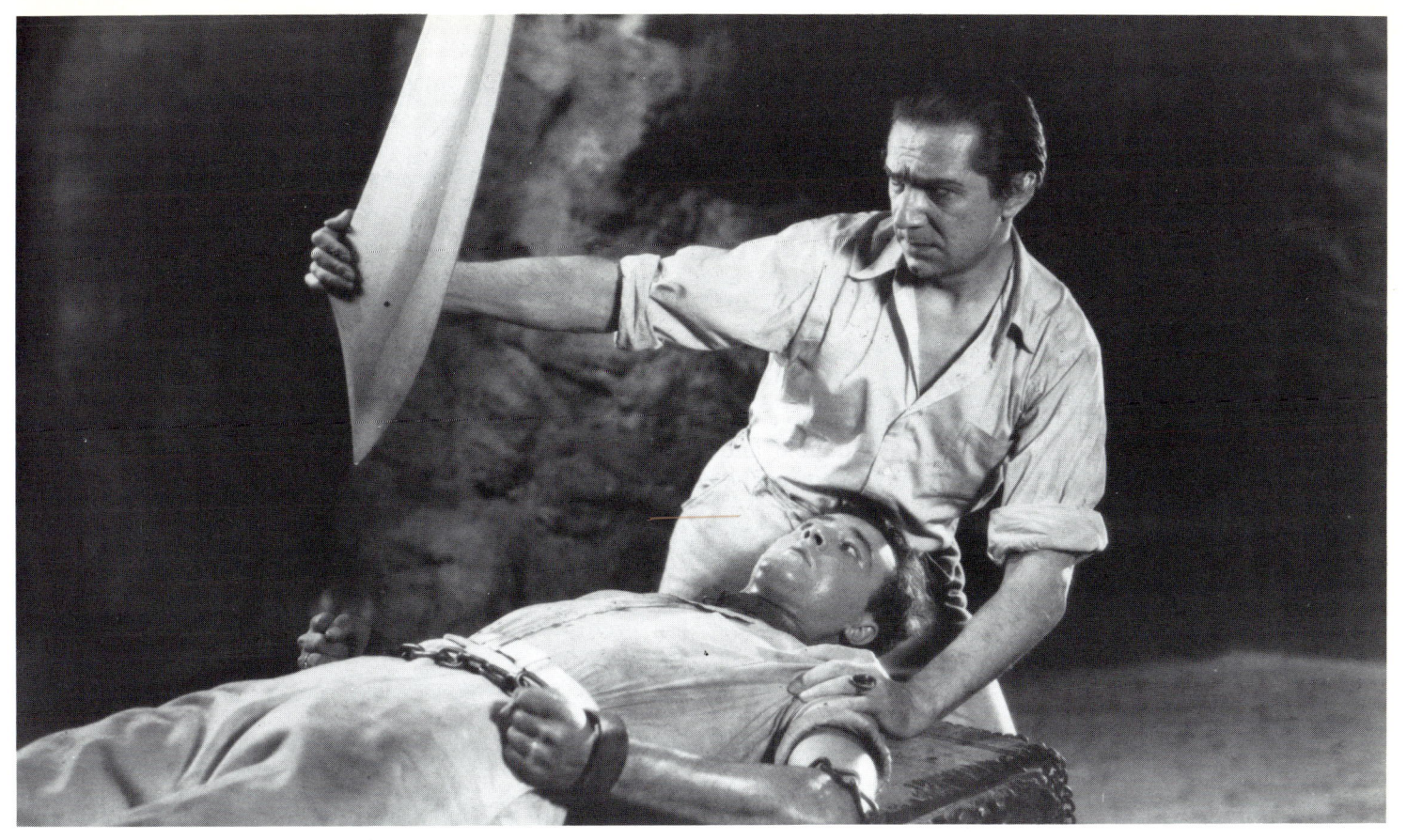

Above: Bela Lugosi as Dr. Frank Chandler, otherwise known as Chandu, a master of the occult in THE RETURN OF CHANDU (1934), a twelve part serial made by Principal Films.

and big bucks that MGM could possibly provide. The same could not be said for the overly dramatic film serial THE RETURN OF CHANDU (1934) in which Bela Lugosi plays Chandu, master of the occult. Lugosi was delighted to be cast in a non-villainous role. In the film, Chandu saves a mysterious princess from death by sacrifice at the hands of a fanatical cult. The film was far-fetched and ludicrous.

One of the 1930's greatest horror thrillers from the vintage era was Fritz Lang's M (1932). The film introduced us to one of the cinema's most demented and mentally-warped characters enacted by Carpathian-born actor Peter Lorre. Lorre's diabolical child murderer who terrorizes the village of Dusseldorf is absolutely brilliant. During the film's exciting climax, the criminals of the underworld hunt Lorre down and do him in. Lorre was indeed a monster in this film and as a result, he became recognized throughout the world for his peculiar characteristics and his bizarre acting style. The Fritz Lang film was based on a true story that appeared in a Berlin newspaper. The film's success led to the actor's international stardom.

THE MOST DANGEROUS GAME (1932) is another classic from the vintage era that featured yet another demented character. In the film, Leslie Banks portrays a Russian game hunter who hunts human game as a sport. Fay Wray and Joel McCrea play the film's hero and heroine and Bank's latest victim. The film, based on Richard Connell's award-winning short story, was produced by David O'Selznick for RKO. O'Selznick was responsible for producing many of the screen's greatest films.

Paramount contributed to the sub-genre with a big budget remake of its own 1920 silent classic DR. JEKYLL AND MR. HYDE (1932). The 1932 remake was the first of many sound versions of the famous Robert Louis Stevenson tale and was directed by Rouben Mamoulian from a brilliant screen adaptation written by Samuel Hoffenstein and Percy Heath. Top billing went to Frederic March, who played the celebrated dual role. In fact, the actor won an Academy Award for his brilliant performance. In addition to the Oscar for best actor of 1932, the film received high recognition for the lavish photography of Karl Struss.

DR. JEKYLL AND MR. HYDE was Paramount's answer to Universal's DRACULA (1931) and

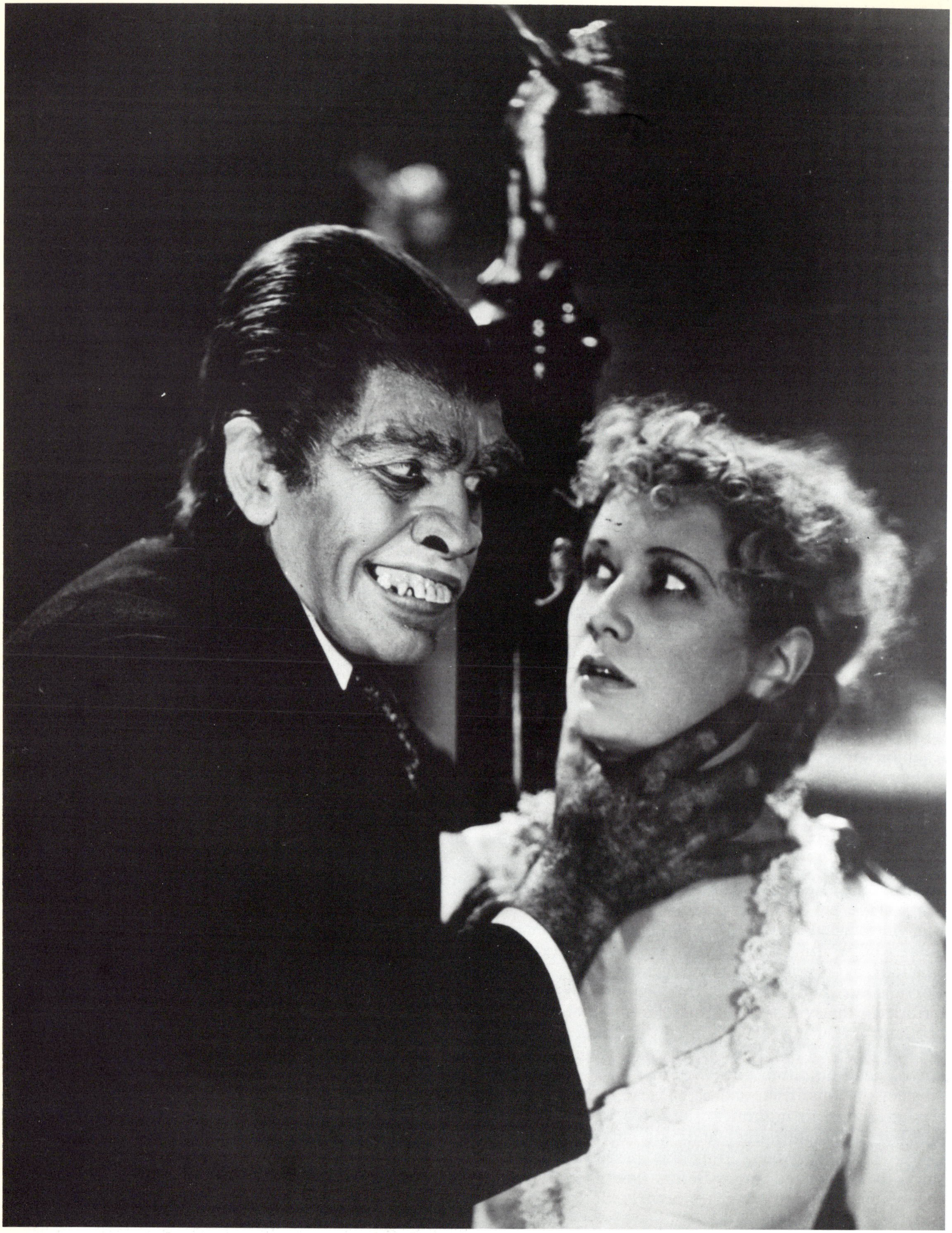

Opposite Page: Frederic March as Mr. Hyde with Miriam Hopkins in Paramount's DR. JEKYLL AND MR. HYDE (1932).
Above: A vintage poster for THE INVISIBLE RAY (1936).

FRANKENSTEIN (1931). In fact, because Paramount still owned the film rights to the Stevenson novel, Universal was unable to produce a version of their own, which is something they terribly hoped to do with Boris Karloff in mind for the dual role (it was not until 1953 when Karloff took on the dual role for Universal in ABBOTT AND COSTELLO MEET DR. JEKYLL AND MR. HYDE - see chapter four). Just as a note of nostalgic interest, actor Irving Pichel was originally chosen to play the dual role for Paramount, but director Mamoulian argued that he wanted an actor who could play the dual role, not just the character of Hyde! In any event, the director made a very wise casting decision by choosing March over Pichel. March's Jekyll and Hyde characterization has gone down in movie history as being brilliant.

MAD LOVE (1935) is yet another brilliant and highly unrecognized horror film from the vintage era. The film, masterfully directed by Karl Freund, was a bizarre contemporary-style thriller based on the classic novel *The Hands of Orlac* written by Maurice Renard. To begin with, the Renard novel was adapted to the screen by some of filmdom's most talented screenwriters: Guy Endore, John L. Balderston and P.J. Wolfson. Furthermore, the film was handsomely produced on a solid budget and featured fascinating set designs and the atmospheric and very fluid photography of Chester Lyons (under the careful supervision of Freund). Finally, the film starred the very talented Peter Lorre in yet another one of his bizarre characterizations. In this film, the actor portrays Dr. Gogol, a very sinister, sadistic figure with the eyes of death and the presence of mental rot and decadence. In the film, the mad Dr. Gogol believes that each man should kill the one person he loves the most.

The basic premise, however, follows the original novel and silent film closely, as Dr. Gogol grafts the hands of a murderer onto the arms of famous concert pianist Stephen Orlac (played magnificently by Colin Clive), whose original hands are destroyed in a horrible train wreck. Gogol commits ghastly murders and makes poor Orlac believe that the murderer's hands have taken control and that he has perpetrated the heinous crimes. Of course, the police authorities do not take kindly to Orlac's story, nor do they believe that such a renown surgeon could ever commit such crimes. The demented surgeon does all this to win the love of Orlac's wife (played by Frances Drake), but during the tension-filled climax, Gogol captures his love and begins to strangle her with her locks of hair. It is ironic that the hands Gogol sadistically grafted onto Orlac are the very devices that Orlac uses to kill the surgeon and save his wife.

MAD LOVE is downright brilliant and is unfortunately one of filmdom's greatest and most underrated horror films. Freund provides images and moments of horror and suspense unequalled to this day. The scene in which Gogol disguises himself as the murderer Rollo is the film's most horrifying moment. Lorre is dressed in black cloak, scarf and hat with a metallic neck brace, metallic hands and a sneer that would make Conrad Veidt's fearsome Gwynplaine from THE MAN WHO LAUGHS (1928) look tame. How could anyone overlook this Karl Freund classic?

After Universal's THE BLACK CAT (1934), THE GIFT OF GAB (1934), and THE RAVEN (1935), Boris Karloff and Bela Lugosi teamed up again to star in THE INVISIBLE RAY (1936), excellently directed by Lambert Hillyer. In this fabulous science fiction thriller from Universal, Karloff portrays a scientist who is inadvertently transformed into a mad killer by way of a toxic poison called Radium X. Lugosi, once again billed under Karloff, played the humanitarian part of Karloff's colleague and friend Dr. Bennett, who attempts to find a cure for Karloff's condition. Although Karloff's compassionate performance is larger than Lugosi's part, Lugosi delivers a restrained performance equally important. The film marked Lugosi and Karloff's final collaborative effort for Universal, cast amidst a backdrop of flashy special effects by John P. Fulton. The film's director cleverly and successfully combined horror with science fiction to create this mild classic, a formula that would endlessly be imitated by later science fiction films.

Prior to THE INVISIBLE RAY, Karloff played twins in THE BLACK ROOM (1935) for Columbia Pictures. In the film, one of the twins is a sadistic murderer that tries to pin the wrap on his brother. The stylish film was directed by Roy William Neill from a screenplay by Arthur Strawn. Curiously, Columbia's quartet of horror films with Karloff that began in 1939 did not match the quality of this earlier vehicle

Opposite: Bela Lugosi as the mad Dr. Orloff with his blind monster (Wilfred Walter) and victim (Greta Gynt) in DARK EYES OF LONDON (1939).
Above: Boris Karloff about to do-in Katherine deMille in THE BLACK ROOM (1935).
Right: Boris Karloff as Mord the executioner from Universal's TOWER OF LONDON (1939).

and the studio never did anything like it again.

Karloff delivers an excellent dual performance and it is unfortunate that the film, an original piece of filmmaking for its time, continues to go unrecognized.

THE DARK EYES OF LONDON (1939) was a superior British film from Pathe directed by Edgar Wallace. The film starred Bela Lugosi as a ruthless and sinister insurance swindler named Dr. Orloff. In the film he drowns his victims and disposes of their bodies in the Thames River and then collects on their insurance. Orloff is aided by a blind, giant monster (played by Wilfred Walter), whose physical ugliness actually mirrors the ugliness of Orloff's own inner soul. What a perfect combination.

The film, released in America as THE HUMAN MONSTER, still holds up rather well today. Lugosi is brilliant as the unsympathetic and diabolical villain, while Walter's performance as the brute monster is sympathetic and moving. The film was one of the better products of the horror cycle of the 1930's produced by the same company that featured Boris Karloff in THE GHOUL (1933), another superior horror film.

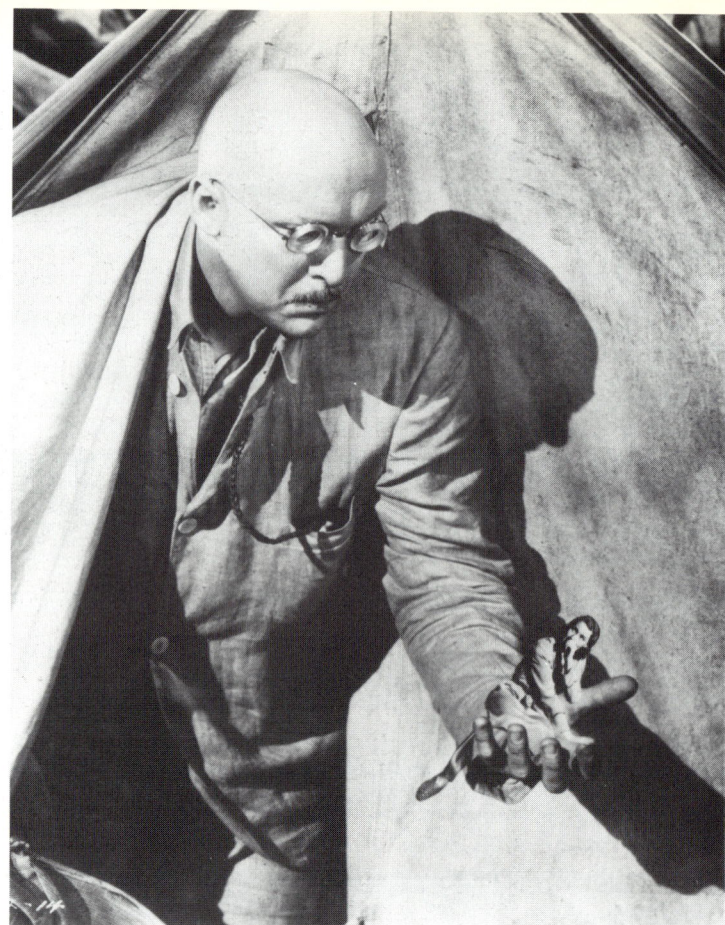

For his next project, Lugosi returned to Universal to film a shoddy 12-part serial entitled THE PHANTOM CREEPS (1939). In the serial, Lugosi plays Dr. Zorka, a completely mad scientist who, like Fu Manchu, has ultimate plans of ruling the world. The shoddy serial was directed on a shoe-string budget by Ford Bebe.

Tod Browning's DEVIL DOLL (1936) and Ernest B. Schoedsack's DR. CYCLOPS (1939 - 1940) were both fascinating and entertaining films that featured some pretty bizarre characters. Both films combined the themes of animal and human miniaturization with madness; a premise that was virtually new during the 1930's.

Tod Browning's DEVIL DOLL is the superior of the two films from a technical point of view. The film was stylishly photographed by Leonard Smith. Smith's combined use of lighting and camera effects with the special set designs created for this film in which oversized furniture was used and matched up with the supposedly miniaturized cast, was innovative and eye-catching. Today we take such effects for granted after having been flooded with a multitude of science fiction and horror films about miniaturization such as THE INCREDIBLE SHRINKING MAN (1957) and HONEY I SHRUNK THE KIDS (1989). DEVIL DOLL was far before its time.

The DEVIL DOLL was the clever story of how a very successful financier (Lionel Barrymore) and a scientist (Henry B. Walthall) escape from their imprisonment on Devil's Island. The pair eventually reach the scientist's hideout where Barrymore learns that Walthall has developed a serum that will miniaturize anything or anyone. Equipped with the powerful potion, Barrymore tracks down his three crooked partners, all three of which were responsible for wrongly and unjustly sending him to prison. With the serum, Barrymore goes a bit off the handle and miniaturizes them to doll size. After completing the task he set out to do, the powerful serum begins to have effects of grandeur and power over the financier's mind, and soon he is contemplating how he could use the potion to rule the world.

DEVIL DOLL is considered by many film

Opposite Left: Bela Lugosi as the mad Dr. Zorka and his diabolical creation in THE PHANTOM CREEPS (1939).
Opposite Right: Albert Dekker as the mad Dr. Cyclops in RKO's DR. CYCLOPS (1939).
Above: A reproduction of a lobby card for the film DR. CYCLOPS.

historians as being Tod Browning's best work, which says a lot when you consider the many fine films he is responsible for.

Unlike Browning's DEVIL DOLL which establishes plenty in the way of well-written dialogue and focuses closely on Barrymore's declining mental state and his bent revenge schemes, DR. CYCLOPS focuses more on special effects and the miniaturization of its characters and less by way of interesting dialogue or character development. No doubt that when director Ernest B. Schoedsack set out to make this film he was mainly concerned with creating another KING KONG (1933). As a result, the film falls short in delivering a very menacing title character- Dr. Cyclops (played by Albert Dekker). Dekker's one dimensional performance as the mad scientist lacks the menace and presence that Boris Karloff or Lionel Atwill would have injected into the role. In trying to create an innovative science-fiction shocker, Schoedsack used a backdrop color of Technicolor green, but the effect did not achieve the mood the director strived for. Instead the poor use of bright green Technicolor robbed the film of its menace and horror overtones. The film would have been better as a flat black and white picture.

In 1939, Boris Karloff signed up at Columbia Pictures to star in several mad scientist films, the first of which was THE MAN THEY COULD NOT HANG (1939). In the film, Karloff plays Dr. Henryk Savaard, an inventor who creates a mechanical heart designed to bring life back to the dead. Savaard tries to revive his dead daughter with the mechanical heart, but the end result only brings destruction to the hapless and devoted scientist. Columbia followed-up THE MAN THEY COULD NOT HANG with THE MAN WITH NINE LIVES (1940), BEFORE I HANG (1940), THE DEVIL COMMANDS (1941) and THE BOOGIE MAN WILL GET YOU (1942), all of which starred Boris Karloff before he defected to Broadway to star in the famous play *Arsenic and Old Lace*.

TOWER OF LONDON (1939) made by Universal featured Boris Karloff as the mad executioner Mord and Basil Rathbone as King Richard III. The film was more of a historical drama and less a horror film, but Karloff's performance as a madman is exquisite.

A NEW STAR ON THE HORIZON

As early as 1937, RKO Pictures and David O'Selznick was planning an elaborate remake of the 1923 silent classic THE HUNCHBACK OF NOTRE DAME with Lon Chaney, Sr. Originally, O'Selznick and famed director William Dieterle had plans of featuring up and coming star Lon Chaney, Jr. in the infamous title role that his father once made famous. At the time, the actor, born on February 10, 1906, had only bits in dozens of films and he had not yet achieved recognition for his performance in John Steinbeck's OF MICE AND MEN (1939). Thus the role went to accomplished actor Charles Laughton. Needless to say, Laughton delivered a magnificent performance as Quasimodo, the hunchback. Laughton's characterization was both horrifying and sympathetic. The film is considered a masterpiece by many film historians and would have been a fabulous beginning for Lon Chaney's career had he won the part. Instead, the actor continued to star in bit roles until the early 1940's, when he finally found stardom as Universal's newest horror film star (see chapter three).

ONE LAST LOOK BACK!

By the closing of the 1930's, it was very clear that the vintage monster movie was a bankable commodity in Hollywood. Furthermore, it was very clear that Lionel Atwill, Bela Lugosi and Boris Karloff were very bankable stars, despite Universal's on-going struggle with Lugosi. It was also very clear that Boris Karloff was King, and both Lugosi and Atwill were second fiddle, although I do not think Atwill really cared, for he mostly enjoyed being involved in horror pictures simply because he relished delivering the meaty dialogue of a raving madman. Finally, it was very clear that Universal was the leading force behind the first cycle of Hollywood horror films. Films like DRACULA (1931), FRANKENSTEIN (1931), THE MUMMY (1932), THE INVISIBLE MAN (1933), WEREWOLF OF LONDON (1935) THE RAVEN (1935) and THE BRIDE OF FRANKENSTEIN (1935) reached heights of popularity unimaginable. These films influenced rival studios to cash in on the horror film market and soon Warner Brothers released THE MYSTERY OF THE WAX MUSEUM (1933) and THE WALKING DEAD (1936); Paramount released DR. JEKYLL AND MR. HYDE (1932) and ISLAND OF LOST SOULS (1932); MGM released THE MASK OF FU MANCHU (1932), MAD LOVE (1935) and MARK OF THE VAMPIRE (1935); and Columbia released THE MAN THEY COULD NOT HANG (1939). And let us not forget the granddaddy of all fantastic films, RKO's KING KONG (1933).

The 1930's was an exciting decade for the horror film, especially for the vintage monster movie. It was a decade of experiments, trial and error and fascinating and innovative cinematic accomplishments. It is undoubtedly one of this author's favorite periods from the genre of horror films. It was the golden era.

One Last look back to the monster movies of 1930's!
Opposite Page: Frederic March as the evil Mr. Hyde in DR. JEKYLL AND MR. HYDE (1932).
Above Left: Boris Karloff (right) in THE MAN THEY COULD NOT HANG (1939).
Above Right: Boris Karloff as THE MAN WHO LIVED AGAIN (1936).
Right: Claude Rains as Jack Griffin in THE INVISIBLE MAN (1933).

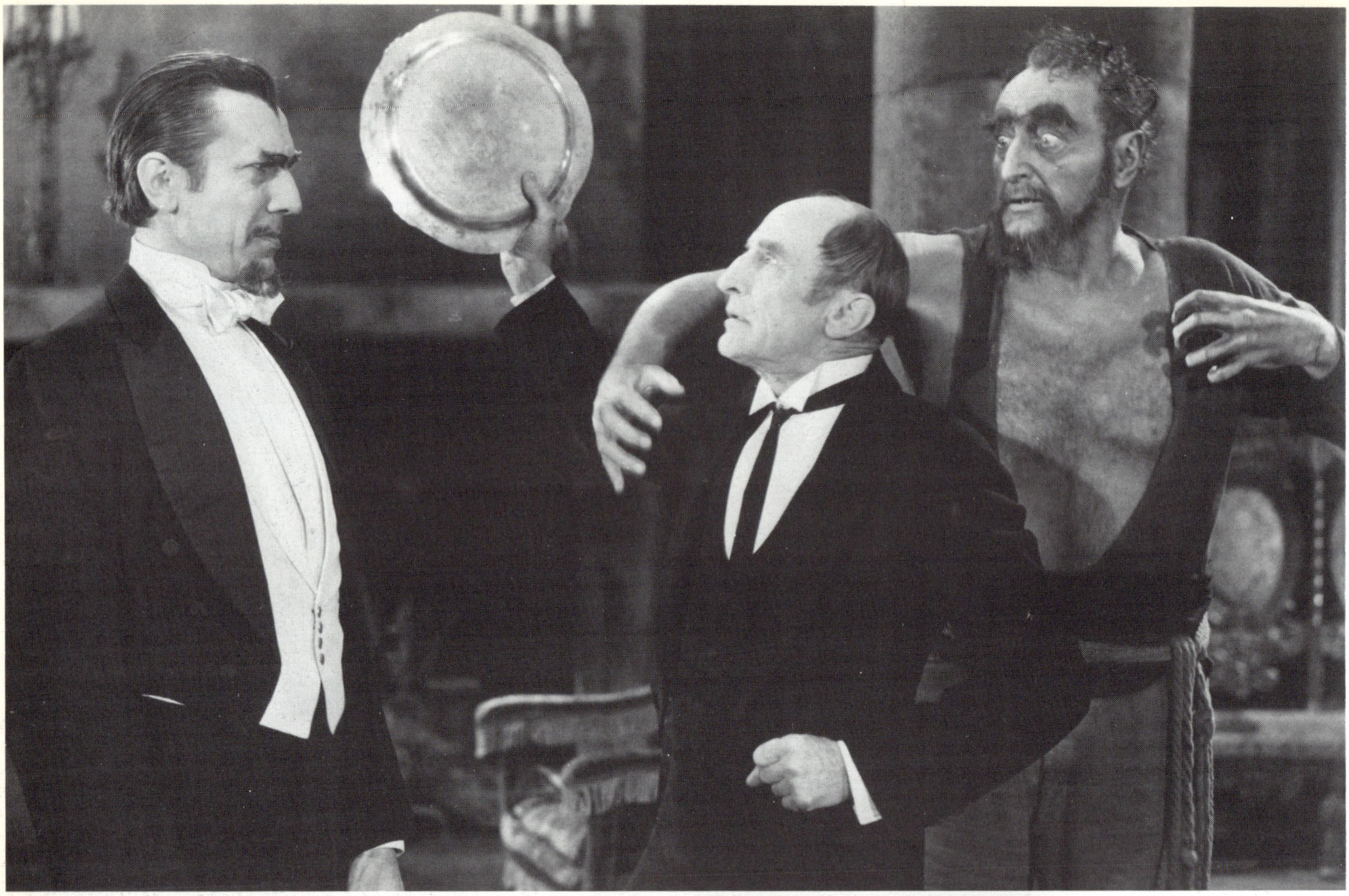

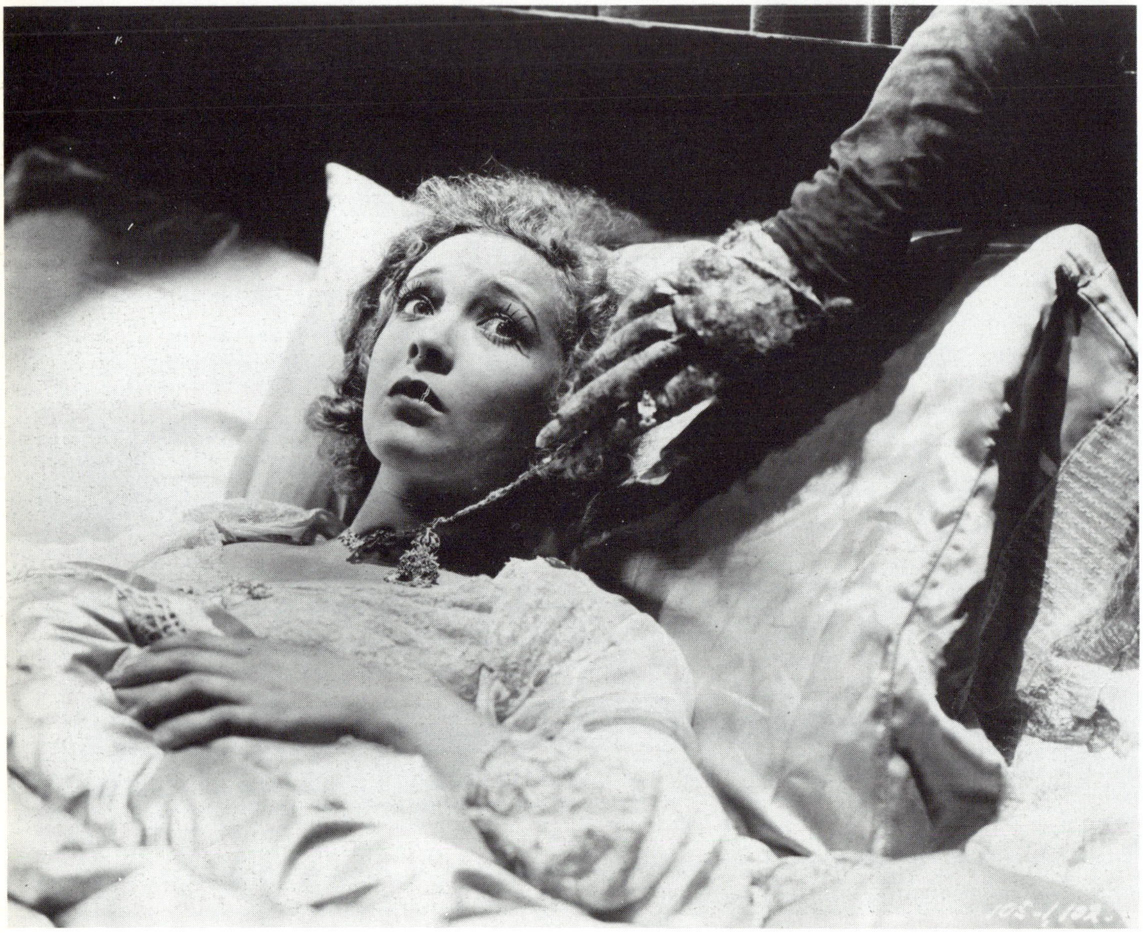

The vintage monster movie holds many moments of suspense.
Opposite Top: Bela Lugosi (right) and his zombie (left) prepare to murder another victim in WHITE ZOMBIE (1932).
Opposite Bottom: A very suspenseful moment from THE CAT CREEPS (1930).
Above: Boris Karloff reaches for Gloria Stuart in THE OLD DARK HOUSE (1932).
Right: Claude Rains (right) tries to hide his identity in this tense moment from THE INVISIBLE MAN (1933).

The first cycle of horror films from Universal Pictures are considered by film historians to be the vintage era's better productions. Among the best of the films from the first cycle are DRACULA (1931), FRANKENSTEIN (1931), THE MUMMY (1932) and DRACULA'S DAUGHTER (1936).
Above: Bela Lugosi's Count Dracula cowers from Professor Van Helsing (Edward Van Sloan) and his crucifix in Tod Browning's DRACULA (1931).
Left: Gloria Holden's vampire dies at the mercy of a wooden arrow in DRACULA'S DAUGHTER (1936).
Opposite Top: Boris Karloff's mummy prepares to sacrifice Zita Johann to the great god Anubis in THE MUMMY (1932).
Opposite Bottom: An incredibly tense moment from James Whale's masterpiece FRANKENSTEIN (1931) in which Colin Clive, Edward Van Sloan and Dwight Frye restrain the monster (Boris Karloff).

67

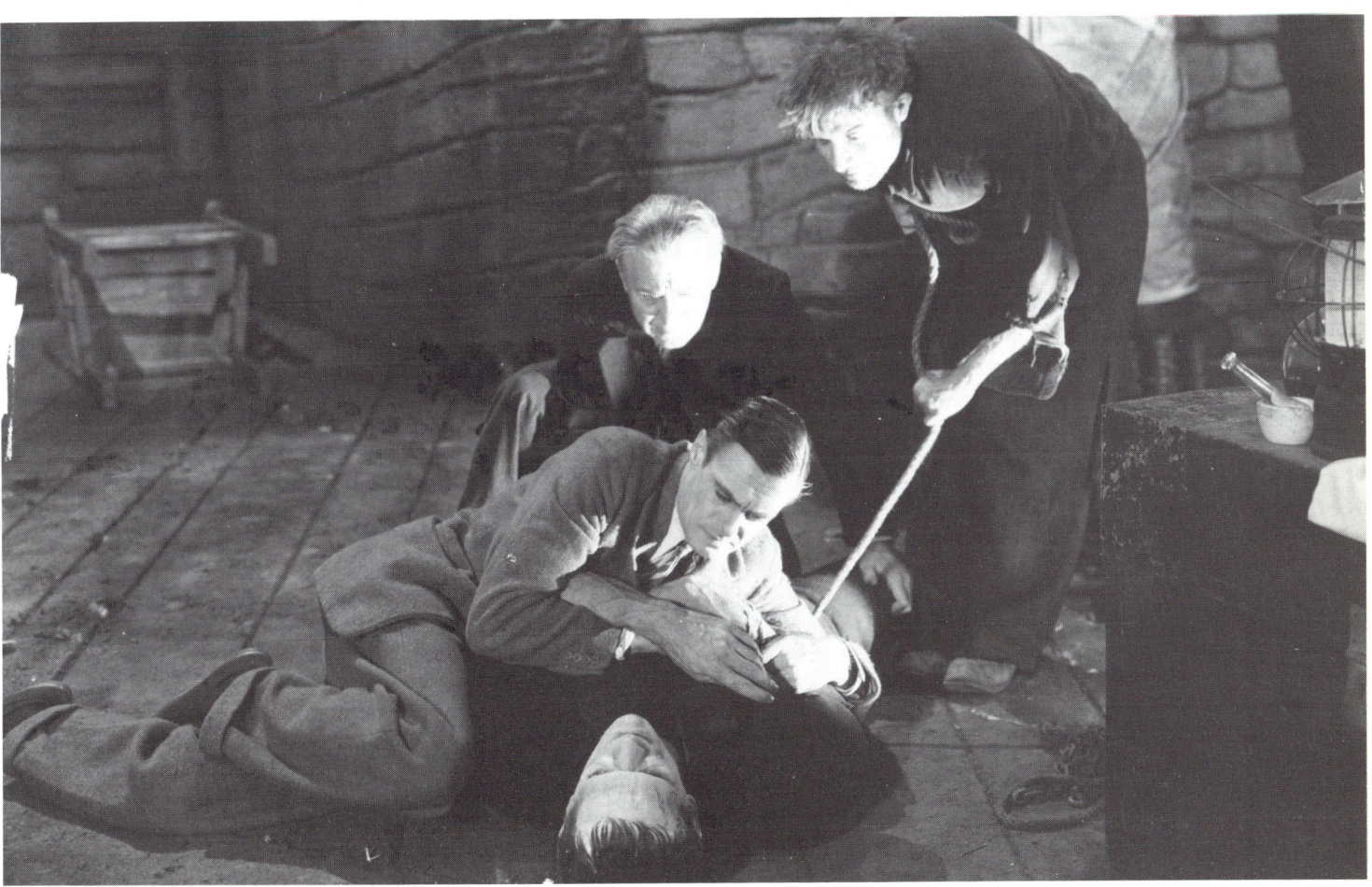

The EDGAR ALLAN POE
MYSTERY SHOW!
Boris KARLOFF
Bela LUGOSI
The RAVEN
IRENE WARE
INEZ COURTNEY
LESTER MATTHEWS
A Realart Picture
Released by
FILM CLASSICS, INC.

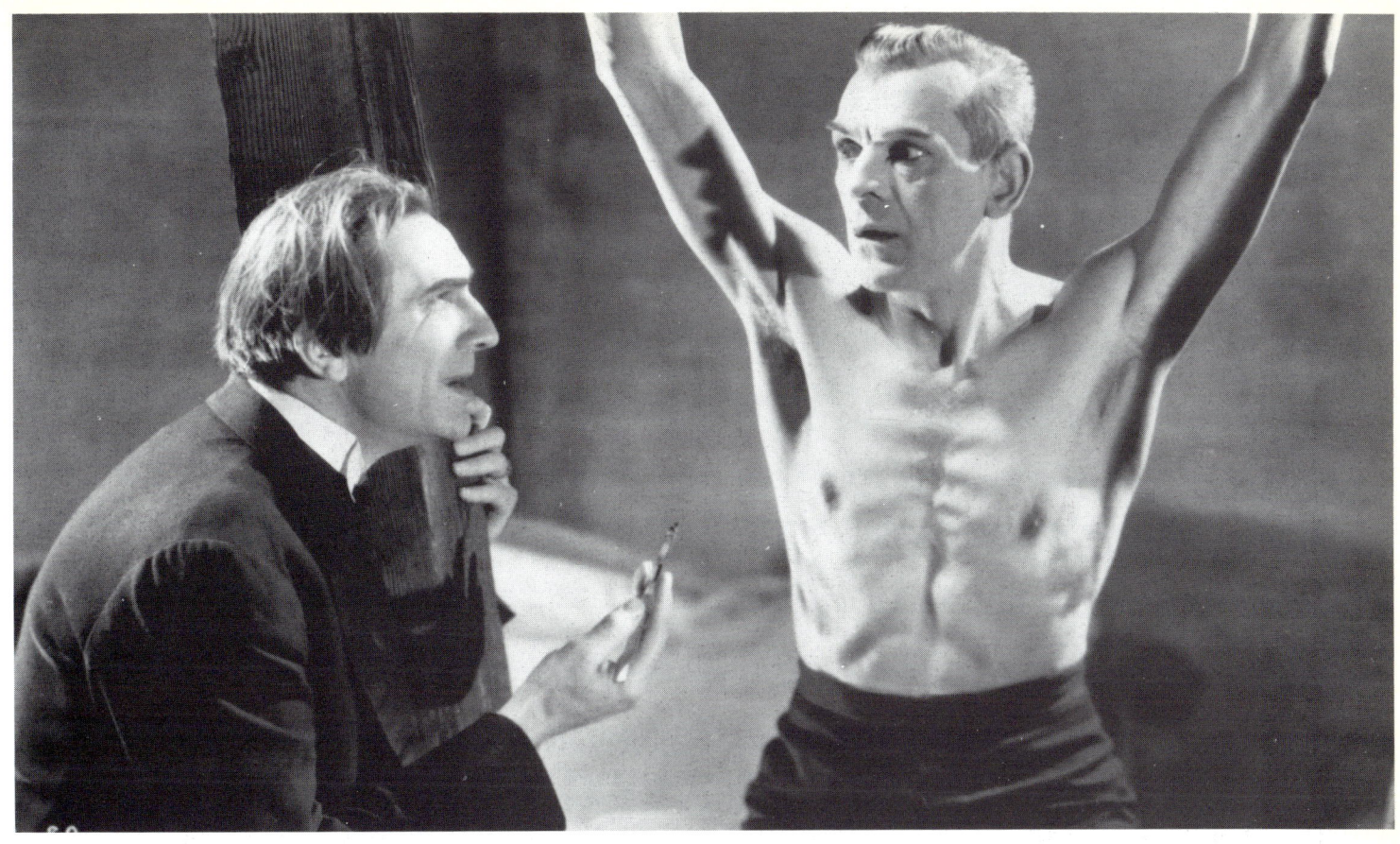

More Edgar Allan Poe horrors!
Opposite Top: A vintage poster for THE RAVEN (1936).
Opposite Bottom: Boris Karloff (Left) and Bela Lugosi (Right) engaged in a battle to the finish in THE BLACK CAT (1935).
Above: The roles are now reversed. Bela Lugosi has Boris Karloff right where he wants him in THE BLACK CAT (1935).
Right: The murderous ape abducts another victim in MURDERS IN THE RUE MORGUE (1932).

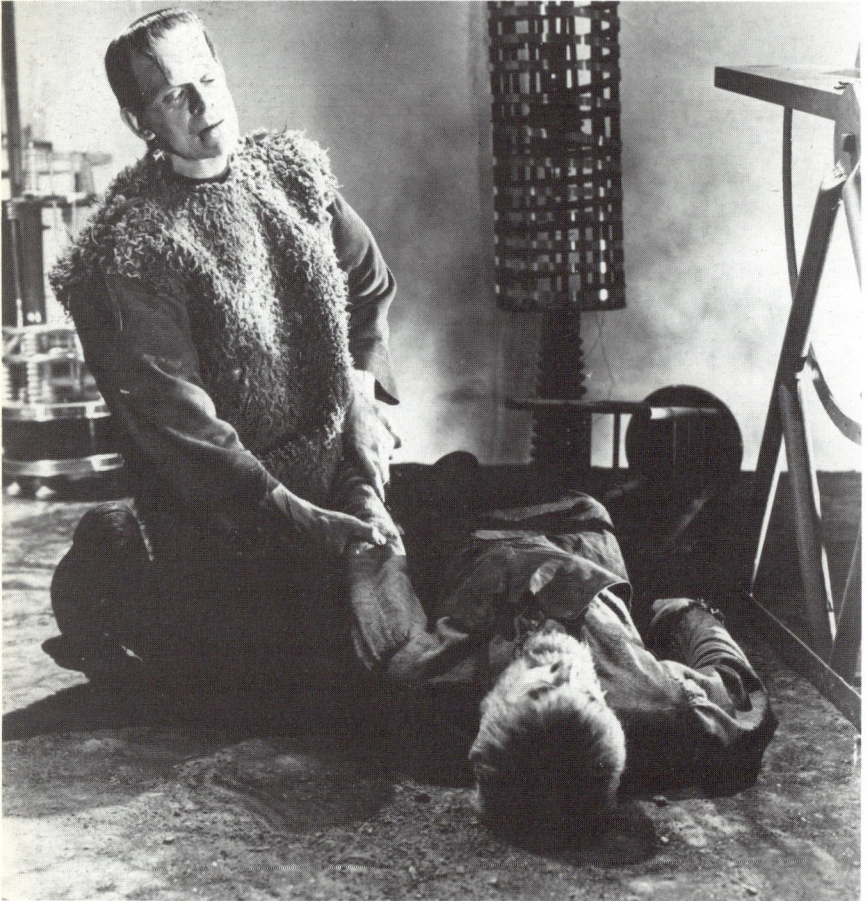

Boris Karloff is undoubtedly the best of all the screen Frankenstein monsters. His characterizations are both frightening and sympathetic. No other actor has ever been able to match Karloff's tragic monster.
Above: The monster (Karloff) tries to befriend his newly created mate (Elsa Lanchester) in THE BRIDE OF FRANKENSTEIN (1935).
Left: The monster (Karloff) mourns the death of his friend Ygor (Bela Lugosi) in SON OF FRANKENSTEIN (1939).
Opposite: The monster (Karloff) from the original masterpiece FRANKENSTEIN (1931).

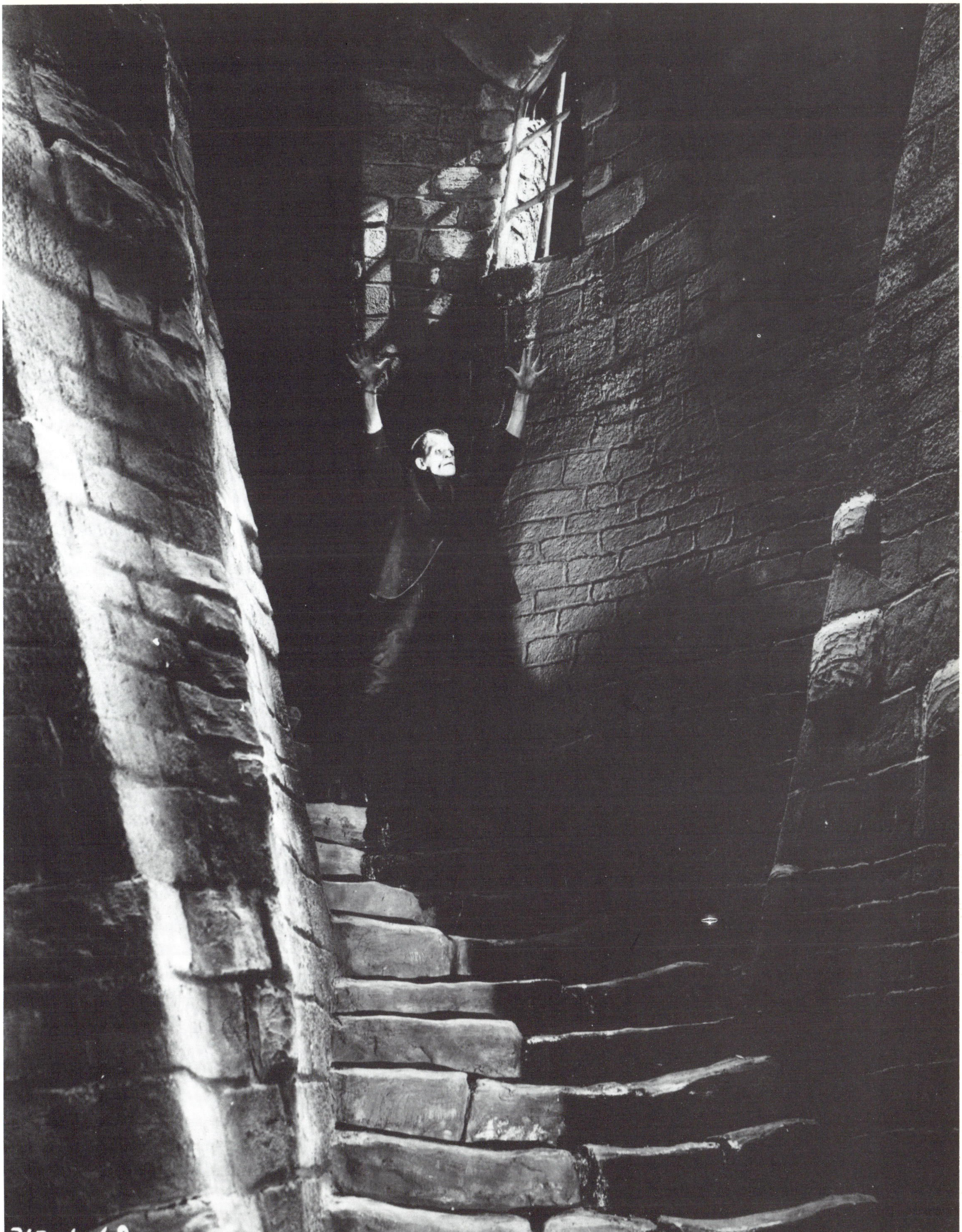
310-1-62

KING KONG (1933) is "The Greatest Story Ever Told" on film. The genre masterpiece has dazzled millions the world over since its initial 1933 release, and continues to do so even up to 1993. No other film can match the horror and the beauty that makes this film a gem from the golden era of cinema.
Above: King Kong, towering nearly fifty-feet tall, prepares to carry miniature Fay Wray (on tree) in his paws.
Opposite: The King of monsters shoves a tree down the throat of a Tyranosaurous Rex in this memorable scene from KING KONG.

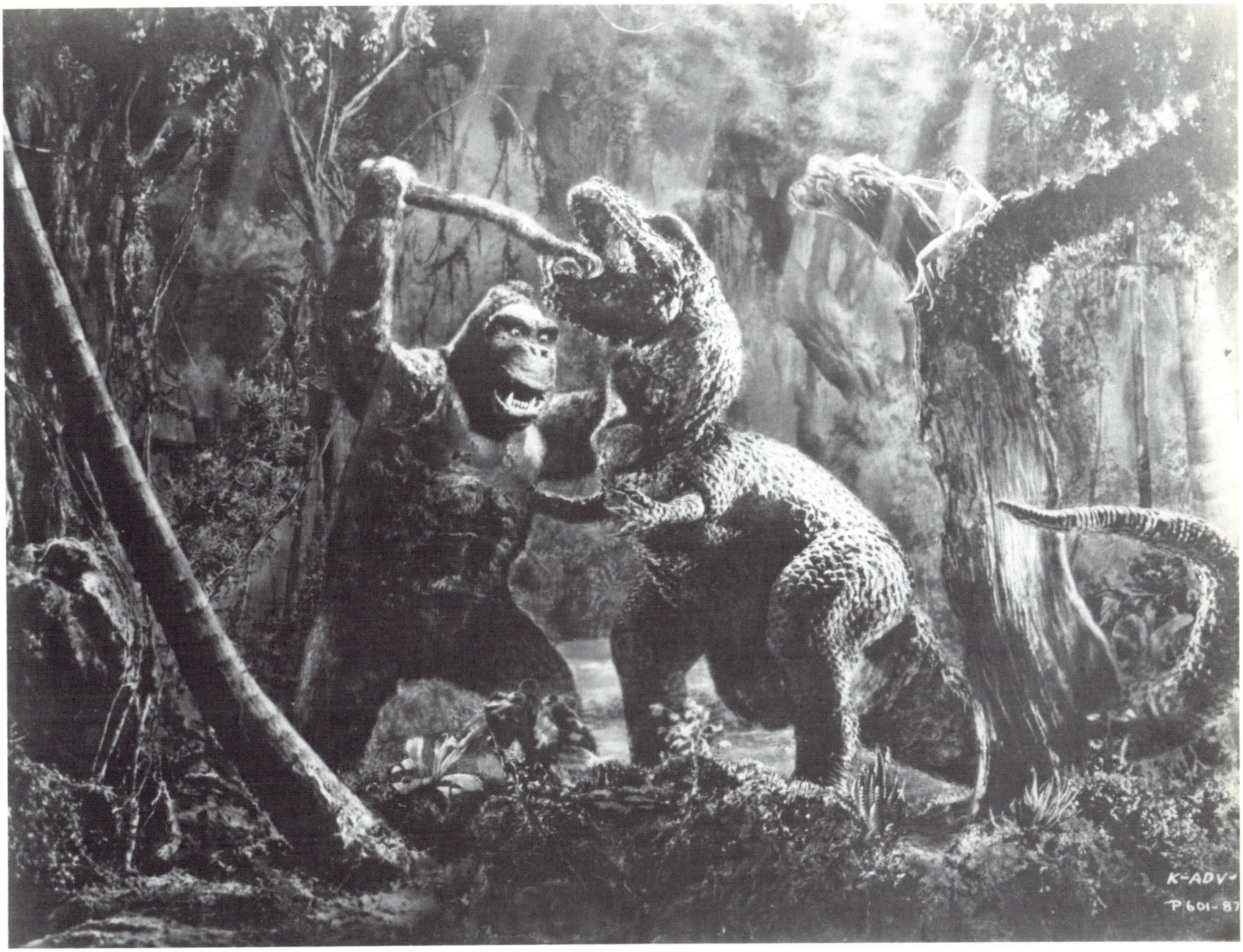

KARLOFF The Uncanny in "The MUMMY"

74

The walking dead!
Opposite Top: Boris Karloff as the living, breathing centuries-old mummy from Universal's THE MUMMY (1932).
Opposite Bottom Left: Bela Lugosi and Carroll Borland portray undead creatures of the night in MARK OF THE VAMPIRE (1935).
Opposite Bottom Right: Gloria Holden as the title character from DRACULA'S DAUGHTER (1936).
Above: Three female vampires roam the night eternally in DRACULA (1931).
Right: Bela Lugosi (Left) and his league of zombies in WHITE ZOMBIE (1933).

75

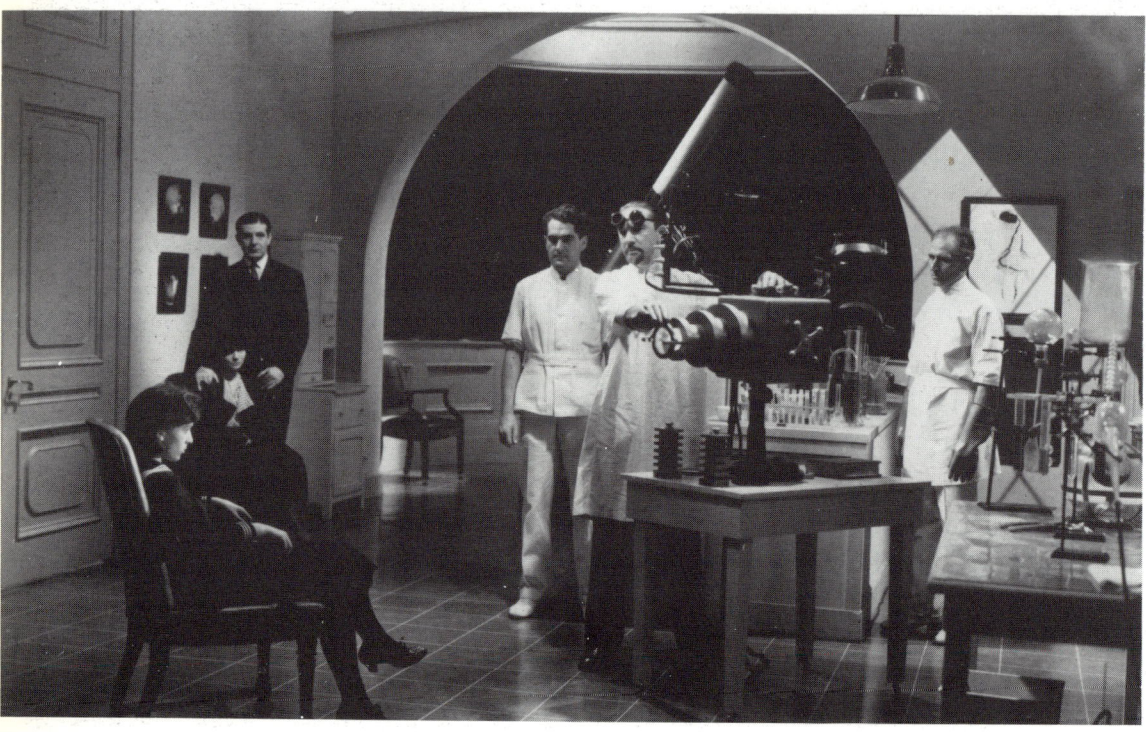

Above: Henry Hull and Warner Oland battle in WEREWOLF OF LONDON (1935).
Left: Scientist Bela Lugosi tries out his new apparatus in THE INVISIBLE RAY (1936).
Opposite Top: vintage poster for THE INVISIBLE MAN (1933).
Opposite Bottom: Colin Clive and Dwight Frye in FRANKENSTEIN (1931).

76

77

78

No other actor from the vintage era could ever match Bela Lugosi's portrayal of a vampire; His most famous characterization and his claim to fame. Curiously, Lugosi only starred in two films during the 1930's as a vampire: DRACULA (1931) and MARK OF THE VAMPIRE (1935).

Opposite Top Left: Lugosi as Count Dracula in DRACULA (1931).

Opposite Top Right: As Dracula, Lugosi advances at Dwight Frye in DRACULA.

Opposite Bottom: Lugosi and Helen Chandler in DRACULA.

Above: Lugosi and Carroll Borland advance on a victim in MARK OF THE VAMPIRE (1935).

Right: Lugosi mesmerizes Helen Chandler in DRACULA.

Above: The Invisible Man (Vincent Price) and love interest in THE INVISIBLE MAN RETURNS (1939).
Left: Boris Karloff and Eva Moore in a touching moment from THE OLD DARK HOUSE (1932).
Opposite Top: Boris Karloff in a moving moment from THE BRIDE OF FRANKENSTEIN (1935).
Opposite Bottom: Bela Lugosi kills his monster-slave in THE DARK EYES OF LONDON (1939).

81

82

Opposite Top: Bela Lugosi from WHITE ZOMBIE (1932).
Opposite Bottom: Lionel Atwill and Jean Hersholt hunt for the graves of the vampires among the decaying ruins of an eerie castle in MARK OF THE VAMPIRE (1935).
Above: A reproduction of a vintage lobbycard from THE MUMMY (1932) that shows the discovery of Boris Karloff's mummy.
Right: A close-up of the Frankenstein monster as portrayed by Boris Karloff taken from FRANKENSTEIN (1931).

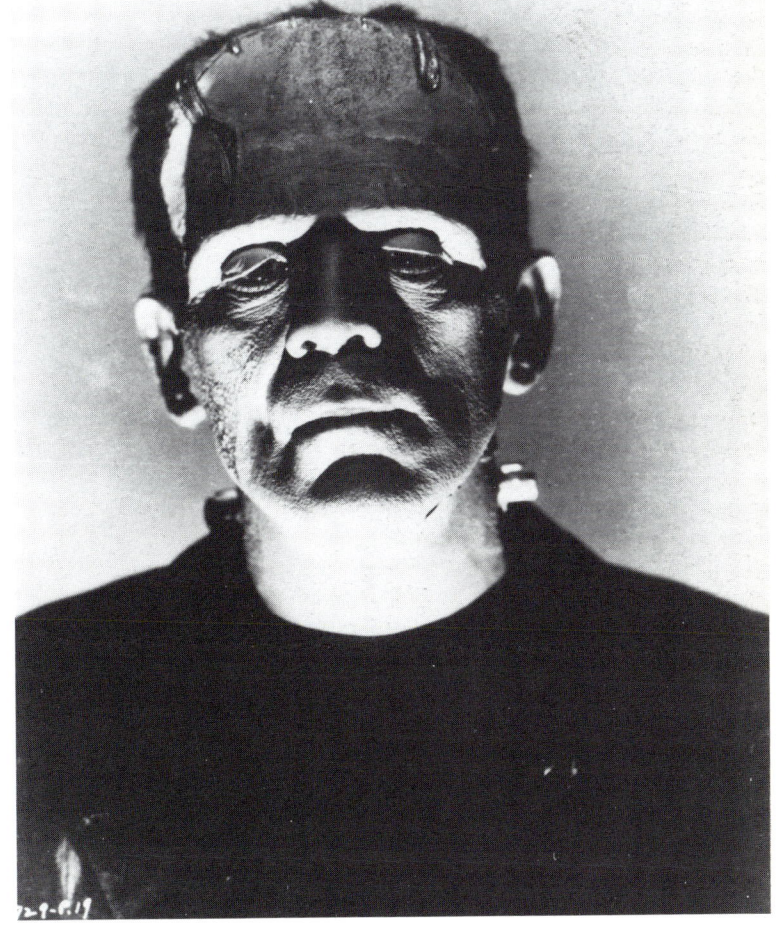

CHAPTER THREE
THE MONSTERS OF THE 1940'S

Opposite Page: A magnificent close-up of Lon Chaney's Wolfman character from Universal's THE WOLFMAN (1941).
Above: A vintage poster for THE GHOST OF FRANKENSTEIN (1942).

LIKE FATHER LIKE SON!

The 1930's ended triumphantly for Universal Studios after a full decade of dominating the monster movie genre. The new decade promised even greater riches for the studio. The first four years allowed Universal to produce some very good monster movies under the direction of an entirely new regime of executive producers, directors, and writers. The director's seat at Universal, once occupied by James Whale and Tod Browning, was now filled by new talent such as Erle C. Kenton and George Waggner, both of whom would direct fresh new material from writers like Robert and Curt Siodmak. The early to mid 1940's was clearly dominated by Universal's monster films, but with the arrival of new talent such as Val Lewton and the surfacing of numerous poverty row studios like Monogram and PRC (Producers Releasing Corporation), the face of horror began to take a change; A change in which the old school of monster movies would become obsolete and a new style of horror would emerge.

Lon Chaney, Sr. was the King Of Monster Movies during the silent era because of his highly celebrated screen characterizations. In addition to leaving us a legacy of famous monster movies, the king also gave us Lon Chaney, Jr., who, not by choice, became a leading star of many of the major Universal monster movies during the 1940's.

Executives at Universal intended on making Chaney the new Boris Karloff, after Karloff had defected to Broadway in 1940 to star in Joseph Kesselring's play *Arsenic and Old Lace*. Chaney, who had worked for Universal as a stunt-man, an extra and as a supporting actor, was the logical choice For Karloff's replacement. Chaney was immediately signed up and his career as a monster movie star began with MAN MADE MONSTER (1941), a film originally written and intended for both Boris Karloff and Bela Lugosi as early as 1936. The role of Karloff's monster was given to Chaney, while the role of the mad scientist, originally intended for Bela Lugosi (who was currently filming for Monogram and thus unavailable), went to horror film star Lionel Atwill.

Atwill was his usual amiable, overzealous self as the mad scientist, this time on a mission to build a race of super electric men to aid America in combat against the German Nazi army. In other words, the actor delivered a perfect performance, the kind that he relished the most. Chaney was near brilliant in his first horror film role as the sympathetic dead man who Atwill pumps up with electricity and restores to life.

Today, film historians view MAN MADE MONSTER as a glorified "B" film directed with all the flashy style of a grade" A" horror film by Erle C. Kenton. The film was unusual for its kind because a larger-than-normal budget was allotted towards its production when, originally, Karloff and Lugosi was slated to star. The film's success convinced Universal executives to give the actor the leading title role in his greatest horror film, THE WOLFMAN (1941).

THE WOLFMAN was directed with great style by George Waggner, the force behind many of the Universal monster movies during the early 1940's. Waggner was one of the few people in Hollywood with a legal contract to produce, write and direct, and he felt that the time was ripe for a new horror sensation that could replace and even top the success of both the Dracula and Frankenstein films from the studio. For this new project, Universal allotted a very impressive budget from day one, most of which went towards the lavish sets, the fantastic Wolfman make-up and the assembly of a first rate cast, headed by Claude Rains, Evelyn Ankers, Bela Lugosi and Ralph Bellamy. What more could one expect for a horror picture?

In THE WOLFMAN, Chaney portrays the young and handsome Larry Talbot, a curse young soul who is attacked by a werewolf (played by Bela Lugosi) and later tormented when he too transforms into a similar beast when the moon is full and the wolfbane blooms. His characterization is both convincing and sympathetic.

Throughout the film, Chaney is given several fabulous transformation scenes from man into werewolf, after which he goes on a murdering spree until confronted by his father (Rains) and destroyed with a silver cane.

THE WOLFMAN is considered the definitive werewolf film of all time. The werewolf make-up by Jack Pierce is literally flawless and some of the effects by John P. Fulton are innovative and trend-setting. Waggner's atmospheric style and Joseph Valentine's extremely fluid camera assist in making this classic horror film Universal's last stable of grade "A" monster movies. In addition to creating one of filmdom's most celebrated monsters, THE WOLFMAN became the studio's biggest hit of the season and boosted the second horror film cycle. The film also established Chaney as a viable actor with star quality, which led to numerous different film roles as monsters during the 1940's and 1950's.

THE NEW FRANKENSTEIN!

After the successful release of SON OF FRANKENSTEIN (1939), Boris Karloff pledged that he would never again take on the role of the Frankenstein monster. The actor stuck to his word when producer George Waggner approached Karloff to play the infamous role of the monster for the fourth time in GHOST OF FRANKENSTEIN (1941). Instead, Chaney was forced into the part (Chaney was never really thrilled about playing movie monsters, at least not in the beginning. The actor had always maintained visions of becoming a Charles Boyer-type leading man in romantic films, but studio executives knew that casting Chaney as a romantic lead would be a disaster because of his clumsy and awkward mannerisms).

The cast of GHOST OF FRANKENSTEIN is headed by distinguished actor Sir Cedric Hardwicke as Dr. Ludwig Frankenstein, another son of the infamous Dr. Henry Frankenstein. Ralph Bellamy was given the role of the film's hero, while Evelyn Ankers was cast as the heroine. Lionel Atwill (who was involved in a sordid rape trial at the time) was cast third as the wicked Dr. Theodore Bohmer while Bela Lugosi returned to his role of Ygor. Poor Chaney was given last billing as the monster, and he was totally outraged by false promises made by Universal. Promises of leading roles in

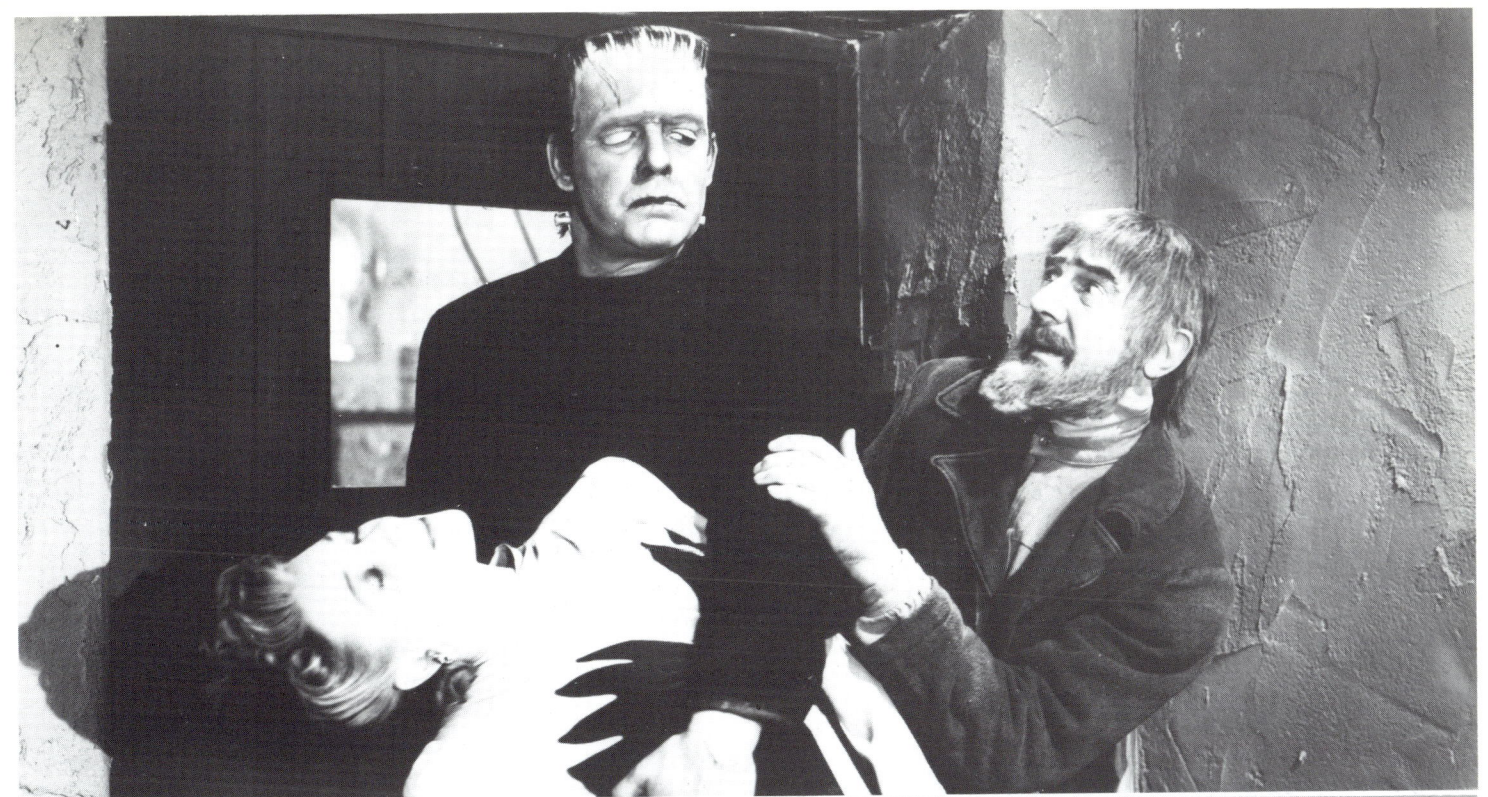

Above: The new Frankenstein monster (Lon Chaney, Jr.) carries an unconscious Evelyn Ankers as Ygor (Bela Lugosi) looks on in THE GHOST OF FRANKENSTEIN (1942).

Right: The monster (Chaney) gives Lionel Atwill a reason to get all choaked-up in THE GHOST OF FRANKENSTEIN.

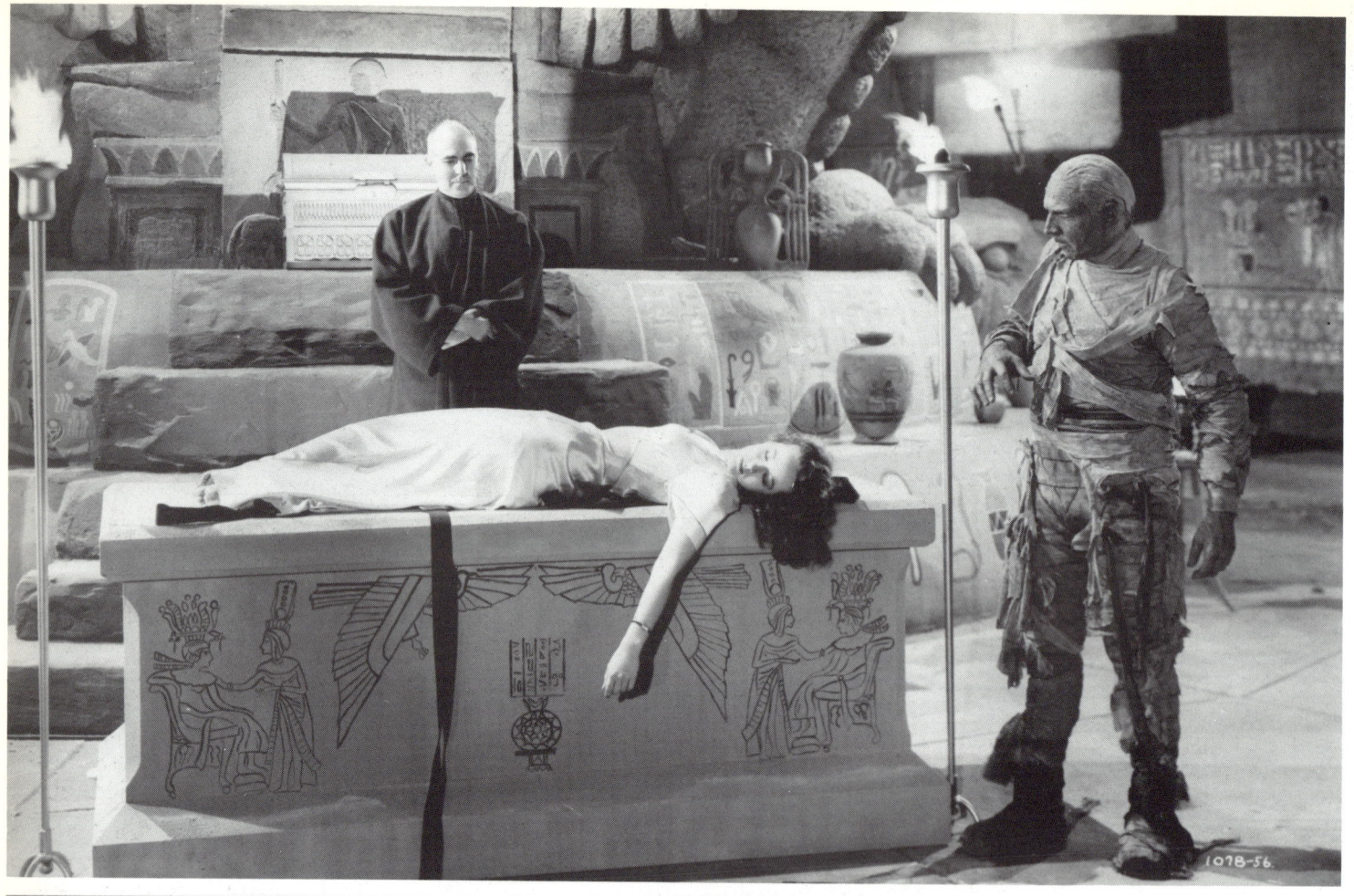

Above: A scene from THE MUMMY'S HAND (1940) with Tom Tyler as Kharis and George Zucco as the evil high priest and the borrowed sets from the adventure film GREEN HELL.
Left: A vintage poster for SON OF DRACULA (1943).

88

romantic films, or, at the very least, top billing in the studio's monster movies. In any event, most film historians agree that GHOST OF FRANKENSTEIN marked the downfall of the Frankenstein series as a result of cheaper sets and the total miscasting of Lon Chaney as the monster. Unlike Boris Karloff's moving and sympathetic performances as the monster, Chaney's characterization is stone cold with little or no emotions. Most of Chaney's monsters are very clearly stereotypical uninteresting, and as a result of which, his monsters are almost always conceived as mindless mechanizations that reflect on both the actor's inability to inject emotions into his characters and the studio's apathy for quality over its assembly-line approach to filmmaking in regards to their monster movies. In short, after THE WOLFMAN (1941), the studio only viewed their monster movies as a quick method of generating income rather than an outlet for artistic talent as in the days of James Whale and Tod Browning. The studio was only concerned with a fast shooting schedule, quick editing and foolish and unreasonable deadlines. Even the script was effected due to budget limitations and the studio's assembly-style of filmmaking. For example, the idea of transplanting Ygor's brain into the monster's body was not a crowd pleaser. Somehow the entire film lacked the conviction the previous Frankenstein vehicles offered.

Despite the film's many flaws, THE GHOST OF FRANKENSTEIN still proved that the new monster was as bankable a commodity as before and still the driving force behind the Universal monster movies. This was mainly due to the enormous publicity created by the studio. Needless to say, the film was Chaney's final performance as the monster.

KHARIS - THE WALKING MUMMY!

The Wolfman and the mummy were part of Universal's second generation of monsters and THE MUMMY'S HAND (1940) was Universal's first sequel to THE MUMMY (1932) with Boris Karloff. The film was produced on a much lower budget than the original but the film's appearance was that of a lavish horror adventure due to the fabulous borrowed sets of GREEN HELL, an elaborate adventure picture from Universal. The film was produced before Chaney had achieved stardom in THE WOLFMAN (1941), therefore the role of Universal's new monster Kharis, the crumbling centuries-old mummy, went to action-adventure star Tom Tyler. Tyler took on the role of the new mummy, who in this film, is given life to by an evil high priest (played by George Zucco) who uses the mummy to destroy the desecrators of the forbidden tomb of Anaka, Kharis's beloved princess of centuries past.

The success of THE MUMMY'S HAND inspired Universal to launch a series of similar but less impressive mummy films in the 1940's. The next film in the short-lived series was THE MUMMY'S TOMB (1942), directed by Harold Young. In this film, Chaney, covered in loads of make-up and bandages, is used by another high priest to kill those who have desecrated the tomb of Anaka. In this film, the mummy goes up in flames during the climax.

THE MUMMY'S GHOST (1944) was the next installment, and probably the best in the series because of its carefully prepared script. But no matter how you change the story around, there is just not much one can do with this subject matter. In any event, Chaney returned as the mummy Kharis, but actors George Zucco and John Carradine played the real villains at large. Together, Zucco and Carradine use the pitiful creature to carry-out their evil bidding.

THE MUMMY'S CURSE (1944) was the final and the least distinguished of the Universal mummy vehicles. The script, written by Bernard Schubert, Dwight Babcock and Leon Abrams, lacked consistency with the previous films and was set in the Louisiana Bayou, of all places. The film, poorly directed by Leslie Goodwins, was Chaney's least favorite in the series because he was covered from head to toe in a rubber suit and the heat in the American South reached the upper nineties during filming. The mummy's destruction comes as a result of being crushed to death by the ruins of an ancient monastery.

All of Universal's mummy films, with the exception of both THE MUMMY (1932) and THE MUMMY'S HAND (1940), were a product of mass production, produced quickly and on a low budget for commercial gain. These were not films of style or cinematic art. Instead, the mummy films of the 1940's were vehicles produced mainly for profit and the directors responsible for these films sacrificed all attempts at logic and character development for cheap thrills and exploited suspense. This is not to say that THE MUMMY'S HAND, THE MUMMY'S TOMB, THE MUMMY'S GHOST and THE MUMMY'S CURSE were not successful at the box office. To say the least, they were very entertaining.

DRACULA RETURNS!

By 1943, Chaney was clearly the new leading star of horror films. The actor had played the electric monster in MAN MADE MONSTER (1941), the werewolf in THE WOLFMAN (1941), the Frankenstein monster in GHOST OF FRANKENSTEIN (1941) and the mummy in THE MUMMY'S TOMB (1942), all for Universal. The only movie monster the actor had not yet portrayed was Count Dracula himself! The role was offered to Chaney by Universal as a partial fulfillment of a long-standing promise. The new film was entitled SON OF DRACULA (1943) and was directed by Robert Siodmak from an original story written by brother Curt Siodmak.

SON OF DRACULA was the studio's first Dracula effort since DRACULA'S DAUGHTER (1936) and DRACULA (1931) before that. The stylishly directed action thriller offers the much improved special effects of John P. Fulton, however, like many of the monster movies produced by Universal during the 1940's, SON OF DRACULA suffers from a number of acute flaws, beginning with the decision to cast Chaney in the role of Dracula. The studio would have done better by casting a much more suave and debonair performer like Claude Rains or even Bela Lugosi. It is quite evident that Universal recognized this major flaw in later years by using actor John Carradine as Dracula in both HOUSE OF FRANKENSTEIN (1944) and HOUSE OF DRACULA (1944). In any event, one may argue that Chaney's Dracula embodied the physical strength of the undead better than his predecessors in the Universal trilogy. Chaney's interpretation of the vampire placed less emphasis on scaring the audience with terror; instead his vampire relied more on action and visual effects.

In addition to casting problems, SON OF DRACULA suffers greatly from an over melodramatic plot and quickly-paced direction. Furthermore, the Gothic character of Count Dracula just does not work in the modern Louisiana Bayou. One can only blame the film's writer, Eric Taylor, for attempting to modernize a Gothic character at a time when moviegoers were far from ready for such a major transition in setting. History has proven time and time again that the best vampire films offer Gothic settings. Screenwriter Taylor changed some things regarding the vampire lore. For example, Chaney's vampire <u>did</u> cast a mirror image. He also transformed into a vampire bat right before startled eyes of the audience. Taylor also changed the name of Dracula to Alucard (Dracula spelled backwards). But the true blame should go to Universal for putting pressure on director Robert Siodmak to quickly shoot this film within a record-setting time. This was the fate of many Universal horror films of the 1940's as a result of Universal's assembly-line production schedule.

True, SON OF DRACULA does not possess the menace and unhurried haunting visuals that make DRACULA (1931) and DRACULA'S DAUGHTER (1936) vintage classics. However, let us just say that SON OF DRACULA, though not a classic in the likes of its predecessors, is the slickest and most entertaining of the trilogy.

THE PHANTOM THAT CHANEY WAS NOT!

It was always true that Universal Studios was on the verge of collapsing since 1931 and that the studio was kept alive primarily by its monster movies. Because of this fact, the studio was not able to allow its leading horror star, Lon Chaney, to play Charles Boyer-type roles; the type of roles the actor demanded from the studio. Instead, they needed his name to promote their horror movies that in return, would keep Universal afloat.

By 1942, executives at Universal decided it was time to pull out all the stops and produce a horror masterpiece that would surpass the successes of DRACULA (1931), FRANKENSTEIN (1931), THE BRIDE OF FRANKENSTEIN (1935) and THE WOLFMAN (1941). Apparently original ideas were sparse, and the studio decided to remake their 1925 silent classic, THE PHANTOM OF THE OPERA as a Technicolor extravaganza.

The new film went into production as early as summer 1942 and was released in 1943. Universal used THE PHANTOM OF THE OPERA to get Chaney to play other monsters such as the Frankenstein monster and the mummy, both monsters that he literally hated to play on film. But because there was a chance to win the role his father, Chaney, Sr., had made famous, Chaney delivered his end of the bargain. Unfortunately, Universal had to renege on their end of the deal. After Chaney's unbecoming portrayal of the Frankenstein monster and his lifeless Dracula and mummy characterizations, the studio realized that they simply could not risk casting Chaney in a role of an intricate romantic such as Erik the Phantom, especially when the studio had over $1,750,000 invested into this project. Thus the role went to honored and distinguished actor Claude Rains, who had delivered brilliant performances in THE INVISIBLE MAN (1933)

Above: Jon Hall plays the Invisible Man in THE INVISIBLE MAN'S REVENGE (1944).

and THE WOLFMAN (1941) and had just been nominated for two Academy Awards for best supporting actor in both MR. SMITH GOES TO WASHINGTON (1939) and CASABLANCA (1942). The studio had made a very wise decision in choosing the talented actor. The role of Erik demanded an actor who had a strong presence since the Phantom would be masked and hooded throughout most of the film.

THE PHANTOM OF THE OPERA received very favorable reviews and the lavish Technicolor remake won the studio two Academy Awards. Rains was absolutely brilliant as The Phantom, and although the film was played for its lavish sets, atmospheric photography and strong performances rather than the traditional action and suspense melodramas that the studio usually pushed in their horror films during that period, THE PHANTOM OF THE OPERA proved that Universal could manufacture quality horror films. The film is a monument and helped to keep Universal on the map during the 1940's.

As for Chaney, loosing the part to Claude Rains came as a hard blow for the actor, especially after loosing to Charles Laughton for the title role of THE HUNCHBACK OF NOTRE DAME (1939), another infamous role his father had made famous. Chaney felt degraded, especially when he was asked to take on the role of Kharis again in THE MUMMY'S GHOST (1944). However, this was one of the few instances in which the studio made a good casting call. The studio was very sorry for Chaney, and promised that they would make it up to him by giving him another werewolf film. The question was how? The werewolf supposedly died at the climax of THE WOLFMAN (1941).

ATTACK OF THE INVISIBLE PEOPLE!

Both THE INVISIBLE MAN (1933) and THE INVISIBLE MAN RETURNS (1939) were both very successful and highly overlooked monster movies, the first of which is considered a major movie classic. In 1940, screenwriter Curt Siodmak developed a story that was slightly diverse from the original H.G. Wells story. The new film, directed by Edward Sutherland, was released as THE INVISIBLE WOMAN (1940).

In this slightly unusual concept on the invisibility theme, John Barrymore portrays an eccentric scientist who develops a serum and an electrical machine that is capable of rendering a human invisible. Virginia Bruce plays an attractive fashion model named Kitty Carroll who answers an advert in a local newspaper sponsored by the scientist, who is looking for a human guinea pig for his invisibility experiment. What follows is an amusing mixture of laughs and suspense as Kitty Carroll goes after those she despises.

Despite its commercial title, which leads us to believe the film is nothing more than a cheap programmer, THE INVISIBLE WOMAN is very competently directed by Sutherland and stars distinguished actor John Barrymore in another brilliant performance. The stylish film is played strictly for laughs and offers some very fabulous special effects by Universal's own technician John P. Fulton. Actress Virginia Bruce is quite good in the title role and the entire film is a refreshing and original variation on the traditional invisible monster theme.

Universal also made a couple sequels to THE INVISIBLE MAN (1933) and THE INVISIBLE MAN RETURNS (1939). THE INVISIBLE AGENT (1942) was based on another story written by Curt Siodmak. The basic concept of this film was designed to combine the invisibility theme so that it coincided with the news of the ongoing War; therefore, the film was more of a propaganda piece that reflected the American people's attitudes during the war rather than a straight-forward monster movie. The espionage thriller stars Jon Hall as Frank Griffin, the invisible agent and grandson of the original Invisible Man. Peter Lorre and Sir Cedric Hardwicke play foreign spies who demand that Griffin give them his grandfather's invisibility formula.

THE INVISIBLE MAN'S REVENGE (1944) was the studio's attempt to infuse horror into the series and back into the character of Griffin (played again by Jon Hall). In the film, John Carradine portrays an eccentric scientist named Dr. Drury. The scientist has invented a formula that can make a man invisible. When Robert Griffin (Hall) is abandoned in the jungles of Africa by his devious partners (Leland Hodgson and Gale Sondergaard) while searching for diamonds, Griffin comes across the isolated home of Dr. Drury. The adventurer agrees to be the scientist's human subject and once invisible, he enjoys his powers to the fullest, killing his enemies and terrorizing the film's heroine (played by 1940's horror starlet Evelyn Ankers).

THE INVISIBLE MAN'S REVENGE was a very fluid, quickly paced "B" programmer that featured some very good special effects by John P. Fulton and some excellent moments of horror. The film was the studio's final Invisible Man film until the 1950's.

THE WILD WOMAN THAT WOULDN'T DIE!

John Carradine holds the record for having starred in more horror films than any other actor. He was born as Richmond Reed Carradine on February 5, 1906 in New York City. During the 1930's, Carradine starred in a variety of horror and monster movies as a supporting actor. His films include Universal's THE INVISIBLE MAN (1933), THE BLACK CAT (1934) and THE BRIDE OF FRANKENSTEIN (1935). In 1942 he appeared with Milton Berle in the pseudo-horror comedy WHISPERING GHOSTS, but it was not until 1943 when Universal Pictures made an attempt to use the actor for the leading role in a new horror series. The new film, CAPTIVE WILD WOMAN (1943), originally slated to star Lon Chaney, would introduce a new monster named Paula Dupree, the world's only ape woman-creature (as created by make-up artist Jack Pierce). In the film, the ape woman is created by mad scientist John Carradine by way of glandular extractions from victim Martha MacVicar. For their new monster, Universal wanted originality in both its creation and its physical appearance. Screenwriter Curt Siodmak felt that by twisting the traditional theme of the monster and the girl by making the monster a female, audiences would react positively to the fresh subject matter and the film would break the stigma of the traditional laboratory-created movie monster.

CAPTIVE WILD WOMAN was successful enough to inspire Universal in launching two sequels. JUNGLE WOMAN (1944), the first sequel, starred actor J. Carrol Naish as the new mad scientist (Carradine was busy making THE MUMMY'S GHOST) who revives the ape woman, while JUNGLE CAPTIVE (1945), the third and final film in the Universal trilogy, starred Otto Kruger as the mad Dr. Stendhal who revives the monster for the third and final time.

JUNGLE CAPTIVE marked the end of Universal's ape-woman series, but for John Carradine, CAPTIVE WILD WOMAN was the beginning of a long-lasting career in fantasy, horror and science fiction movies. A career that would last through the 1990's.

WHEN THE WOLFMAN MET FRANKENSTEIN, DRACULA AND EVERYONE ELSE!

By 1943, Universal had literally exhausted and overplayed all of its original monsters. Around that time, writer Curt Siodmak and producer George Waggner developed the idea of combining the studio's two most successful screen monsters into one film. The film's title during production was THE WOLFMAN MEETS FRANKENSTEIN because the script, as promised by Universal to Lon Chaney, devoted more time to the actor's Wolfman character than to the Frankenstein monster. Another hollow promise made by the studio. The film was released as FRANKENSTEIN MEETS THE WOLFMAN (1943) and the final, edited version is dominated mostly by the Frankenstein monster.

Producer George Waggner and director Roy William Neil originally planned on having Chaney play both the Wolfman and the Frankenstein monster, allowing the actor to enjoy an avalanche of publicity as well as keeping him from making unreasonable demands, but mostly to make him happy again after the PHANTOM OF THE OPERA (1943) ordeal. They later scrapped the idea of having Chaney play the dual monsters due to costly production time and fear of Chaney's erratic behavior displayed during the production of previous films. But as history has it, Chaney was eventually content just playing the role of the Wolfman, which he did ever so well. However, the big question still remained. Who would take on the role of the Frankenstein monster?

Boris Karloff was the logical choice to play the Frankenstein monster in FRANKENSTEIN MEETS THE WOLFMAN, unfortunately, in addition to having vowed to never play the monster again, the actor was simply unavailable. This left only one choice: Bela Lugosi. But before choosing the actor, Universal even considered their newest horror star, John Carradine. However, Carradine was far too gaunt an actor to undertake such a characterization, at least in the image of Karloff and Chaney's monsters. Furthermore, the studio had much admiration for the talented Shakespearean actor to allow him to be buried under layers of uncomfortable make-up. Thus the studio gave into their discontentment with Lugosi and offered him the very same part he once refused in 1931.

Once the decision was made, producers argued for days that the declining talents of Lugosi would prevent him from playing the part. Lugosi had created one character, that of Count Dracula! That character had stuck with the actor. Furthermore, Lugosi was nearing the age of sixty and would require additional stunt persons, which in turn would require more capital from the studio. Stunt-man Eddie Parker doubled for Lugosi. Still Lugosi seemed to be the logical choice since the brain of Ygor in GHOST OF FRANKENSTEIN (1941) had been transplanted into the body of the monster during the film's ending and that the monster in FRANKENSTEIN MEETS THE WOLFMAN would have dialogue like never before. The idea was to have the monster speak in the voice of Ygor (Lugosi) and even resemble the madman to a degree. Whatever significance this held, producers finally agreed to cast Lugosi as the new Ygor-speaking Frankenstein monster!

FRANKENSTEIN MEETS THE WOLFMAN was advertised as "The Battle of The Century!" The film opened with good reviews and reaped record breaking profits as a result of Universal's enormous marketing campaign. The "Battle of The Century" proved to be everything it was hailed to be and even a little more. But when viewed today, the once fierce battle appears docile in comparison to many of the violent scenes featured in modern horror films. I must say, however, from a nostalgic viewpoint, the clash between the screen's legendary monsters still sends shivers up my spine.

The film opens during a moon-lit night with two grave-robbers breaking into the crypt of Lawrence Talbot. The full moon shines on the young man's corpse and fully restores the Wolfman to life and the killings begin. In his human form, Talbot (Chaney) and his old gypsy woman friend Maleva (Maria Ouspenskaya) travel to Vasaria to locate Dr. Ludwig Frankenstein with hope that they will find a cure to his condition. Unfortunately, Frankenstein has died in a fire and all hope is lost. There only hope is Dr. Mannering (Patrick Knowles), the film's hero, but he refuses to believe in werewolves. The film, as a result of poor editing, moves quickly from this point, with more killings at the claws of the Wolfman, the discovery of the Frankenstein monster (Bela Lugosi) and the location of the book *The Secrets Of Life And Death by Dr. Frankenstein* in the ruins of the old Frankenstein castle in Vasaria. Eventually Dr. Mannering (played by Patrick Knowles) is educated on the concept of lycanthropy and he promises to help Talbot by destroying both the Wolfman and the monster. To accomplish this, he must begin by draining their energy and

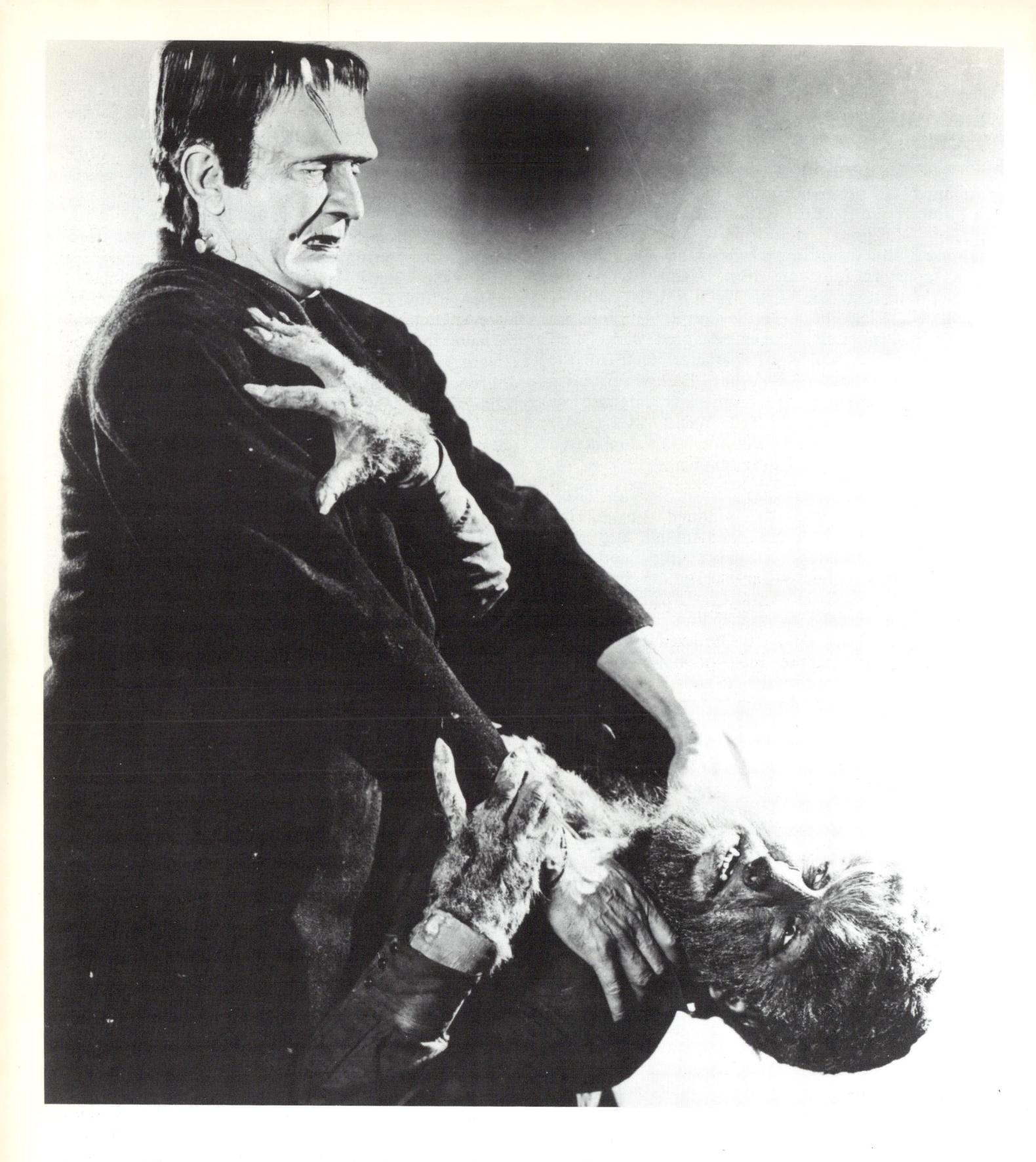

Above: Two titans of terror, the Frankenstein monster (Bela Lugosi) and the Wolfman (Lon Chaney), in mortal combat in this spine-tingling scene from FRANKENSTEIN MEETS THE WOLFMAN (1943).
Opposite Page: The Wolfman (Chaney) on the prowl in FRANKENSTEIN MEETS THE WOLFMAN (1943).

transmitting it elsewhere. But during the film's climax, which is staged within the fabulous ruins of the old Frankenstein laboratory, Dr. Mannering begins to display traits of Universal's mad scientists and instead of destroying the horrid monster, he blasts the beast with energy, insisting that he cannot destroy Frankenstein's creation without seeing it at its full strength! The monster, who had been strapped to a platform alongside Talbot to this point, breaks his bonds and attacks Dr. Mannering and his assistant Elsa Frankenstein (Ilona Massey). Meanwhile, Talbot falls under the influence of the full moon and transforms into the dreaded Wolfman. He, too, breaks free from his straps and what follows is the battle of the century. Both monsters engage in a fierce battle until a wall of water, released from a dam as a result of an explosion set off by two villagers, engulfs both monsters in a torrent current that wipes out the entire ruins of the Frankenstein castle. It is presumed that both monsters are destroyed and Vasaria is once again released from the horrors that plagued them.

For Chaney, FRANKENSTEIN MEETS THE WOLFMAN certainly enhanced his career as the leading horror film actor of the 1940's- playing the role that he did best. Chaney carries the film from start to finish, delivering a performance of pathos that conveys the tragedy and melodrama of his character. But for poor Bela Lugosi, the film proved to be ddisastrousto his career as a result of some poorly edited sequences throughout the film regarding the monster. For example, the script originally called for Lugosi to speak in the voice of Ygor. In the final print Lugosi's dialogue was cut completely from the film, therefore you have the actor flapping his mouth mutely throughout the entire film. As a result of this atrocity, what could have been a comeback performance for the actor was described by critics as being blatant and ludicrous. Secondly, the monster was originally supposed to be blind. But any mention of the monster's blindness is eliminated from the final print, thus you have Lugosi's monster walking around with his eyes closed and waving his arms aimlessly in the air. Still, despite all of this, Lugosi's monster characterization is far more impressive than anything Chaney did in GHOST OF FRANKENSTEIN (1941). In any event, as a result of the numerous edits made throughout the film, there are moments in FRANKENSTEIN MEETS THE WOLFMAN that simply do not make sense.

Despite the many changes made in the film, FRANKENSTEIN MEETS THE WOLFMAN broke box office records for the studio and proved to executives that the public still demanded more appearances by the Wolfman and the Frankenstein monster.

By 1944, Universal was fighting rival studios to maintain its reign as the world capital of monster movies. At the time, RKO Pictures was producing intelligent, well-crafted psychological horror films such as THE CAT PEOPLE (1943) and I WALKED WITH A ZOMBIE (1943), and Columbia was turning out some pretty good genre films as well such as THE DEVIL COMMANDS (1941), RETURN OF THE VAMPIRE (1944) and CRY OF THE WEREWOLF (1944) with Boris Karloff and Bela Lugosi in top billing and in good form. To stay on top, Universal executives hired Curt Siodmak to come up with some really good horror material for their next monster extravaganza. The result was a story called THE DEVIL'S BROOD, a monster epic that featured the Wolfman (played by Lon Chaney), the mad scientist-Doctor Gustav Von Niemann (played by Boris Karloff), the evil hunchback assistant (played by J. Carroll Nash), the mighty Frankenstein monster (played now by Glenn Strange) and the new Count Dracula (played by John Carradine). This film was to be the greatest assembly of monsters in one film (originally, the mummy and the invisible man were somehow written into the plot, but later dropped).

The film was paced quickly, beginning during a stormy night with Dr. Niemann and his hunchback assistant Daniel escaping a prison and masquerading as the proprietor of a Chamber of Horrors traveling caravan. Included in the circus of horrors are the skeletal remains of Count Dracula himself. Niemann removes the wooden stake from the skeleton's heart, and the cadaver of Count Dracula materializes. Niemann threatens to send the vampire's soul back to limbo, but if the vampire does as he asks, he promises to serve him eternally faithful. Dracula agrees to destroy the men who wrongly imprisoned the scientist and after doing so the vampire sets his lusts towards actress Anne Gwynne. However the Count's plans are thwarted when his identity is discovered and in a cross country horse chase, the vampire is destroyed by the dooming rays of the early morning sun. Eventually, Niemann and Daniel arrive in the village of Frankenstein (changed from Vasaria) and happen upon the ruins of Frankenstein's castle. Their they discover the frozen remains of the Frankenstein monster and the Wolfman. Fascinated by the prospect of restoring the monster to its full power as opposed to helping Larry Talbot from his lycanthropy curse and transplanting Daniel's brain from his horrendous body to that of Talbot's, Niemann brings about his own destruction. The Wolfman is destroyed by the silver bullet fired from a pistol held in the hand of the woman that loves him; Daniel is strangled by the Frankenstein monster and tossed out of a window to his death; and Niemann is carried into a bog by the Frankenstein monster where they both meet their horrid deaths.

THE DEVIL'S BROOD was released as HOUSE OF FRANKENSTEIN (1944), directed by Erle C. Kenton. The opening scene in which Karloff and Nash escape from a prison and kill George Zucco to sabotage his Chamber of Horrors Traveling Circus was quite clever and impressive, as well as how the duo happen to stumble across the Wolfman and the Frankenstein monster, both of whom are remarkably still alive! Strange is quite good as the monster, but his performance lacks the vibrance and charisma that Karloff's monster possessed. In any event, Strange's Monster was just what the studio ordered, a tall lumbering, lifeless brute. Most impressive was John Carradine's suave and debonair Count Dracula. Carradine's vampire was very physical and menacing and yet he managed to maintain a romantic and lustful aura that Lon Chaney's Dracula in SON OF DRACULA (1943) lacked. Even the supporting players were brilliant in their roles: Lionel Atwill played the cameo of Inspector Arnz while George Zucco played Professor Bruno Lampini.

HOUSE OF FRANKENSTEIN still manages to provide pure enjoyment, decades after its initial release. Although most of the trappings are predictable and dated, the film has indeed endured the years and has become a classic, so-to-speak, of the 1940's style of horror films from Universal.

HOUSE OF FRANKENSTEIN was originally intended to be the studio's final vehicle in which the Wolfman, the Frankenstein monster, the mad scientist and Count Dracula would share the screen in the same film. However, the film received great reviews and did extremely well at the box office, inspiring the

Above: In this magnificent scene from Universal's HOUSE OF FRANKENSTEIN (1944), Boris Karloff (left) and J. Carroll Naish descend upon a helpless George Zucco.
Right: Poster art for the film HOUSE OF FRANKENSTEIN.

studio to cash in on its monsters once more.

HOUSE OF DRACULA (1945), written for the screen by Edward T. Lowe and directed by Erle C. Kenton, was a sequel to HOUSE OF FRANKENSTEIN in which all five monsters were squeezed back together again one more time after their alleged destruction in the previous film (Universal always had a knack for bringing their monsters back from the dead).

HOUSE OF DRACULA finally gave Lon Chaney, Jr. the top billing that he so often demanded in his previous films (the actor received second billing under Boris Karloff in HOUSE OF FRANKENSTEIN). Chaney was back as the Wolfman, while John Carradine returned as Dracula and Glenn Strange as the Frankenstein monster. Replacing Karloff as the mad scientist was actor Onslow Stevens, and the new Hunchback assistant was played by Jane Adams.

97

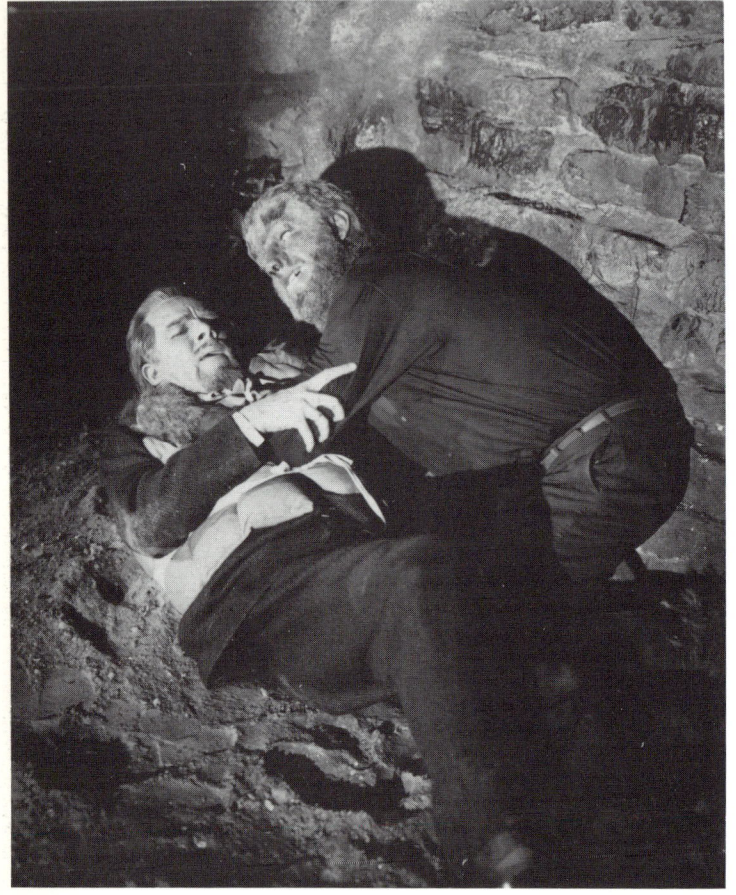

Above: Count Dracula (John Carradine) has a confrontation with Onslow Stevens in HOUSE OF DRACULA (1945).
Left: Onslow Stevens is attacked by the Wolfman (Lon Chaney) in HOUSE OF DRACULA.

Of course, Lionel Atwill, who had always been associated with every Frankenstein film the studio produced beginning with SON OF FRANKENSTEIN (1939), was cast as Inspector Franz Holtz. The film was a final reunion for the old Universal monster movie stars from the 1930's and 1940's.

In this film, Count Dracula arrives at the castle of Dr. Edelmann seeking a cure for his vampiric state. The scientist agrees to help him as well as Larry Talbot, who is also fully revived without explanation by writer Edward T. Lowe. The scientist feels that the trouble with both Dracula and Talbot has nothing to do with curses. He proceeds to give Dracula transfusions of his own blood, but the vampire,

Above: A vintage poster for the film ABBOTT AND COSTELLO MEET FRANKENSTEIN (1948).
Right: The Wolfman (Lon Chaney) about to make mince-meat out of Costello in ABBOTT AND COSTELLO MEET FRANKENSTEIN.

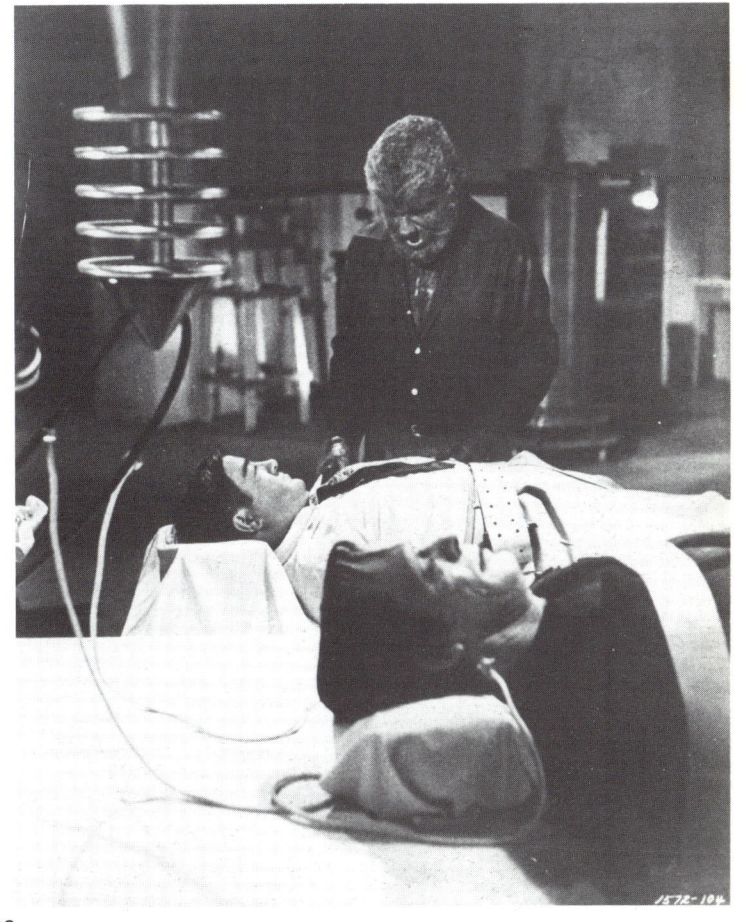

up to his old tricks, hypnotizes the scientist and reverses the blood flow. Meanwhile, Talbot revives Edelmann from his trance and together he and the doctor chase the vampire to his coffin, the only sanctuary for the fiend during the daylight hours. There, they open the lid and allow the sunlight to reduce the creature to bones once again. The scientist also happens across the body of the Frankenstein monster and recharges it for the sake of science. To make matters even worse, Dr. Edelmann becomes possessed by the blood of Dracula as a result of the reverse transfusion. The contaminated blood causes the scientist to transform into a Jekyll-Hyde monster with no reflection and with a taste for the jugular veins of his victims! But the madden scientist does manage to cure Talbot of his curse during a spell of sanity. Soon after, the doctor is back to his hideous self, recharging the monster to its fullest capacity of strength. During the climax, an angry mob of villagers descend onto the Edelmann castle where the Frankenstein monster is set on fire and Dr. Edelmann is shot to death by Talbot.

HOUSE OF DRACULA suffered from economic trouble, however, despite its financial difficulties, the film has aged nicely and is a fitting end to the monster sagas of Universal. For Chaney, the film allowed his character to be cured from lycanthropy, and the final destruction of the Frankenstein monster in flames somehow seemed permanent. The use of shadows by director Kenton, especially the enlivened performances of John Carradine, Lon Chaney and even Lionel Atwill in his supporting role as Inspector Holtz and the pathetic demises of both Onslow Stevenson's Edelmann and Jane Adams' hunchback make this film a league above HOUSE OF FRANKENSTEIN.

ABBOTT AND COSTELLO MEET THE MONSTERS OF UNIVERSAL!

HOUSE OF DRACULA seemed to mark the demise of the great Universal monsters, and in essence, this is true. Since ABBOTT AND COSTELLO MEET FRANKENSTEIN (1948) must be taken on its own farcical terms and not as part of the classic Frankenstein legend Universal adapted to the screen, it is thus considered the final chapter in the studio's saga. Therefore writers Robert Lees, Frederic I. Rinaldo and John Grant did not have to explain the re-existence of the film's monsters: The Wolfman, the Frankenstein monster, Count Dracula and others.

Bud Abbott and Lou Costello were recognized as legends of show business. By 1948, the comedy team had put together several comedy outings for Universal International. Somehow, the brainstorm of teaming Universal's top comedy team with the studio's legendary movie monsters originally came to be known as THE BRAIN OF FRANKENSTEIN. Producers loved the idea, but Lou Costello did not and he refused to work in that type of "crap," as he called it. "My five year old daughter can write something better than that," proclaimed Costello about the script. The brainstorm of resurrecting Frankenstein's monster, Count Dracula, The Wolfman, Kharis the mummy, Dracula's son Alucard and the invisible man just did not appeal to Costello. It could have been that the actor was insecure with the notion of starring alongside of or billed under several horror screen legends. With some redrafting in the script, in which Alucard and Kharis were eliminated, and a $50,000 advance to Costello from the film's producer, the uncooperative actor became ever-so-happy. Costello was even happier when he film's title was changed to ABBOTT AND COSTELLO MEET THE FRANKENSTEIN.

The new horror comedy was actually a blessing for most of the veteran horror actors, with the exception of Boris Karloff, who was enjoying a wonderful later career in horror films from RKO Pictures. Many of the original stars were re-hired for the film, after having been dropped after the release of HOUSE OF DRACULA. Bela Lugosi rightfully won the part of Count Dracula over John Carradine, while Lon Chaney was given his Wolfman role back. Glenn Strange repeated his role as the Frankenstein monster. The veteran horror actors were very grateful and content with their parts and the film offered them a chance to reminisce on the old days when their monsters were king. The project offered nostalgic meaning to the actors.

The plot was very feeble as far as these films go, but very enjoyable to fans of this fare non-the- less. In the film, Count Dracula arrives in Florida with the Frankenstein monster, both of whom are concealed in crates. This is how two baggage clerks (Abbott and Costello) come across the monsters. As the film develops, we learn that Dracula has plans of giving the monster a new brain, that of Costello's! The film's climax is set in an eerie castle believed to belong to Dracula. It is there where the operation is set to take place, but the Wolfman is also on hand, and both he and the vampiric count engage in a cat and mouse battle while the Frankenstein monster menaces the comedy team. The death of the monsters comes fast. First, the Wolfman leaps off a balcony as he tries to catch Count Dracula in his bat form as the vampire attempts to escape. Both monsters fall to their demise on the cliffs below, while the Frankenstein monster is destroyed once again by fire.

ABBOTT AND COSTELLO MEET FRANKENSTEIN was a very big success, but all hopes of reviving the vintage movie monsters in a new series of horror films was just a glimmer that faded away very quickly. ABBOTT AND

Above: Boris Karloff in Columbia's THE DEVIL COMMANDS (1941).

COSTELLO MEET FRANKENSTEIN was truly the last outing for Universal's beloved monsters: Frankenstein's monster, the Wolfman and Count Dracula. As for Abbott and Costello, they still had Dr. Jekyll and Mr. Hyde, the mummy and the mad doctor (Boris Karloff) to meet.

BORIS KARLOFF - THE MADDEST DOCTOR!

While Universal Pictures was keeping its main horror attractions busy, other studios jumped on the band wagon to cash in on the monster - horror movie boom of the 1940's, primarily RKO Pictures and Columbia Pictures.

By 1940, Universal was in the midst of grooming their new horror star Lon Chaney, Jr., while Boris Karloff was fulfilling his contractual obligations over at Columbia. Karloff signed up to make five "mad doctor" movies for Columbia, beginning with THE MAN THEY COULD NOT HANG (1939). Between 1940 and 1941, Karloff filmed THE MAN WITH NINE LIVES (1940), BEFORE I HANG (1940), THE DEVIL COMMANDS (1941) and THE BOOGIE MAN WILL GET YOU (1942).

THE MAN WITH NINE LIVES (1940), directed by Nick Grinde, featured Karloff as a rather mild

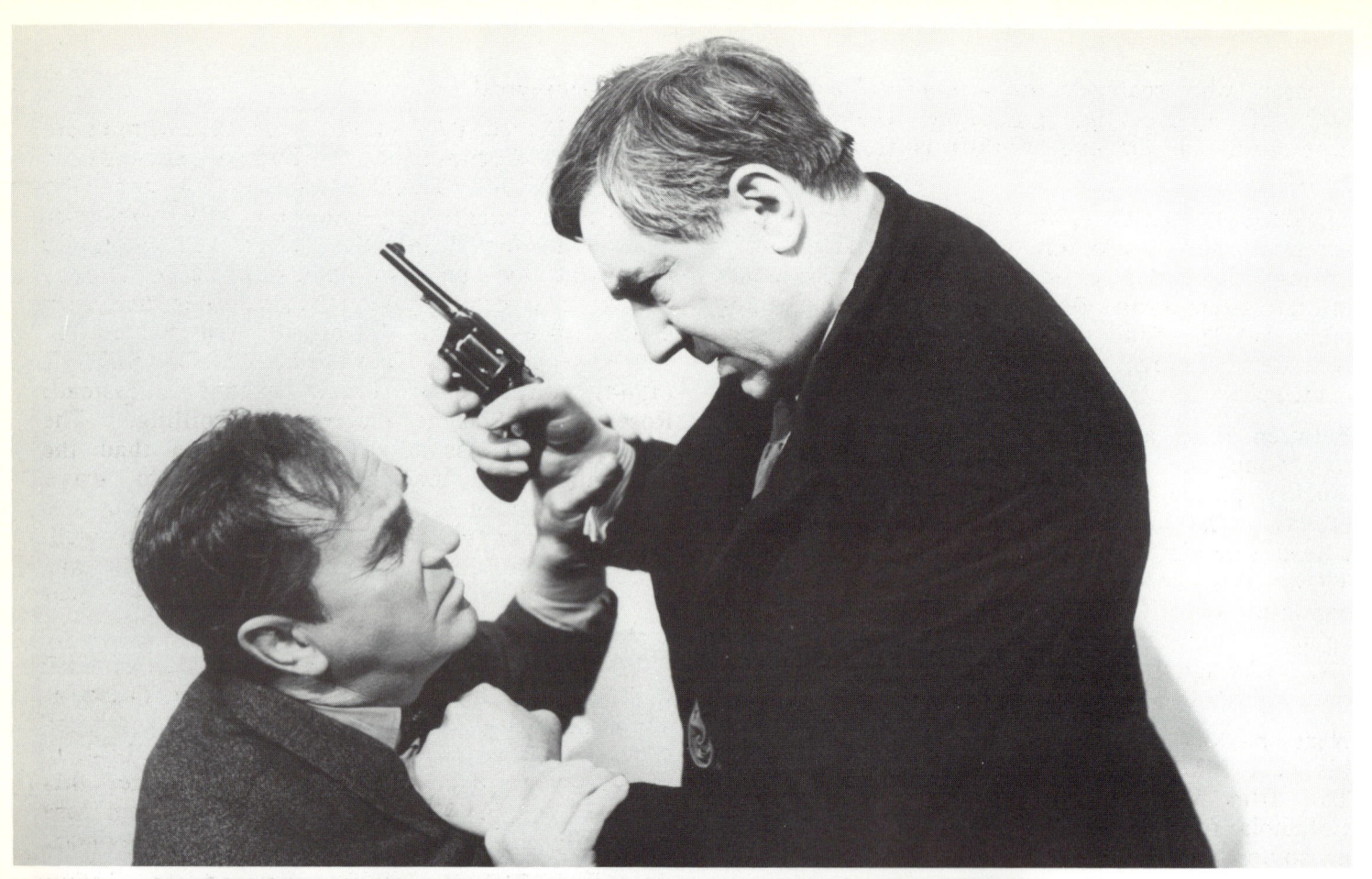

Above: Bela Lugosi struggles with Stanley Ridges in BLACK FRIDAY (1940).
Left: Bela Lugosi as mad scientist Carruthers in THE DEVIL BAT (1941).

scientist who searches for a cure to cancer by way of a freezing technique that he has developed. In the end, Karloff is frozen for ten years.

BEFORE I HANG (1940) starred Karloff as a scientist and murderer who commits ghastly killings in order to continue his experiments in an attempt to find a cure for the aging process. The film, directed by Nick Grinde, was remade several times throughout movie history.

Between films at Columbia, Karloff jumped over to Monogram Pictures where he made the quickly pieced together monster film THE APE (1940). The low budget film featured Karloff as a mad scientist who searches for a cure to polio. To do this, he disguises himself as an ape and commits ghastly murders to obtain a certain spinal fluid required to cure a poor crippled girl. As always, Karloff's good intentions are outweighed by his ghastly methods.

Next, Karloff jumped back to Columbia to make his next film, THE DEVIL COMMANDS (1941). The film was by far superior to the other Columbia films, with Karloff as Dr. Julian Blair, a somewhat mad but devoted scientist who develops an apparatus that allows him to communicate with the dead. For the film, Karloff was in top form, and the stylish and atmospheric direction of Edward Dmytryk is compellingly good.

THE BOOGIE MAN WILL GET YOU (1942) was actually filmed and completed in 1941 prior to Karloff's departure to Broadway. The film marked the end of Karloff's mad doctor series at Columbia. The film teamed Karloff and Peter Lorre, both of whom had just completed a Kay Kyser vehicle for RKO Pictures along with Bela Lugosi entitled YOU'LL FIND OUT (1940). THE BOOGIE MAN WILL GET YOU starred Karloff as Dr. Nathaniel Billings and Peter Lorre as Dr. Lorentz. Together they attempt to create a race of electrical superman to aide in the war against Germany. The premise was a rip-off of Universal's MAN MADE MONSTER (1941) with Lon Chaney, Jr.

MORE FAMOUS MAD SCIENTISTS!

Bela Lugosi, like Boris Karloff, certainly had his share of good roles during the 1930's. However, during the 1940's, the actor had to accept inept roles in poorly written and directed low budget thrillers from poverty row studios like Monogram, PRC and Screen Guild Pictures. The actor would occasionally land a role for the big studios like RKO, Columbia or even Universal.

In THE DEVIL BAT (1940) from PRC (Producers Releasing Corporation) Lugosi starred as Physician Paul Carruthers, a mad doctor who creates an electrically-enlarged killer vampire bat. In the film, the actor is eventually destroyed by his own monster bat, but not before delivering some meaty dialogue with sinister glee. Bela Lugosi did not star in the film's sequel, THE DEVIL BAT'S DAUGHTER (1944), directed by Frank Wisbar. Instead, Rosemary LaPlanche received top billing. The sequel was less of a horror movie than the original, as a mad scientist tries to drive LaPlanche mad by making her believe the killer bat her father created is alive and well. Finally, the original Bela Lugosi vehicle was re-issued to theaters as KILLER BATS just around the time the sequel was released.

THE DEVIL BAT was remade by PRC as THE FLYING SERPENT (1946) with George Zucco as an insane archaeologist who discovers an Aztec treasure and uses a giant prehistoric bird to protect his discovery and to murder his victims. As in THE DEVIL BAT, the giant bird eventually does its master in during the climax.

BLACK FRIDAY (1940), directed by Arthur Lubin, was Universal's final Boris Karloff and Bela Lugosi vehicle. The film was based on the original screenplay by Curt Siodmak and Eric Taylor about a kind doctor, Dr. Sovac (played by Karloff) who transplants the brain of his kind friend into the body of a gangster named Kingsley (Stanley Ridges). Lugosi was given the role of rival gangster Marnay. Originally, Lugosi was to have Ridges's part, but the footage of Lugosi in that part was simply not as effective as director Lubin had hoped for and the footage was shelved. BLACK FRIDAY marked one of the few films in which Karloff played a benevolent doctor. In this case, the real monster was the doctor's patient, who goes on a murder spree. For those faithful aficionados of horror films, BLACK FRIDAY was the movie in which reporters were invited onto the set by the studio to watch Lugosi being hypnotized for his death scene. Unfortunately, BLACK FRIDAY did not fare well as a follow-up to SON OF FRANKENSTEIN (1939).

Lionel Atwill received top billing in Universal's THE STRANGE CASE OF DR. RX (1942), a part originally intended for Lon Chaney. In the film, Atwill plays a mad scientist (which is what the actor did very well, hence the reason why he won the part over Chaney) who drains the blood of the living to aid him in his morbid experiment involving the transplantation of a gorilla's brain into the body of a man. The film was a lessor-known variation on the studio's earlier film MURDERS IN THE RUE MORGUE (1932). The actor also starred in Universal's THE MAD DOCTOR OF MARKET STREET (1942) in which the actor discovers a potion that will revive the dead. Both films were unfortunately a flop for the studio next to the big commercial successes of THE WOLFMAN (1941) and GHOST OF FRANKENSTEIN (1942) mainly because Universal allotted a low production budget on both films. THE STRANGE CASE OF DR. RX and THE MAD DOCTOR OF MARKET STREET marked the actor's final performances in a leading role. From this point on, the actor would receive supporting assignments in monster movies, but considering the situation surrounding the actor and his sordid rape trial at the time, Atwill was just happy to be working.

George Zucco (1886-1960) made his screen debut by starring in minor roles in such fantasy films as THE MAN WHO COULD WORK MIRACLES (1937), THE CAT AND THE CANARY (1939) and THE HUNCHBACK OF NOTRE DAME (1939). The actor also starred as the evil high priest in both THE MUMMY'S HAND (1940) and THE MUMMY'S GHOST (1944). Zucco, like Lionel Atwill, John Carradine, Boris Karloff and Bela Lugosi, made most of his horror film appearances as a mad scientist. The actor, who usually received a supporting role, was given top billing for Paramount's THE MONSTER AND THE GIRL (1941), not to be confused with Republic's THE LADY AND THE MONSTER (1944). In the Paramount film, Zucco stars as a mad doctor who surgically transplants the brain of a wrongly executed man into the head of a vicious ape. The result of which produces a raging monster who goes on a killing spree destroying those who originally sentenced him to death. The film was a remake of the 1920 silent film GO AND GET IT. Zucco proved to be quite good in this effort, and the film's minor success led the actor to many supporting roles in Universal and poverty row horror films.

Metro Goldwyn Mayer also got into the swing of things and produced a very respectable version of Robert Louis Stevenson's DR. JEKYLL AND MR. HYDE (1941). The Grade "A" production produced and directed by Victor

Fleming starred Academy Award winning actor Spencer Tracey in the infamous dual role alongside of Ingrid Bergman and Lana Turner. Although the MGM film lacked the enthusiasm and vigor of both the 1920 and 1939 versions and although Tracy's Hyde was not as physically monstrous a beast as that of both Barrymore and March's Mr. Hyde characterizations, the film offered great dialogue, beautiful photography, stylish direction and very strong performances by the cast.

George Zucco returned in yet another leading role for Fox. The film was entitled DR. RENAULT'S SECRET (1942), a sound remake of the silent classic THE WIZARD (1927), in which actor Gustav Von Seyffertitz played a mad doctor who uses his ape monster to kill his enemies. Zucco, equally menacing as his predecessor, replaced the role of Von Seyffertitz, while actor J. Carrol Naish played the new ape-man. The remake was produced on a minuscule budget and, considering the limited finances, was directed rather well by Virgil Miller.

Bela Lugosi starred in THE CORPSE VANISHES (1942). In this programmer from Monogram directed by Wallace Fox, Lugosi stars as orchid fancier Dr. Lorenz, who kidnaps and restrains his female victims and then proceeds to remove their mysterious fluids to restore his aged wife's youth and beauty. The film, being that low budget thriller that it is, offers some rather good moments, one of which features Lugosi's assistants, a sinister old woman (played well by Minerva Urecal) and her demented son (Frank Moran), up to no good in an underground mortuary. The script, written by Harvey Gates, Gerald Schnitzer and Sam Robins, played the film for entertainment rather than credibility.

Lugosi, fulfilling his contract at Monogram, also starred in the much superior film BOWERY AT MIDNIGHT (1942). In the film, the actor plays Professor Brenner, at least by day! By night the professor becomes the sinister Mr. Hyde-type Karl Wagner. Both characters are destroyed during the film's climax by a cellar full of the living dead victims that Lugosi put there and that a crazed doctor restores to life. BOWERY AT MIDNIGHT was loosely based on Lugosi's earlier horror film, DARK EYES OF LONDON (1939). The film, directed by Wallace

Opposite Page: A vintage poster for the Spencer Tracy film DR. JEKYLL AND MR. HYDE (1941).
Right: Bela Lugosi as Dr. Lorenz and Minerva Urecal in Monogram's THE CORPSE VANISHES (1942).

Fox is above average for Monogram, with numerous characters and subplots floating about.

PRC's THE MONSTER MAKER (1944) starred J. Carrol Naish as a mad doctor who turns Ralph Morgan into a hideous monster. The film was slightly above the average standards for a programmer from PRC and Monogram.

THE MAN ON HALF MOON STREET (1944) was yet another film about a mad scientist who finds a method of arresting the aging process. As always, the scientist's true age is revealed during the climax. The film was remade by Hammer Studios as THE MAN WHO COULD CHEAT DEATH (1959).

Much more impressive was Republic's THE LADY AND THE MONSTER (1944), starring Erich Von Stroheim, "The Man You Love To Hate!" In the film, Stroheim plays the diabolical mad scientist Dr. Franz Mueller. Mueller extracts the brain of a freshly dead financier and keeps it alive in a tank. Eventually, the brain grows to control and influence all those around it. THE LADY AND THE MONSTER was the first of many " Brain in the tank" films to be based on Curt Siodmak's very popular story, *Donovan's Brain*. The film is stylishly directed by George Sherman.

Of course there were other lesser known "mad doctor" films in the 1940's, such as VALLEY OF THE ZOMBIES (1946) and FACE OF MARBLE (1945) as well as the Invisible Man and Frankenstein films from Universal Studios. But for all the sub-genre's assets, no performer could ever match the brilliance and conviction of Boris Karloff's mad scientist characterizations for Columbia Pictures. He was the greatest and the maddest of all the mad scientists.

THOSE CREEPY OLD DARK HOUSES!

The 1940's offered many old house chillers about creepy cats, spooks, haunted houses and beasts with five fingers. These films were usually great fun to watch and very entertaining because of their tongue-in-cheek suspense.

Universal's THE BLACK CAT (1941), directed by Albert S. Rogell, starred actors Bela Lugosi, Basil Rathbone, Broderick Crawford, Gale Sondergaard and Anne Gwynne in what is perhaps the best of the old house romps made in Hollywood during the 1940's. The film is complete with secret passages, yowling cats, greedy relatives, wills, murders, a gloomy old mansion in which a sinister old lady keeps a crematorium for her beloved cats and some very sinister characters, primarily that of Rathbone's. The film was Universal's attempt to deviate from the straight forward horror formula by concocting a mixture of horror and comedy. The film works well, and although THE BLACK CAT has less to do with Poe than its 1934 namesake, the film is very enjoyable.

HORROR ISLAND (1941) was another old house romp with spooks that starred Peggy Moran, while THE NIGHT HAS EYES (1942), stylishly directed by Leslie Arliss, featured James Mason in a powerful rehashing of Universal's OLD DARK HOUSE (1932) from director James Whale.

THE UNINVITED (1944) was one of the few ghost chillers to be played for straight horror rather than laughs. Even today, the film remains far superior to many of the more contemporary ghost films released like THE HAUNTING (1963), THE INNOCENT (1965), THE LEGEND OF HELL HOUSE (1973), GHOST STORY (1980) and even POLTERGEIST (1981). To begin with, the film is of a separate school altogether, and must be judged by its own standards, however THE UNINVITED was far before its time and is technically brilliant in lieu of the limitations a film of its kind was up against. By today's standards, THE UNINVITED is a simple, old fashion but brilliant ghost tale from director Lewis Allen made in the similar style of Carl Dreyer's classic VAMPYR (1931). Allen produced an eerie feeling as if there was always something lurking behind you throughout the film, beginning when actors Ray Milland and Ruth Hussey first step into the big house. The horror film relies on dialogue and the superb photography of Charles Lang, with little emphasis on the special visual effects of Ferciot Edouart. In any event, the film is incredibly good and must not be missed by fans of quality vintage horror.

DEAD OF NIGHT (1945), like THE UNINVITED, was another quality tale of ghosts, madness and haunted old houses. The anthology film consisted of five ghost stories told in the course of an evening by a group of guests at an old house. The most striking of the tales are *The Ventriloquist Story* and *The Haunted Mirror*. The first tale tells how a ventriloquist's dummy comes to life and drives his owner to madness. This segment was effectively directed by Alberto Cavalcanti. The later told the story of a mirror bought from an antique store as a wedding present. The newly wed husband is soon influenced and seduced by the mirror to the point where he begins to

Above: A vintage poster from Universal's star-studded horror film THE BLACK CAT (1941).
Right: Ray Milland and Ruth Hussey in THE UNINVITED (1944).

murder, even his own wife. This segment was directed by Robert Hamer and is the most striking of the segments. DEAD OF NIGHT was clearly influenced by the Val Lewton horror films made at RKO at the time in which the film avoids outright statements of horror, and concentrates on suggestion.

Finally, the best of all the old dark house chillers from the 1940's was undoubtedly the classy little horror film, THE BEAST WITH FIVE FINGERS (1946).

THE BEAST WITH FIVE FINGERS in its suggestive ways literally pokes fun at its own horror subject matter in a melodramatic way. The plot tells of a partially paralyzed concert pianist (Victor Francen) who has retired to his gloomy mansion in a small Italian village. There he is looked after by only his secretary (Peter Lorre), who is on the borderline of madness, and a private nurse (Andrea King) as he continues to play his beloved Bach with his usable left hand. Suddenly, we are faced with the pianist's death, followed by a profane, unexplained horror. We soon discover that the corpse's decapitated left hand is alive and well and out for revenge against the sole inhabitants of the manor.

THE BEAST WITH FIVE FINGERS is unquestionably writer-director Robert Siodmak's best screenplay. Together with William McGann's brilliant cinematic effects and Peter Lorre's sensational paranoia induced performance, the film is unsurpassed as one of the better old house chillers from the 1940's. Director Robert Florey uses shadows and dark, gloomy sets to create the film's cold atmosphere and a feeling of entrapment. Even the supporting cast, which includes J. Carrol Naish and Charles Dingle, is above par.

COLUMBIA'S MONSTER MASH!

It has been said that the Columbia horror films of the 1940's were classics of the "B" film genre. If anything, they provided Universal Pictures with some competition. Columbia launched a series of horror and monster films that began with the "mad doctor" movies of Boris Karloff. The studio also produced RETURN OF THE VAMPIRE (1944), CRY OF THE WEREWOLF (1944) and THE SHEWOLF OF LONDON (1946). These films were pretty basic in premise but they also provided good, well-mounted entertainment non- the- less.

RETURN OF THE VAMPIRE (1944) was a promotional and experimental piece from Columbia. The film was an attempt to capitalize on the career of Bela Lugosi as the vampire king as well as a test to see how well the film would be received by moviegoers and critics. The film was Lugosi's best screen role since his characterization of Ygor in GHOST OF FRANKENSTEIN (1941). Based on the idea by Kurt Neumann, the script by Griffin Jay updated the vampire lore by setting the film against a war-torn London. A Nazi bombardment of London frees the centuries-old vampire Armand Tesla from his crypt and once revived, the vampire seeks revenge against the man who destroyed him with a little help from his werewolf assistant (played by Matt Willis).

Lugosi was afforded plenty of rich dialogue to his character and he received several close-ups and entrances throughout the film, not to mention the fact that he is destroyed twice. The actor, in later interviews, once commented how please he was with the project. For his services, Lugosi was paid a mere $3,500. The entire film cost Columbia nearly $75,000 but during its initial release, RETURN OF THE VAMPIRE grossed over $500,000.

Because Universal still owned the film rights to Bram Stoker's *Dracula*, Columbia was forced to changed the name of Lugosi's character to Armand Tesla. However, had one not known about the name change, one would swear that Lugosi was reprising his role of Count Dracula. It was quite clear that the script was written around Lugosi's screen image. Like Lugosi's Dracula, Tesla could be destroyed by a wooden stake and sunlight and he did not cast a reflection in mirrors. Universal also insisted that the world "Dracula" not be used anywhere in the script.

The impressive "B" movie was well directed by Lew Landers in a style reminiscent of the old Universal vampire films from the 1930's. In addition to Bela Lugosi, the film stars Frieda Inescort as the film's Professor Van Helsing character and Matt Willis as the werewolf, the latter a clear attempt on Columbia's behalf to capitalize on the success of Lon Chaney's sympathetic Wolfman characterization. Executives also felt that by combining both monsters effectively they could also cash in on the highly successful market that Universal launched with FRANKENSTEIN MEETS THE WOLFMAN (1943) and HOUSE OF FRANKENSTEIN (1944).

In CRY OF THE WEREWOLF (1944), Columbia's next monster film, actress Nina Foch (who also starred in RETURN OF THE VAMPIRE) inherits a

Above: Matt Willis confronts vampire Bela Lugosi in Columbia's stylish "B" horror film RETURN OF THE VAMPIRE (1943).

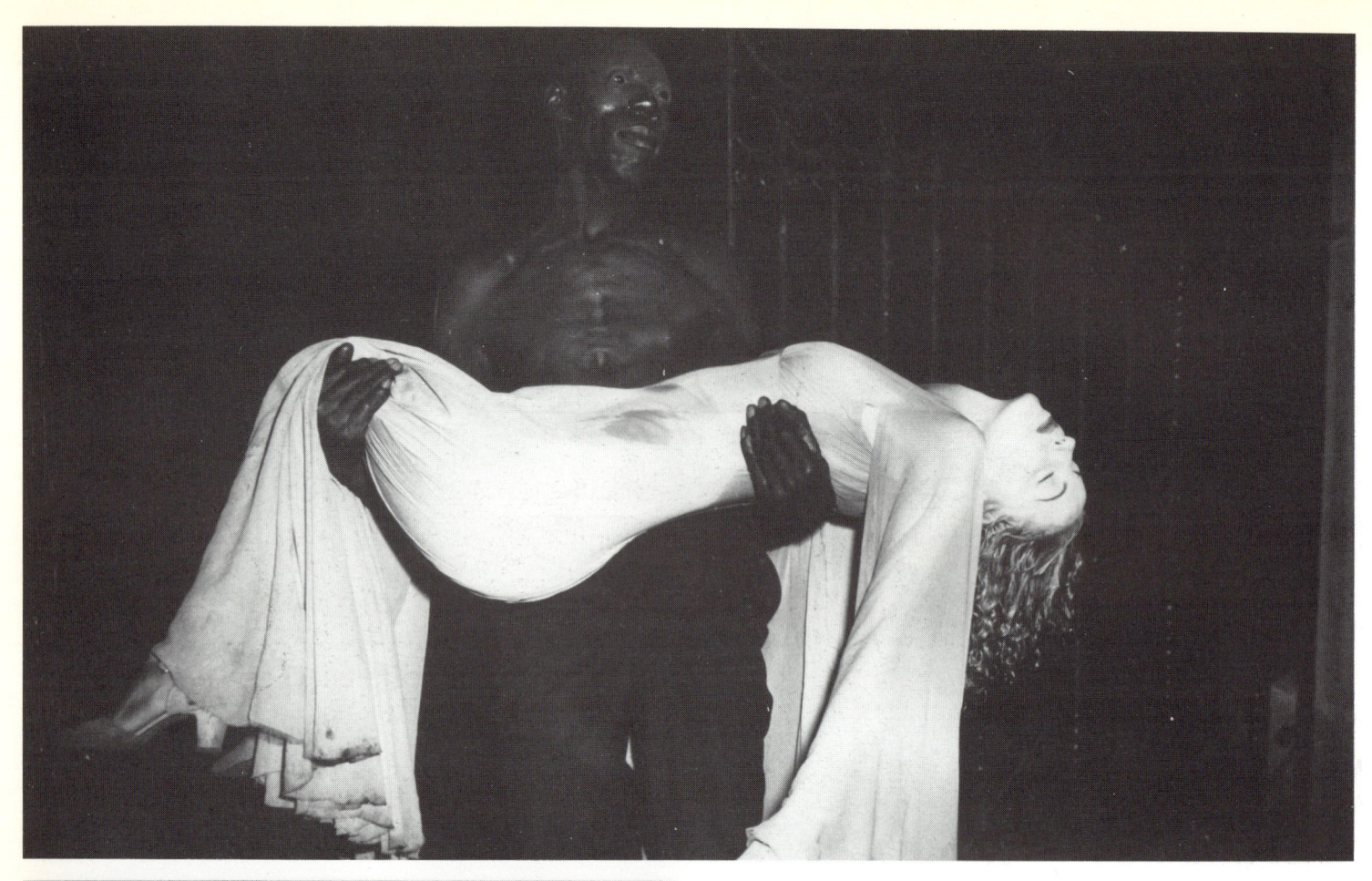

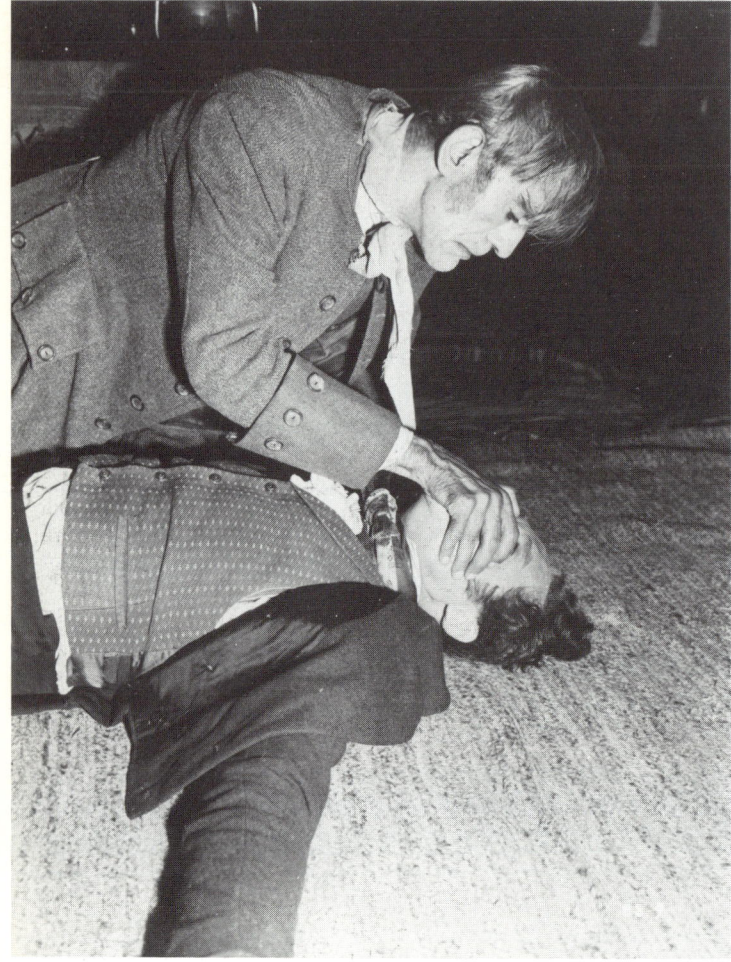

lycanthropy curse from her mother and shape-changes into a murderous werewolf. The film was directly influenced by Val Lewton's more successful horror film THE CAT PEOPLE (1943), but unfortunately for Columbia, the film was not as stylish a vehicle as the Lewton film nor the studio's previous horror efforts.

THE SHEWOLF OF LONDON (1946) was a revamping of Universal's THE WEREWOLF OF LONDON (1935). The Columbia film starred June Lockhart as another woman who inherits a curse that compels her to transform into a shewolf by night. Jean Yarbrough directed and it is Yarbrough's talent that creates some interesting scenes of the shewolf stalking its victims at night. The supernatural occurrences of this film are explained away as being pretend Both CRY OF THE WEREWOLF and THE SHEWOLF OF LONDON could have done better at the box office had Columbia invested in a bankable name like Bela Lugosi or Boris Karloff.

VAL LEWTON'S CHAMBER OF HORRORS!

The year 1942 introduced a new era in horror movies. Val Lewton, a producer at RKO Pictures with a lot of influence, introduced a

Val Lewton's horror films for RKO Pictures were both stylish and influential.
Opposite Top: Francis Dee is carried off by a zombie in I WALKED WITH A ZOMBIE (1943).
Opposite Bottom: Sadistic grave-robber and murderer Boris Karloff does in another victim in THE BODY SNATCHER (1945).
Above: Another scene from Val Lewton's I WALKED WITH A ZOMBIE (1943).
Right: Boris Karloff is bed-strickened in ISLE OF THE DEAD (1944), another Lewton horror classic.

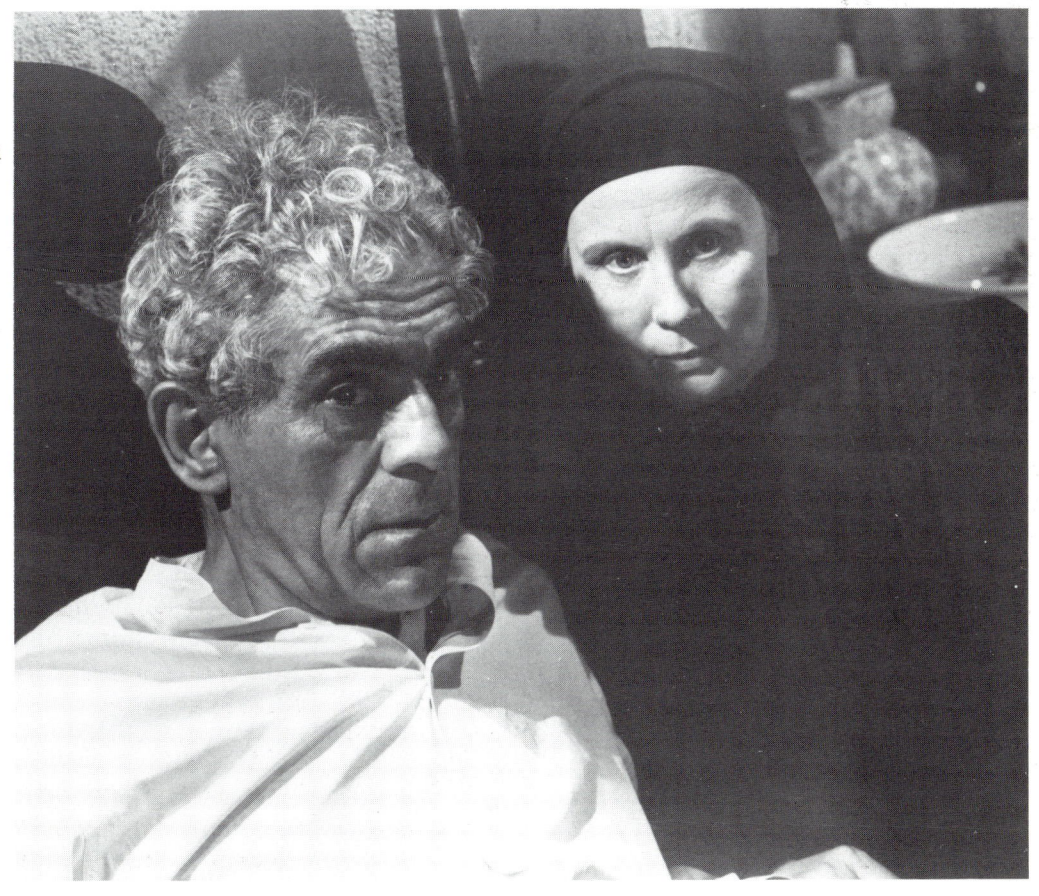

new style of horror and reshaped the way monsters would be portrayed on the screen. Lewton's monsters would take on a new dimension as opposed to the regular one-dimensional monsters from the Universal movies. Lewton believed that horror spawned from the imagination as a result of suggestion was more frightening than physically showing the monster on the screen. With this "new" suggestive technique, Lewton produced a series of stylish horror films that include: THE CAT PEOPLE (1942), I WALKED WITH A ZOMBIE (1943), LEOPARD MAN (1943), THE SEVENTH VICTIM (1943) THE GHOST SHIP (1943), ISLE OF THE DEAD (1944) CURSE OF THE CAT PEOPLE (1944), THE BODY SNATCHER (1945) and BEDLAM (1946). Then there are the quartet of horror films that followed that were influenced by Lewton's horror thrillers.

For his quartet of psychological horror films, Lewton usually worked with three skilled directors, Jacques Tourneur, Robert Wise and Mark Robson. Together, the three filmmakers proved that a horror film produced on a low budget could be made to appear as a lavish, big budget production. Furthermore, Lewton's low budget horror films generated a hefty return at the box office, which was most important to RKO executives.

THE CAT PEOPLE (1943), stylishly directed by Jacques Tourneur, was the first of Lewton's films. The movie dealt with supernatural events concerning a woman (Simone Simon) who fears she is a were-cat (half human-half cat). Furthermore, the lady weds the man she loves, but is unable to give herself to him sexually in fear that her orgasmic release will cause her to transform into the beast she really is.

The lurid tale of romance and sexual repression was a treat for the intellectual horror movie fan, and although Tourneur only gave us one glimpse of the panther woman in full transformation, THE CAT PEOPLE reaches heights of suspense and horror unequalled by the more traditional Universal monster movies. Tourneur's stylish use of shadows and images (originally used by the great filmmaker of the silent era) were quite effective even in 1942. THE CAT PEOPLE literally changed the face of the horror cinema forever, and because of this, the film is considered a milestone in the genre by horror film critics and film historians alike.

Just as a short note of reference, THE CAT PEOPLE was remade in 1983 with Nastassja Kinski and Malcolm McDowell and was the basis for the shoddy Stephen King contemporary thriller SLEEP WALKERS (1992).

I WALKED WITH A ZOMBIE (1943) was as misleading a title as THE CAT PEOPLE. The film, directed by Jacques Tourneur, implies by its title that it is a traditional zombie movie similar to the zombie films produced at the time by the poverty row film company Monogram. This was certainly not the case. Instead, I WALKED WITH A ZOMBIE was a psychological thriller with strong supernatural overtones. The story, created and written by Curt Siodmak, was modeled after the traditional "Jane Eyre" story. In the film, actress Francis Dee portrays a nurse hired to look after the wife of a sugar plantation owner (Tom Conway). The wife, as we later discover, has been zombified by her own mother-in-law. Francis Dee also has some very frightening encounters with the plantation workers, some of who have also been zombified. Quite frankly, the film is near brilliant and superior at times to THE CAT PEOPLE in evoking horror by suggestive means; a style that filmmaker Tourneur had perfected. Tourneur turned an old subject matter into fresh material by using his innovative style of filmmaking (years before I WALKED WITH A ZOMBIE there was WHITE ZOMBIE of 1932, a film that dealt with the same basic subject matter).

Both Tourneur's THE LEOPARD MAN (1943), an excellent adaptation of Cornell Woolrich's *Black Alibi* about a series of murders attributed to an escaped leopard, and Mark Robson's GHOST SHIP (1943), considered lost because of a plagiarism suit, were both superior horror thrillers patterned along the lines of THE CAT PEOPLE and I WALKED WITH A ZOMBIE.

Boris Karloff even starred in three separate horror films from producer Val Lewton: THE BODY SNATCHER (1945), ISLE OF THE DEAD (1945) and BEDLAM (1946) all of which are superior to the kind of films the actor was turning out at Universal and Columbia. For fans of Karloff, it was quite refreshing to see Karloff cast in fresh and innovative material.

THE BODY SNATCHER, directed by Robert Wise and based on the famous Robert Louis Stevenson story of the same title, was a horror tale that relied heavily on dialogue and characterization rather than physical violence, cheap shock scenes, and monsters. Both Boris Karloff and Bela Lugosi carry their lines well (the film proved that Lugosi, who had normally been stuck with a streak of bad casting, could hold his own in delivering his dialogue with great effectiveness contrary to the beliefs of Universal executives. In fact, it was his performance in this film that actually broke the stigma of the actor's ineffectiveness as a performer in the minds of Universal executives which in turn led to his winning the part of Count Dracula in ABBOTT AND COSTELLO MEET FRANKENSTEIN of later years).

In the film, Karloff is clearly the villain, playing a sinister grave-robber named Mr. Gray who supplies a fresh batch of newly buried corpses to Dr. MacFarlane (Henry Daniell) for his experiments in his medical school. THE BODY SNATCHER is a brilliant film about grave-robbing and manipulation and Karloff is great as the film's diabolical and monstrous killer, while Lugosi, on the other hand, plays Joseph, Dr. MacFarlane's snooping houseman who is killed off halfway through the film.

It was a fact that Lugosi's role in THE BODY SNATCHER was actually manufactured into the script so that his name alongside of Karloff's could create more publicity. Had Lugosi refused the role, the part would have been scratched out as quickly as it was created. Despite the small part, Lugosi made it stand out quite effectively.

ISLE OF THE DEAD (1945) and BEDLAM (1946), both directed by Mark Robson, were equally good in comparison to THE BODY SNATCHER. ISLE OF THE DEAD was set during the Balkan war of 1912. In the film, Karloff plays General Nikolas Pherides. The general returns to a small island to visit the grave-site of his wife and discovers that the island is besiezed by the plague. The general believes the plague to be the cause of a vampire, and the events of the film even lead us to believe the same. Karloff is convincing and strong in this role as he delivers some meaty, authoritative dialogue. The film was well acted by its cast and the manipulation of the audience by the use of shadows and images by the director is stylishly clever. ISLE OF THE DEAD is perhaps RKO's most overlooked horror film, and the film leads us to believe that the monster is first, the plague; second, a vampire; and ultimately, Karloff's madness and paranoia!

BEDLAM (1946) is also magnificent little horror film carried mostly by Karloff's brilliant performance. In fact, many film historians believe Karloff's performance in BEDLAM to be his best work to date. The premise was simple, yet disturbing, as Karloff portrays a cruel chief warden named Master George Sims, head of an insane asylum. The authentic film was more of a psychological account of how such prisons were operated and the many atrocities involved, and Karloff was purely evil as the chief warden; a true monster of the worst kind.

BEDLAM marked Lewton's final film for RKO and Karloff's final film for Lewton. Lewton died in 1951, but his stylish and artistic legacy remains an example of the quality horror films made during the vintage 1940's. His style of filmmaking, though innovative by vintage standards, has influenced hundreds of horror films made during and after the release of his first and last film.

BEAUTY AND THE BEAST, OR, HOW I LEARNED TO LOVE THE BEAST!

Universal's THE WOLFMAN (1941) was responsible for setting off a chain reaction of sub-genre films dealing with transformation and beasts. The popularity of the Universal film prompted other studios to cash in on the werewolf legend in a variety of different forms. The first of these was THE UNDYING MONSTER (1942) from Fox.

THE UNDYING MONSTER is unfortunately one of vintage Hollywood's most overlooked horror films. The film was literally overshadowed by the success and popularity of Universal's THE WOLFMAN (1941) and has been ever since. In fact, the film is believed to be lost, since it has not surfaced since its initial release in 1942, which is a shame. Many who have seen the film when it was originally released remember it to be a stylish and atmospheric rendition of the werewolf legend. Several film historians have even called the film as being the equivalent of THE WOLFMAN. The modest little film was directed by John Brahm and adapted from the very good mystery thriller written by Jessie Douglas Kerruish. The film supposedly told the tale of a family cursed by lycanthropy. John Howard played the role of the monster, who is shot in the moors during the film's climax. The film was released heavily censored in England as THE HAMMOND MYSTERY.

PRC's THE MAD MONSTER (1942) was another low budget monster film made to capitalize on the success of THE WOLFMAN (1941). The film starred George Zucco as Dr. Lorenzo Cameron who transforms actor Glenn Strange into a werewolf-type creature via blood transfusions with wolves (this theme would later evolve into the more successful films THE WEREWOLF of 1957 and I WAS A TEENAGE WEREWOLF also of 1957).

Left: A rare poster for the very stylish werewolf film THE UNDYING MONSTER (1942).
Above Right: Bela Lugosi is attacked by his own gorilla in Monogram's THE APE MAN (1943).
Opposite Top: A scene from Jean Cocteau's classic BEAUTY AND THE BEAST (1946).
Opposite Bottom: A scene from monogram's shoddy sequel RETURN OF THE APEMAN (1944).

THE APEMAN (1943) was Monogram's version of the increasingly popular werewolf legend. The film was an attempt to create a new monster by using the reputation and name of Bela Lugosi. Lugosi, as half-man, half-ape James Brewster, struggles to deliver the poor dialogue of the weak script through loads of hairy make-up. Only the fresh fluid obtained by killing innocent victims at night can cure his horrid condition. The film suffers from hammy performances and Karl Brown's weak adaptation of the original story *They Creep In The Dark*. Despite these flaws, Monogram immediately launched a sequel entitled RETURN OF THE APEMAN (1943), in which Lugosi and John Carradine play scientists who discover a

115

Above: The "Creeper" himself, Rondo Hatton, in a publicity shot for Universal Pictures.
Opposite: A poster for MIGHTY JOE YOUNG (1949)

prehistoric man (Frank Moran). As guessed, the Neanderthal beast goes on a senseless killing spree. The film was inconsistent with the original.

Finally, BEAUTY AND THE BEAST (1945) is the classic allegory about the beautiful girl who sacrifices her life by giving herself to the beast in order to save her father from a horrid death. The heroine, at first, is repulsed by the beast, but eventually, in a strange erotic way, she finds herself falling in love with the inner kindness of the supreme ruler. The theme of "Beauty and The Beast" is as timeless as the horror film and the basis for so many vintage monster movies, primarily KING KONG (1933). The fantasy takes place in the Magic Kingdom (Not Disney!) and is directed with awe-inspiring atmosphere, costumes and cinematic style by Jean Cocteau. BEAUTY AND THE BEAST is the ultimate monster and romance film; it is THE BRIDE OF FRANKENSTEIN and DRACULA rolled into one. The Cocteau version is a milestone of the genre, although the film is recognized more for its poetic beauty rather than its horror overtones.

ATTACK OF THE CREEPER!

The Creeper, as created and portrayed by actor Rondo Hatton (born 1894), emerged during the mid 1940's. Here was an actor the studios loved because of his physical appearance and brute size. The actor was ideal in roles of killers, madmen and monsters without ever having to apply any make-up on his face. The actor was nicknamed The Creeper as a result of a really good role in the Sherlock Holmes thriller, PEARL OF DEATH (1944). The actor also had a role in Universal's JUNGLE CAPTIVE (1945) as Otto Kruger's assistant.

In HOUSE OF HORRORS (1946), Universal cast the actor in the leading role of the Creeper (again), a brute killer! In the film, a demented artist (played by Martin Kosleck) saves the Creeper from drowning. In return, however, the Creeper kills off most of the artist's enemies.

Universal was so pleased with the audience's reaction to the image of the Creeper and featured the actor in yet another Sherlock Holmes thriller, THE SPIDER WOMAN STRIKES BACK (1946), a sequel to THE SPIDER WOMAN (1944) in which actress Gale Sondergaard repeats her title role. In the film, Hatton plays a pseudo-type Creeper who aids the mad woman in extracting blood from female victims in order to make a potion.

Hatton next appeared in THE BRUTE MAN (1946), the actor's final movie role. In the film, the actor plays a handsome (with make-up?) scientist whose face is disfigured and scared by acid in a laboratory explosion (remember THE

John Ford and Merian C. Cooper Present
"MIGHTY JOE YOUNG"
starring
TERRY MOORE
BEN JOHNSON
and
ROBERT ARMSTRONG
with
FRANK McHUGH
Directed by
ERNEST B. SCHOEDSACK
TECHNICAL CREATOR WILLIS O'BRIEN
SCREEN PLAY BY RUTH ROSE
DISTRIBUTED BY
RKO Radio Pictures
AN ARKO PRODUCTION
MERIAN COOPER'S AMAZING ADVENTURE IN THE UNUSUAL!

PHANTOM OF THE OPERA and THE DARKMAN)? As a result of his disfigurement, the scientist becomes a disfigured madman and killer.

Rondo Hatton only contributed very briefly to the genre of vintage monster movies because of his untimely death in 1946. His popularity, though, was immense and the image he created of the Creeper continues to last in the memories of vintage moviegoers around the world.

AN APE CALLED JOE!

The success of KING KONG (1933) continued to linger even through the 1940's. As early as 1942, RKO had been planning another KING KONG film which originally became known as MR. JOSEPH YOUNG OF AFRICA. The film, which bore a strong resemblance to KING KONG in its premise, was finally produced and released in 1949 as MIGHTY JOE YOUNG.

MIGHTY JOE YOUNG was another tale that centered around an oversized gorilla with the use of stop-motion photography. The effects were that of newcomer Ray Harryhausen, a young man who worshipped the special effects of Willis O'Brien. O'Brien actually did some fifteen percent of the animation in MIGHTY JOE YOUNG, while Harryhausen completed the remaining eighty-five percent. And I must add, Harryhausen's dynamic effects dazzled the pants off of Hollywood. The effects were much smoother than that in KING KONG, earning the studio and O'Brien an Academy Award. Though more lovable than his predecessor Kong, Joe was more adventurous and quicker in movement, and the script involved the ape in more moments of peril in the modern city.

The premise is basically the same with some moderate disguises. An African native trades the infant gorilla to a young child named Jill Young. In return she gives him a flashlight. Jill names the gorilla Joe, and together they spend their youth in the African forest. Eventually, the ape grows up to be nearly forty-feet tall (sometimes less), but Jill maintains her relationship with the ape until the day American Max O'Hara arrives in Africa with the idea of roping wild animals for his sheik new nightclub The Golden Safari. Naturally, O'Hara is overwhelmed with Joe's size and presence and he cunningly convinces Jill into allowing him to transport the oversized gorilla to America. What follows is a dazzling display of special effects in the league of the original KING KONG. Unlike Kong and his son, Joe survives the ordeal and is able to live his life in peace in the jungles of Africa.

MIGHTY JOE YOUNG was the only effort of giant movie monsters in the 1940's, and the film, oddly enough, never inspired a sequel.

THE MONSTERS AND MADMEN OF POVERTY ROW!

Many of the quality horror and monster movies from the 1940's originated from the major Hollywood studios such as Universal Studios, RKO Pictures, Columbia Pictures, Fox and MGM. However, Hollywood had its share of what was known as poverty row studios; film companies that usually produced horror and adventure programmers on a relatively low and unheard of budget in the amount of time it took the major studios to film one complex scene from a big budget film.

The poverty row studios at the time were namely Republic Pictures (the largest of the entire lot), Monogram, Screen Guild and, of course, PRC (Producers Releasing Corporation). The major poverty row films of greatest recognition were the vehicles that featured Bela Lugosi, George Zucco, Lionel Atwill, John Carradine and, of course, Boris Karloff. Films like THE APE (1941), THE DEVIL BAT (1941), THE CORPSE VANISHES (1942), and THE APEMAN (1943). The following describes the horror films of poverty row, some good and some bad. But still, these films kept the genre very much alive.

Monogram's KING OF THE ZOMBIES (1941) starred Henry Victor as Dr. Strange, a voodoo sorcerer who commands a force of zombies on a Caribbean island. Much better was I WALKED WITH A ZOMBIE (1943) and even WHITE ZOMBIE (1932) with Bela Lugosi.

THE INVISIBLE GHOST (1941) was Monogram's version of Robert Louis Stevenson's *The Strange Case of Dr. Jekyll and Mr. Hyde*. The film, directed by Joseph H. Lewis, starred Bela Lugosi in the dual role. By day, he was the kind Dr. Kessler, but by night, he turned into a prowling killer.

Lugosi also starred in Monogram's SPOOKS RUN WILD (1941) as the monster who terrorizes the East Side Kids. In the film, Lugosi wore a cape and evening clothes and traveled with coffins and was hunted by a Van Helsing-type character. Was all this to imply that his character was Dracula?

PRC's DEAD MEN WALK (1942) starred George Zucco in the dual role of both Dr. Harold Clayton and his twin brother; one of which is a vampire. The film, released on a double bill with THE MAD MONSTER (1942), suffered from a

Above: Bela Lugosi (seated center), George Zucco (face painted & standing) and John Carradine (left, rear & standing) in VOODOO MAN (1944).
Bottom Right: Bela Lugosi and Angelo Rossitto abduct Gladys Blake in SCARED TO DEATH (1947).

weak script and a low, low, low budget. Need I say more?

John Carradine starred in Monogram's REVENGE OF THE ZOMBIES (1943) as a mad doctor located somewhere in the Louisiana swamp lands who develops an army of zombies for the Nazi army. Didn't we see this before with Bela Lugosi in the lead role?

Next, George Zucco returned along with Bela Lugosi and John Carradine in Monogram's VOODOO MAN (1944). In this low budget effort directed by William Beaudine from a shoddy screenplay written by Robert Charles, the triple terrors (literally waisted) construct an army of zombies by kidnapping young women and then they use their voodoo powers to sustain the life of a long-dead woman. The script, originally titled TIGER MAN, was a rip-off of THE CORPSE VANISHES (1942) with

Bela Lugosi also from Monogram. Nevertheless, the film offered the entertaining performances of the talented trio.

Carradine returned to Monogram to make FACE OF MARBLE (1946). The actor played a scientist who revives the dead. Meanwhile Bela Lugosi starred with George Zucco in Screen Guild's SCARED TO DEATH (1947), the actor's only color film. The film featured the actor in another red herring role, this time in an old dark house where a woman is literally scared to death! The film was loaded with the usual and predictable trappings of its type and Lugosi and Zucco are old hands at this kind of stuff. As with most poverty row films, SCARED TO DEATH suffers from a low budget ($135,000 to be exact) and even the use of Cinecolor (an inexpensive coloring process used by all the independents) could not save the film from its own horrible premise.

If one did not know better, anyone looking at Universal's THE MAD GHOUL (1944) would think the film came from a poverty row studio rather than a major companies. The awful film stars George Zucco as a mad doctor who turns poor David Bruce into a monster-like murderer with a serum. In the film, Zucco uses Bruce as his henchman, but I ask, haven't we seen this before?

Finally, PRC, the same company that produced THE DEVIL BAT (1941) and THE FLYING SERPENT (1946), put together a modest little "B" picture that, for its time, was quite impressive. None could believe the film emerged from a poverty row studio. The film is STRANGLER IN THE SWAMP (1945) and it is perhaps the studio's best horror film outshining even Universal's THE MAD GHOUL (1944). Directed by Frank Wisbar from his own screenplay based on his own original story in a fashion reminiscent of the Val Lewton horror films from RKO, STRANGLER IN THE SWAMP proved that the little poverty row studio could occasionally turn out quality material.

In the film, Charles Middleton (known for his performance as Ming The Merciless in Universal's FLASH GORDON series) plays a man who is wrongly executed for a crime he did not commit. Somehow, Middleton is revived and during the film's climax, the walking corpse confronts the real killer, but not after some very effective shock scenes staged in the Louisiana Bayou. The film was a feast for the eyes to behold from one of Hollywood's little poverty row establishments.

ONE LAST LOOK BACK!

The 1940's was indeed a very busy decade as the second cycle of monster movies emerged ever-so-gallantly onto the screen. THE WOLFMAN (1941) was by far Universal's crowning achievement, technically speaking that is, and that FRANKENSTEIN MEETS THE WOLFMAN (1943) was the studio's most successful in terms of box office receipts. The arrival of new horrors such as Val Lewton's modest and restrained horror films for RKO changed the face of horror forever, and at that point, the popularity of the Universal monster movie began to decline as audiences enjoyed an avalanche of more intelligent and sophisticated horror films like THE CAT PEOPLE (1942) and I WALKED WITH A ZOMBIE (1943) from Val Lewton and films like THE UNINVITED (1944) and DEAD OF NIGHT (1945) from Great Britain. Still, Hollywood continued with its original monsters and ghouls up through the year of 1948 when Universal's ABBOTT AND COSTELLO MEET FRANKENSTEIN marked an end to an era that would soon diminish with the decade known as the 1940's. What did the 1950's hold for the genre?

Opposite Page: Evelyn Ankers is tormented by George Zucco and David Bruce in THE MAD GHOUL (1944).
Above: Another scene from Universal's THE MAD GHOUL with George Zucco (left) and David Bruce (right).
Right: Another poverty row epic that dealt with zombies. From Monogram's KING OF THE ZOMBIES (1941).

121

122

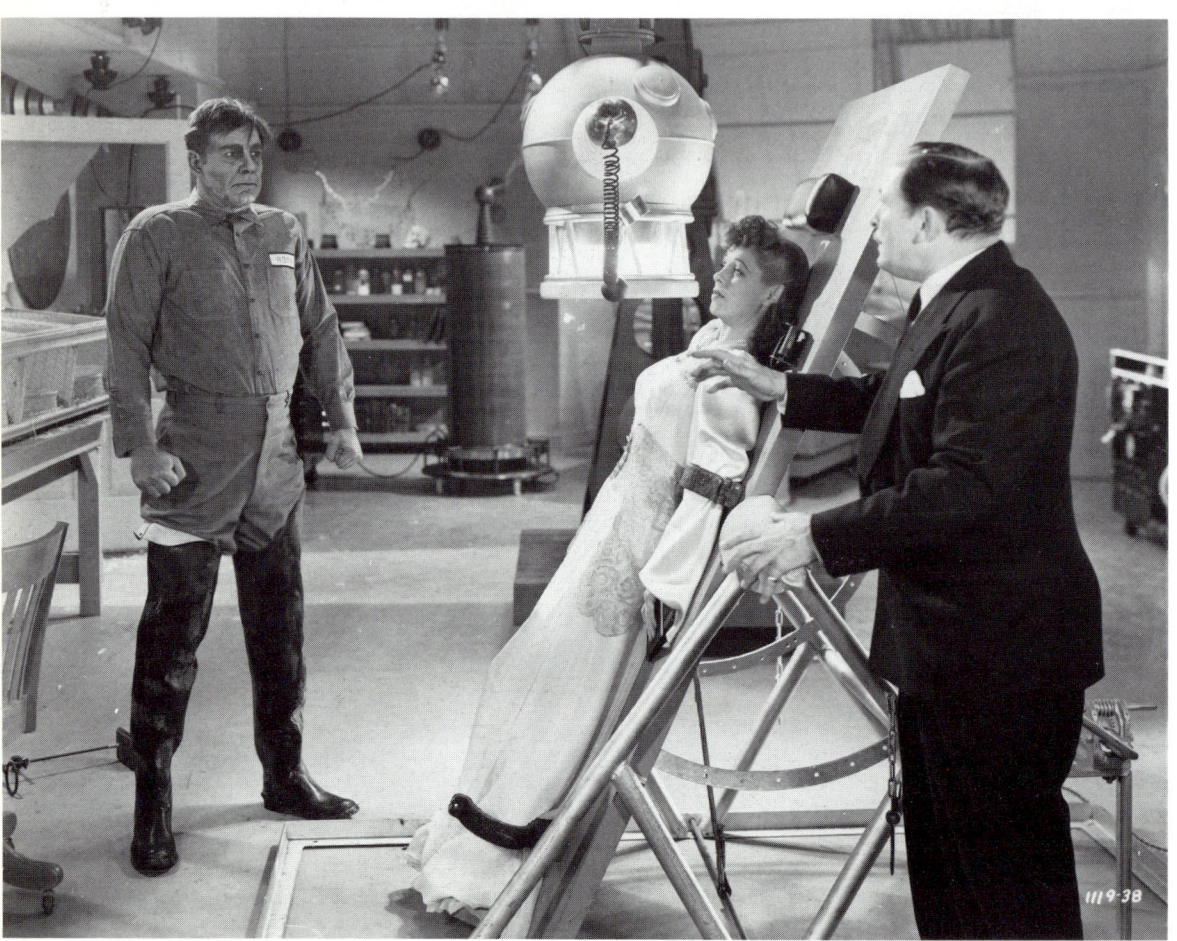

Confrontations with vintage monsters!
Opposite Top: Lon Chaney as Kharis in THE MUMMY'S TOMB (1942).
Opposite Bottom: The monster (Lon Chaney) advances towards Anne Nagel and Lionel Atwill in Universal's MAN MADE MONSTER (1941).
Above: Claude Rains confronts the Wolfman (Lon Chaney) in THE WOLFMAN (1941).
Right: The Frankenstein monster (Glenn Strange) pushes Lionel Atwill (right) and friend aside in HOUSE OF DRACULA (1945).

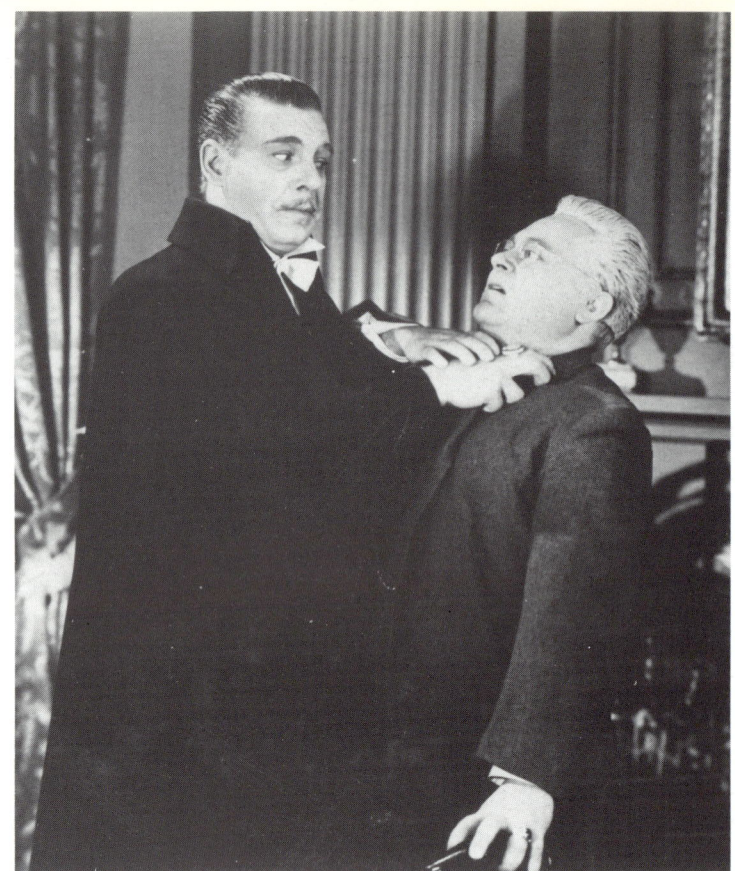

Above Left: Lon Chaney is Kharis in THE MUMMY'S GHOST (1944).
Above Right: Lon Chaney as Count Alucard (Dracula) in SON OF DRACULA (1943).
Left: Boris Karloff as a madman in THE CLIMAX (1944).
Opposite Top: Lon Chaney strangles Boris Karloff while the monster (Glenn Strange) looks on in HOUSE OF FRANKENSTEIN (1944).
Opposite Bottom: From THE MUMMY'S HAND (1940).

125

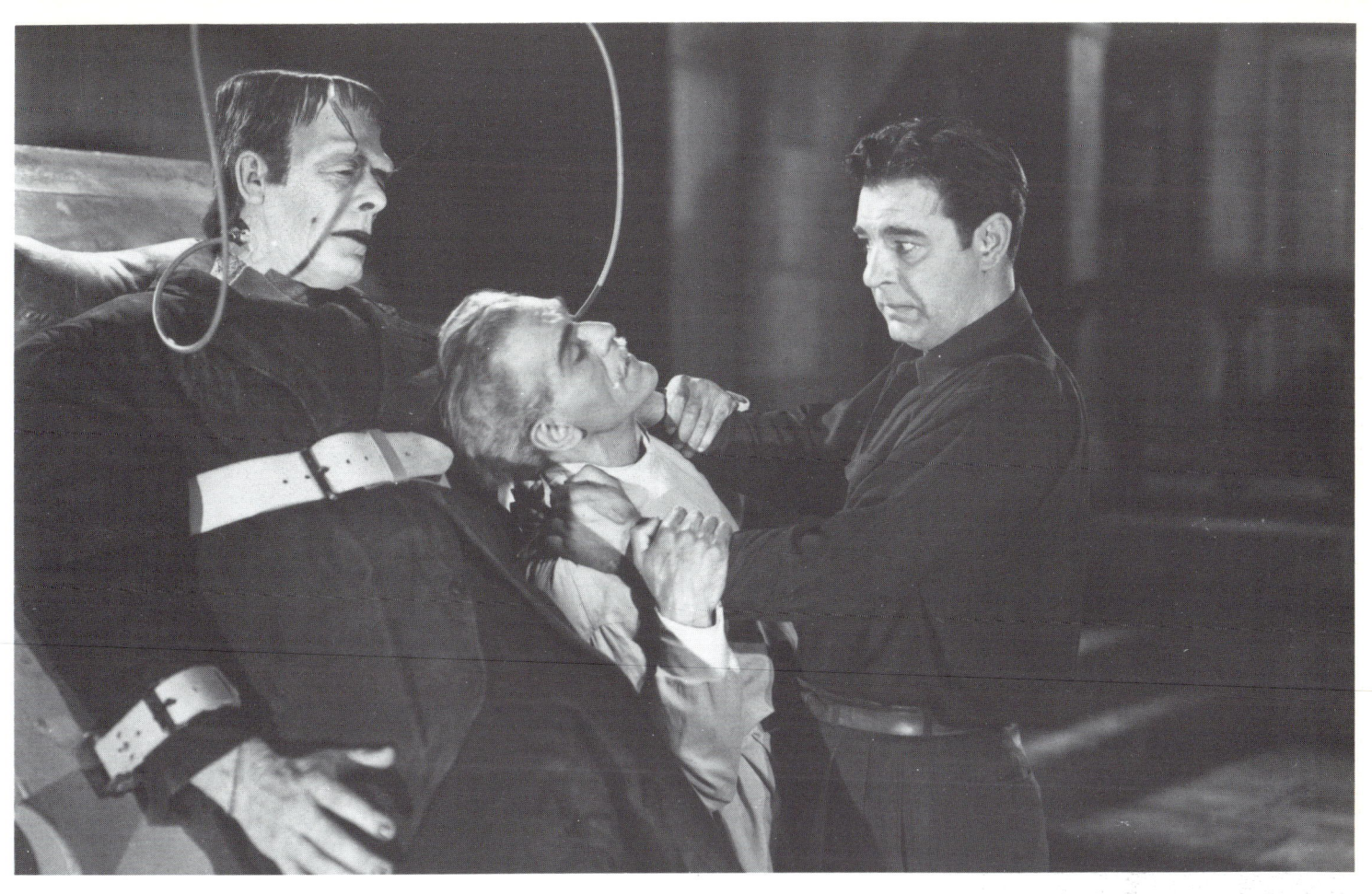

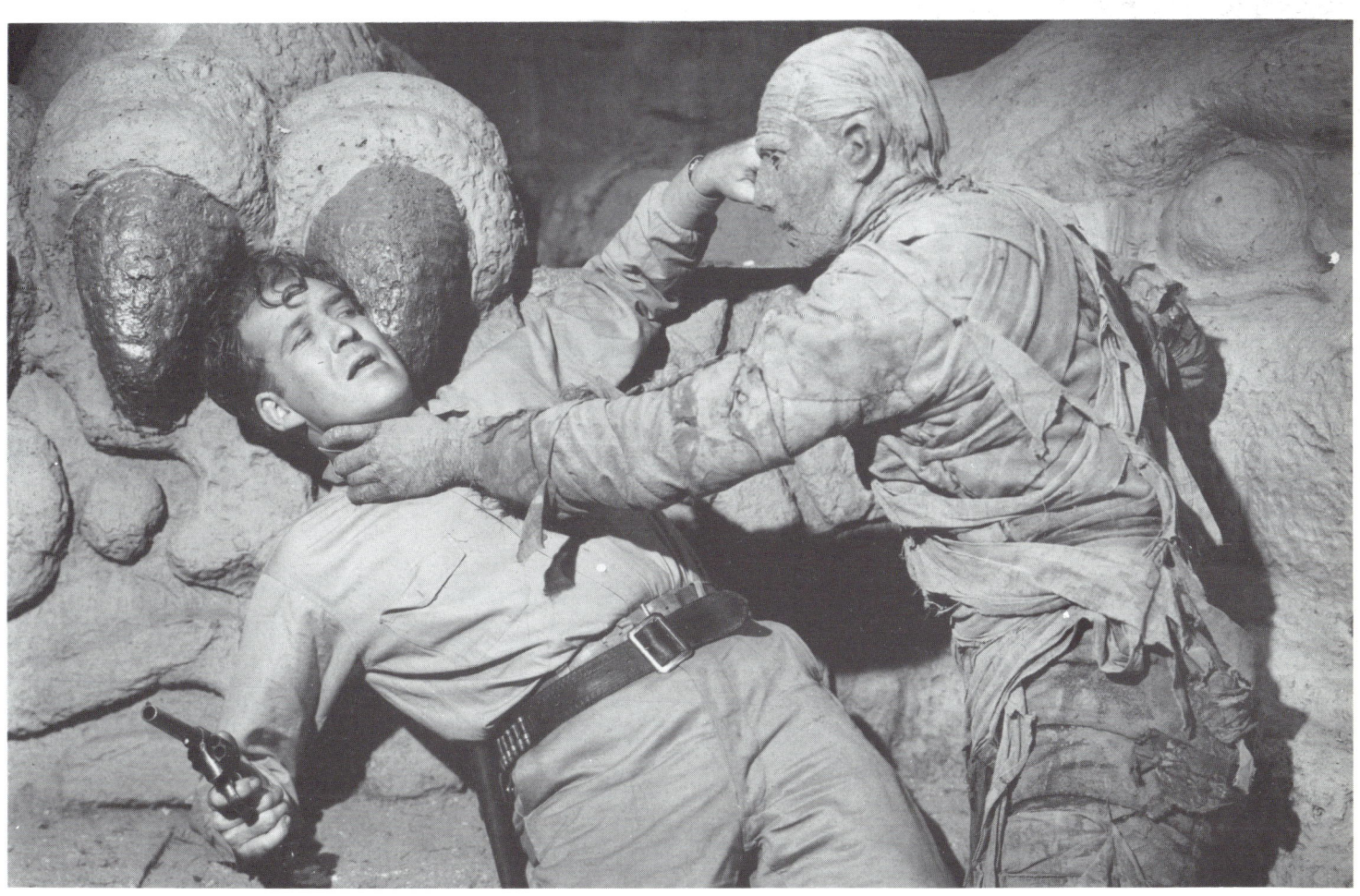

126

Opposite Top: Susanna Foster (right) and Claude Rains in THE PHANTOM OF THE OPERA (1943).
Opposite Bottom Left: Evelyn Ankers is startled by the Wolfman (Lon Chaney) in THE WOLFMAN (1941).
Opposite Bottom Right: The Wolfman (Chaney) attacks the one it loves in HOUSE OF FRANKENSTEIN (1944).
Above: Lon Chaney carries the film's heroine in THE MUMMY'S GHOST (1944).
Right: Another scene from Universal's THE MUMMY'S GHOST (1944).

127

Above: A vintage poster for THE PHANTOM OF THE OPERA (1943).
Left: Claude Rains as the Phantom in THE PHANTOM OF THE OPERA (1943).
Opposite Top: Count Dracula (Bela Lugosi) and the legendary Frankenstein monster (Glenn Strange) in ABBOTT AND COSTELLO MEET FRANKENSTEIN (1948).
Opposite Bottom: Count Alucard (Lon Chaney) cowers at the sight of a crucifix in SON OF DRACULA (1943).

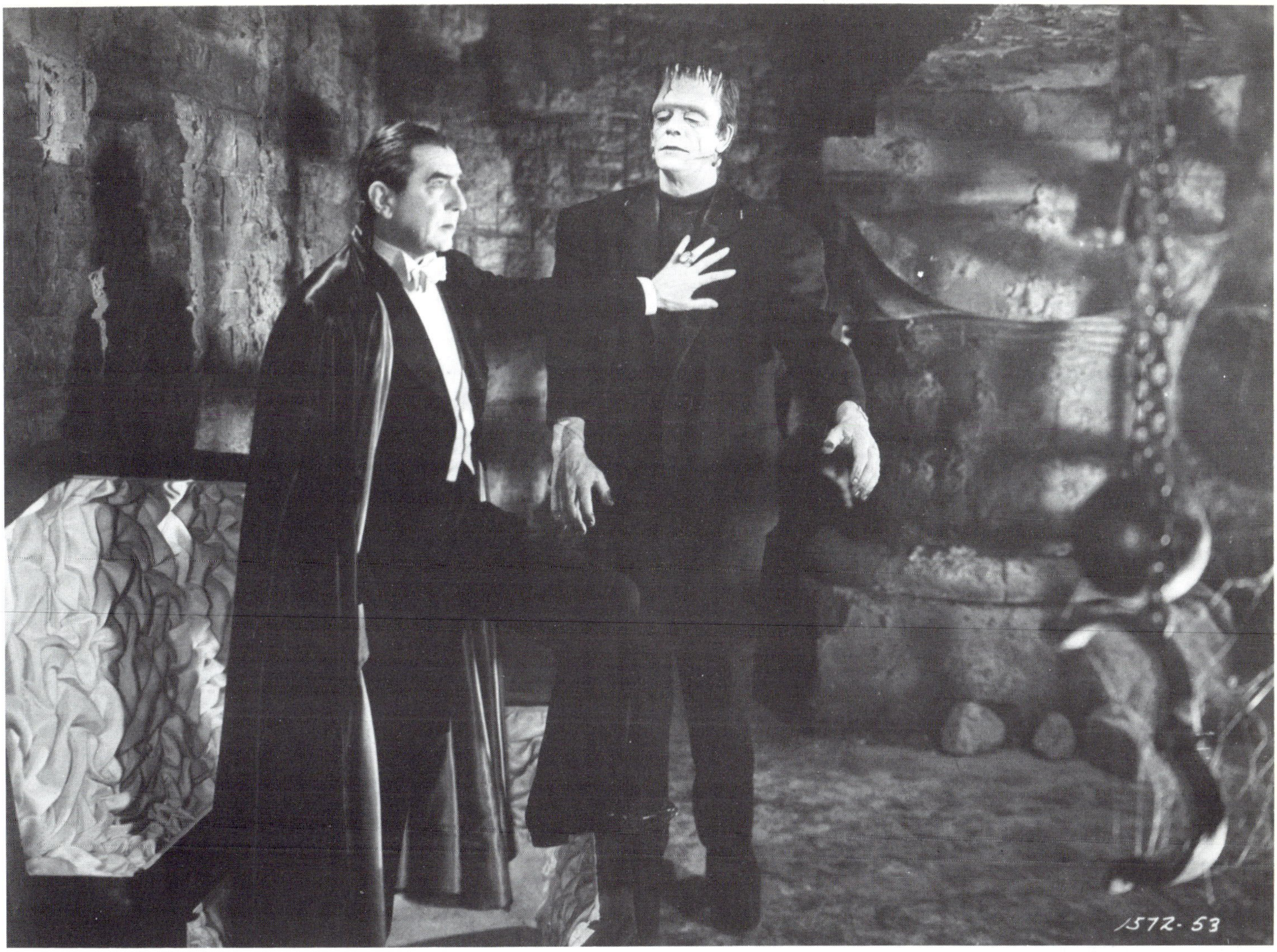
1572-53

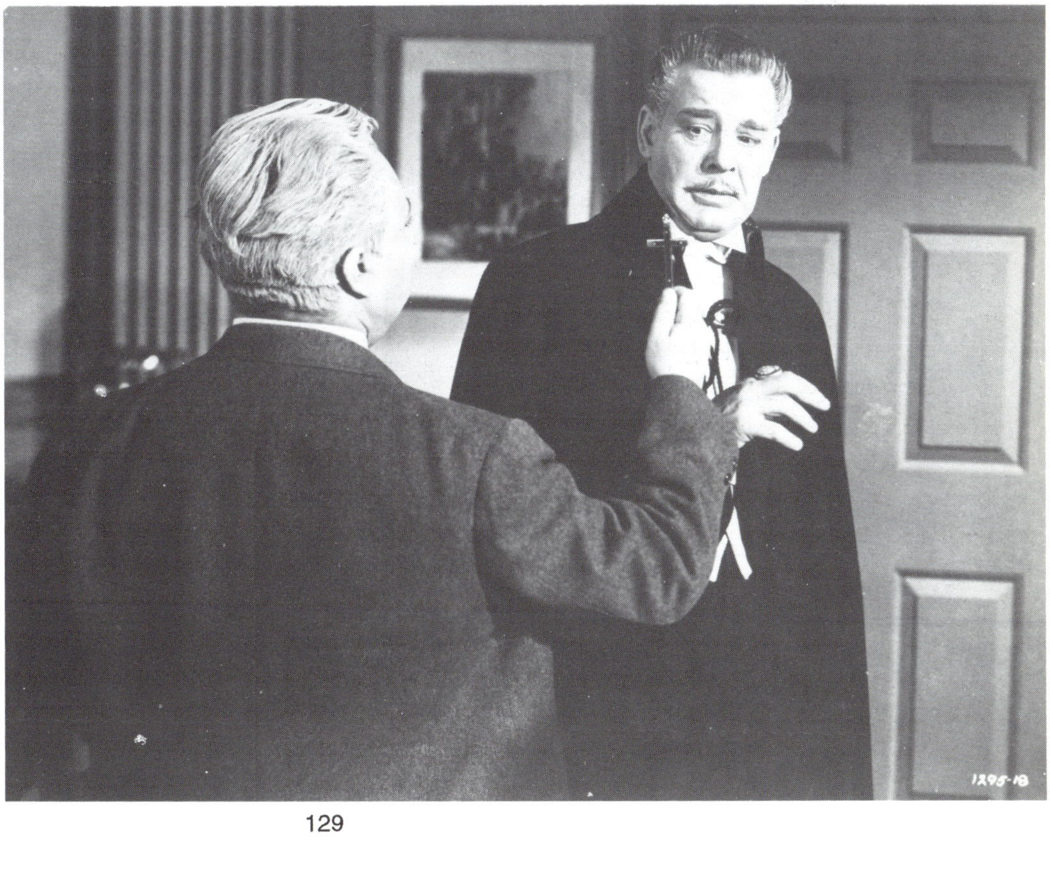
1295-18

CHAPTER FOUR
THE MONSTERS OF THE 1950'S

THE ATOMIC AGE!

The 1950's signaled the birth of the atomic age in both film and history. The good old fashion monster movie that dominated the 1930's and most of the 1940's had lost most of its steam. Moviegoers of the 1950's were younger and much more intelligent and the new crowd of film buffs demanded a fresh new scientific approach to the horror film. As a result of the demands, Hollywood delivered new monsters. From this change emerged a new genre of films that became known as science fiction with such magnificent classics as DESTINATION MOON (1950) about space travel; THE THING (1951) about an alien monster that arrives on Earth; THEM (1954) about giant, radioactive ants; FORBIDDEN PLANET (1956) in which we were able to see the landscape of a foreign planet. These were just a few of the many (hundreds) influential science fiction films that shaped the look of movies during the 1950's.

THE GILL MONSTERS FROM PLANET HOLLYWOOD!

The monsters of the 1950's were either radioactive or atomic creatures or extraterrestrial in nature. The Wolfman, the

Opposite Page: Julie Adams and the Creature. **Top Left:** Julie Adams is abducted by the Creature. **Top Right:** Poster from the film. **Above:** The Creature advances towards Julie Adams. All stills from the original Universal film - THE CREATURE FROM THE BLACK LAGOON (1954).

mummy, Count Dracula and the Frankenstein monster as Hollywood had come to know them were pretty much just a memory. Furthermore, the once ever-present Universal Pictures, now known as Universal-International, was once again on the verge of bankruptcy. Universal needed another horror sensation that would save the studio from financial disaster.

In an attempt to revive the genre with original monster movies and to compete with other studios (primarily RKO Pictures), Universal enlisted producer and director Jack Arnold to create a new wave of horror films. The studio believed that if RKO and producer Val Lewton could reshape the horror film genre in the 1940's, they could do the same in the 1950's.

Jack Arnold, who was born in New Haven, Connecticut in 1916 and was a former stage and film actor during the 1930's and 1940's, began making low budget science fiction vehicles during the 1950's. In fact, Arnold was responsible for producing some of the most fascinating science fiction and horror movies during that glorious decade. The first was the classic science fiction-horror film IT CAME FROM OUTER SPACE (1953), intended to capture the same market that made RKO's THE THING (1951) an overnight sensation. Arnold's film was a big hit and Universal prompted the filmmaker to create another low budget masterpiece. However, this time the studio "demanded" a film with shock appeal and a monster! Arnold proceeded and the result of which created one of filmdom's greatest monster figures of all time and perhaps one of the top ten money-making genre films during the 1950's. The new film was released as THE CREATURE FROM THE BLACK LAGOON (1954). In the 1930's there was DRACULA (1931) and FRANKENSTEIN (1931). In the 1940's there was THE WOLFMAN (1941). In the 1950's THE CREATURE FROM THE BLACK LAGOON replaced the old horrors and became the new sensation! The Creature, for all practical purposes, was the studio's newest and most bankable commodity.

THE CREATURE FROM THE BLACK LAGOON was the creation of producer William Alland. The monster was brought to life by make-up artist Bud Westmore (who replaced Jack Pierce). Its appearance was really frightening for 1950. The creation of the creature was indeed a challenge for Westmore. Equipped with sharp fin-like claws, bulging eyeballs, gills at the side of its neck and a completely scaled body, the creature was an impressive sight to behold. The creature was actually in origin a bizarre

132

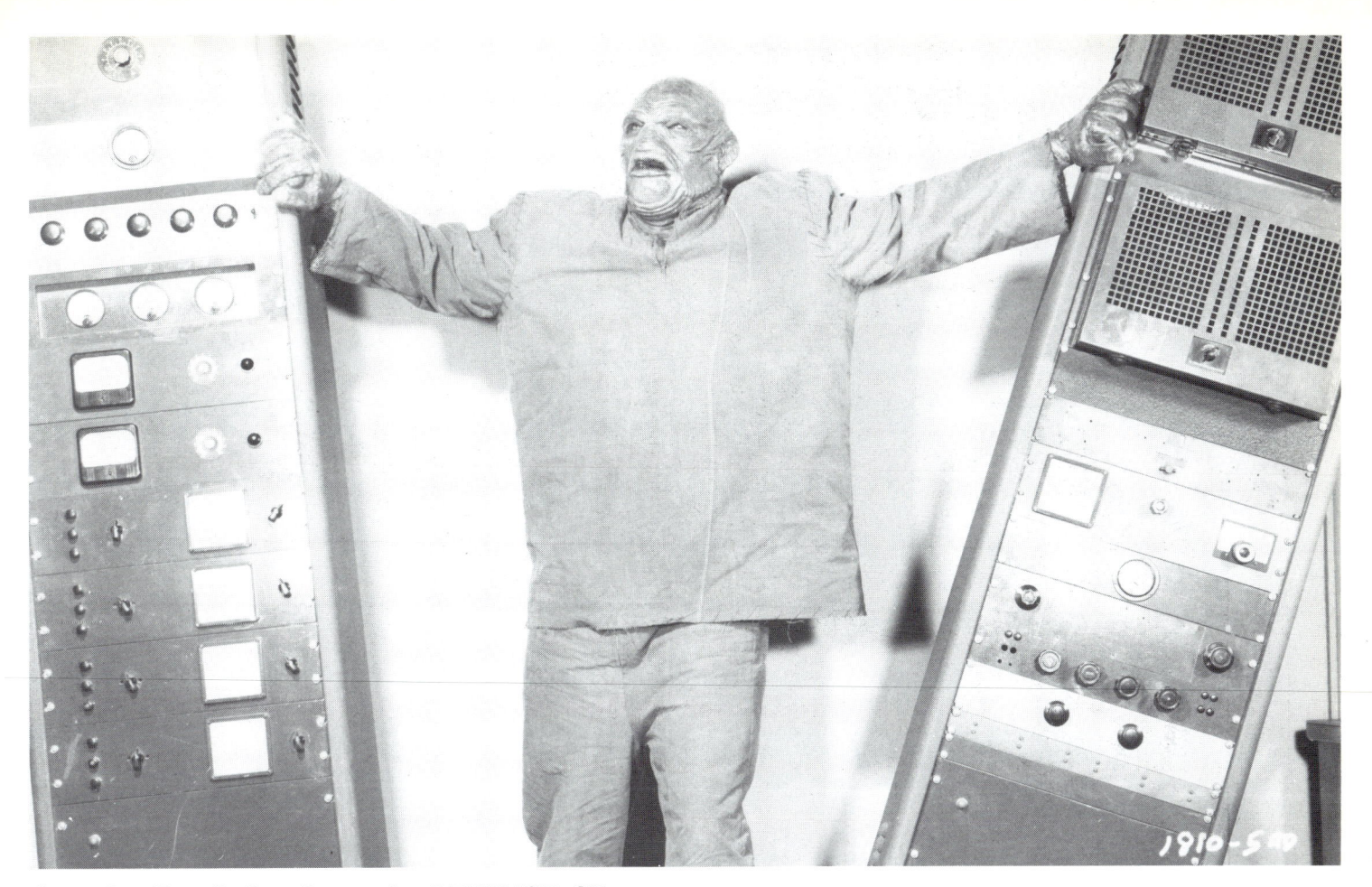

Opposite Top Left: Poster for REVENGE OF THE CREATURE (1955).
Opposite Top Right: Poster for THE CREATURE WALKS AMONG US (1956).
Above: The creature goes on a rampage in THE CREATURE WALKS AMONG US (1956).
Right: The beast from THE MONSTER OF PIEDRAS BLANCAS (1954).

combination of a fish, turtle, alligator and a human from the Devonian Period that dates back some five-hundred million years ago. Universal allotted a whopping $12,000 towards the creation of the gill man suit, worn by stunt-man Ben Chapman.

The film takes place in the Amazon River (actually, the film was shot in the Florida Everglades due to the budget restrictions) and depicts the incredible story of how a expedition crew's (led by actors Richard Carlson, Richard Denning, Julie Adams and Whit Bissel) search for fossil evidence of a reptilian-like man that once existed in that area millions of years ago. During the expedition up the river, the crew have a close encounter with the only

The Screen's Master of the WEIRD... IN HIS NEWEST and MOST DARING SHOCKER!

BELA LUGOSI

More Horrifying than "DRACULA"..."FRANKENSTEIN!"

BRIDE OF THE MONSTER

TOR JOHNSON · TONY McCOY

with LORETTA KING · HARVEY DUNN

surviving gillman. To the crew's dismay, the prehistoric creature turns out to be very hostile. In the eyes of the creature, the expeditioners are looked upon as intruders who intend on doing bodily harm, thus the gillman reacts accordingly. What follows is an incredibly suspenseful and very exciting battle to the finish between the crew and the highly intelligent creature.

As hoped for by Universal, THE CREATURE FROM THE BLACK LAGOON was a big success (mainly as a result of Arnold's stylish and fast paced direction and the film's suspenseful underwater photography). The film grossed over $3 million worldwide by the closing of 1954. Today, THE CREATURE FROM THE BLACK LAGOON still manages to frighten and thrill even the newest generations of moviegoers and the film is regarded as one of Universal's greatest monster movies among the ranks of DRACULA (1931), FRANKENSTEIN (1931) and THE WOLFMAN (1941).

The studio placed Jack Arnold in charge of reviving the supposedly dead gillman for a sequel that was appropriately entitled REVENGE OF THE CREATURE (1955). The sequel was directed by Arnold and the Creature was now played by Rico Browning, who had performed the creature during all of the underwater sequences in the original movie.

In the sequel actor John Agar leads another expedition back into the Amazon only to discover that the creature is miraculously very much alive! The gillman, who was unable to be trapped for examination during the original film, is captured, restrained and transported to an aquarium in Florida where it is contained for close observation. Of course, as any fan of monster movies can tell you, a horror film is not classified as a good old-fashion monster movie unless you have an exciting climax in which the monster escapes its restraints and runs rampant, killing a few people and causing a little havoc. Therefore the screenwriters concocted an escape for the creature that actually works convincingly well.

The climax which has the monster running rampant in Florida was not Jack Arnold's idea. Prior to the film's final editing, Universal executives with all their wisdom at hand insisted that the sequence in which the creature learns to communicate with its captures be completely scratched and replaced by the more dramatic, senseless and commercial scenes of the creature escaping only to be cornered and killed again. It was a formula that worked very successfully the first time therefore it should work as well the second time around. Arnold was discontent with Universal's decision, but his contract forbid him to dispute the matter. Had Universal shared the foresight and intelligence that the film's director had, REVENGE OF THE CREATURE could have become a major classic like its predecessor. Instead, REVENGE OF THE CREATURE is today considered nothing more than a very entertaining "B" film.

THE CREATURE WALKS AMONG US (1956), directed by John Sherwood, attempted to elevate the gillman to the ranks of near human. Actor Don MeGowan played the more humanized gillman in this third and final installment in the Universal trilogy and Jeff Morrow played the scientist appointed to study the creature. Apparently, the creature is discovered to be alive and hiding in the Florida Everglades. During a series of examinations, Morrow discovers the gillman has human-like skin beneath its scales and that its lungs are not unlike that of a human's. But as the final bastardization of the creature unfolds, he is operated on by Morrow so that it may evolve to the next step on the scale of life and is even given a set of clothes to wear! To make matters even worse, MeGowan wore an unfinished-looking gillman mask. Somehow the creature had lost its impact through its short evolution on screen.

THE CREATURE WALKS AMONG US was not nearly as successful as its predecessors, thus the third film ended a series that prompted numerous spin-offs and imitations about amphibious monsters. Two such sequels were THE SHE CREATURE (1957) and THE MONSTER OF PIEDRAS BLANCAS (1958).

THE SHE CREATURE was directed by Edward L. Cahn for American International Pictures (AIP quickly became Universal's counterpart in the horror genre during the mid to late 1950's and up through the early 1970's). The film was actually the story of reincarnation. Actress Marla English plays a lovely young woman who is actually the reincarnation of a hideous amphibious creature from prehistoric times.

In the film, an evil hypnotist puts Marla under his hypnotic spell to recall the horrid creature from the haunted sea and to use this creature to kill-off his own enemies. The impressive She Creature rubber suit was created and worn by Paul Blaisdell. The film was actually remade by AIP as THE CREATURE OF DESTRUCTION in

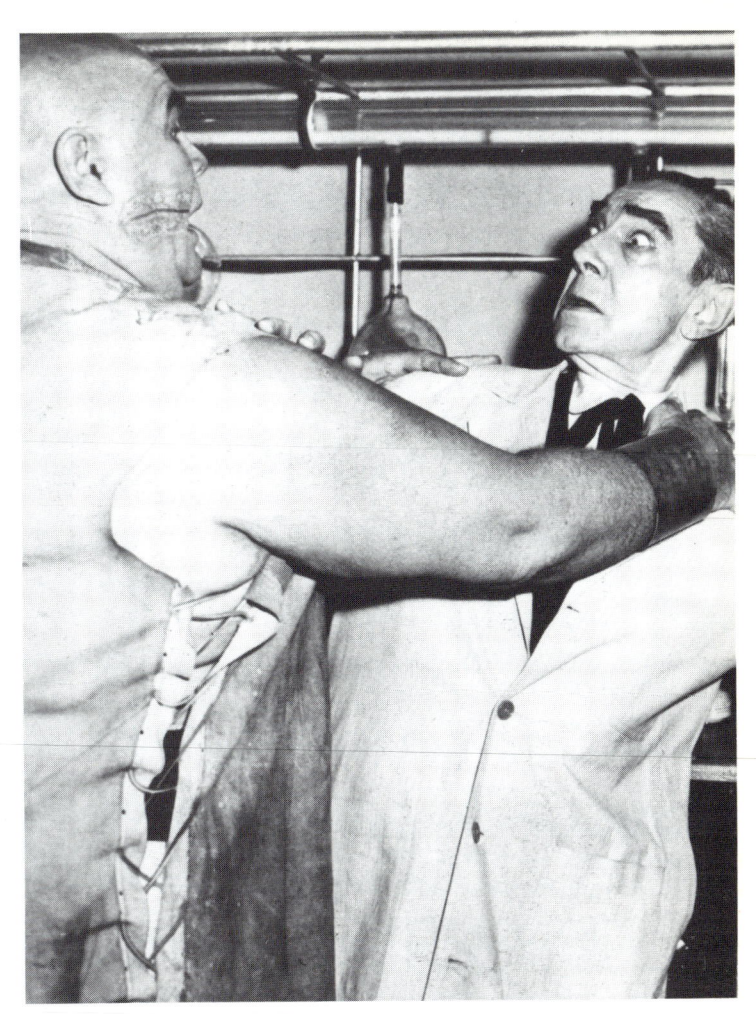

Opposite Page: Poster for BRIDE OF THE MONSTER (1955).
Above: Tor Johnson attacks his master (Bela Lugosi) in BRIDE OF THE MONSTER.

1967.

THE MONSTER OF PIEDRAS BLANCAS was the final film during the 1950's to feature an amphibious monster. The film, also inspired by the success of THE CREATURE FROM THE BLACK LAGOON, was created by Jack Kevan, who was on the Universal-International payroll in 1953 and who also assisted in the creation of the original Universal creature's rubber suit. His talents enabled him to create a very scary-looking monster who, in the film, haunts a sea-side village where the monster actually tears off the heads of its victims. THE MONSTER OF PIEDRAS BLANCAS was directed by Irvin Berwick on a relatively low budget.

As a final note, THE CREATURE FROM THE BLACK

Above Left: A poster for Allied Artists' THE INDESTRUCTIBLE MAN (1956) with Lon Chaney.
Above Right: Steven Ritch as the chemically-transformed werewolf in THE WEREWOLF (1956).
Opposite Top: John Beal perishes in this scene from United Artists' THE VAMPIRE (1957).
Opposite Bottom: Lon Chaney is THE INDESTRUCTIBLE MAN (1956).

LAGOON was Universal's last great vintage monster movie. The studio occasionally dabbled in the science fiction genre, but mostly concentrated on westerns, melodramas, musicals, comedies, etc.; the type of films that won Academy Awards and kept them from bankruptcy. American International Pictures became the new monster capital of the world along with the British-based Hammer Studios in the late 1950's and 1960's. The once grand monsters of Universal had, by 1956, fully diminished in popularity, making room for the radioactive, atomic and teenage monsters of a new era!

I WAS A RADIOACTIVE MONSTER!

Many of the monster movies from the 1950's based their premise on radioactive fallout and atomic energy rather than the traditional supernatural origin. Audiences of the 1950's were a bit too sophisticated to believe in bloodsucking vampires from Transylvania or mummies that could simply rise from the dead. Moviegoers wanted scientific explanations to their famous and not-so-famous movie monsters.

THE ATOMIC KID (1954) starred Mickey Rooney as a kid who is transformed into a radioactive mess, while in THE CREATURE WITH THE ATOM BRAIN (1955), nuclear-created zombies bump off the people who testify against a mad scientist. The film, directed by Edward L. Cahn from a screenplay written by Curt Siodmak, starred Richard Denning and Angela Stevens.

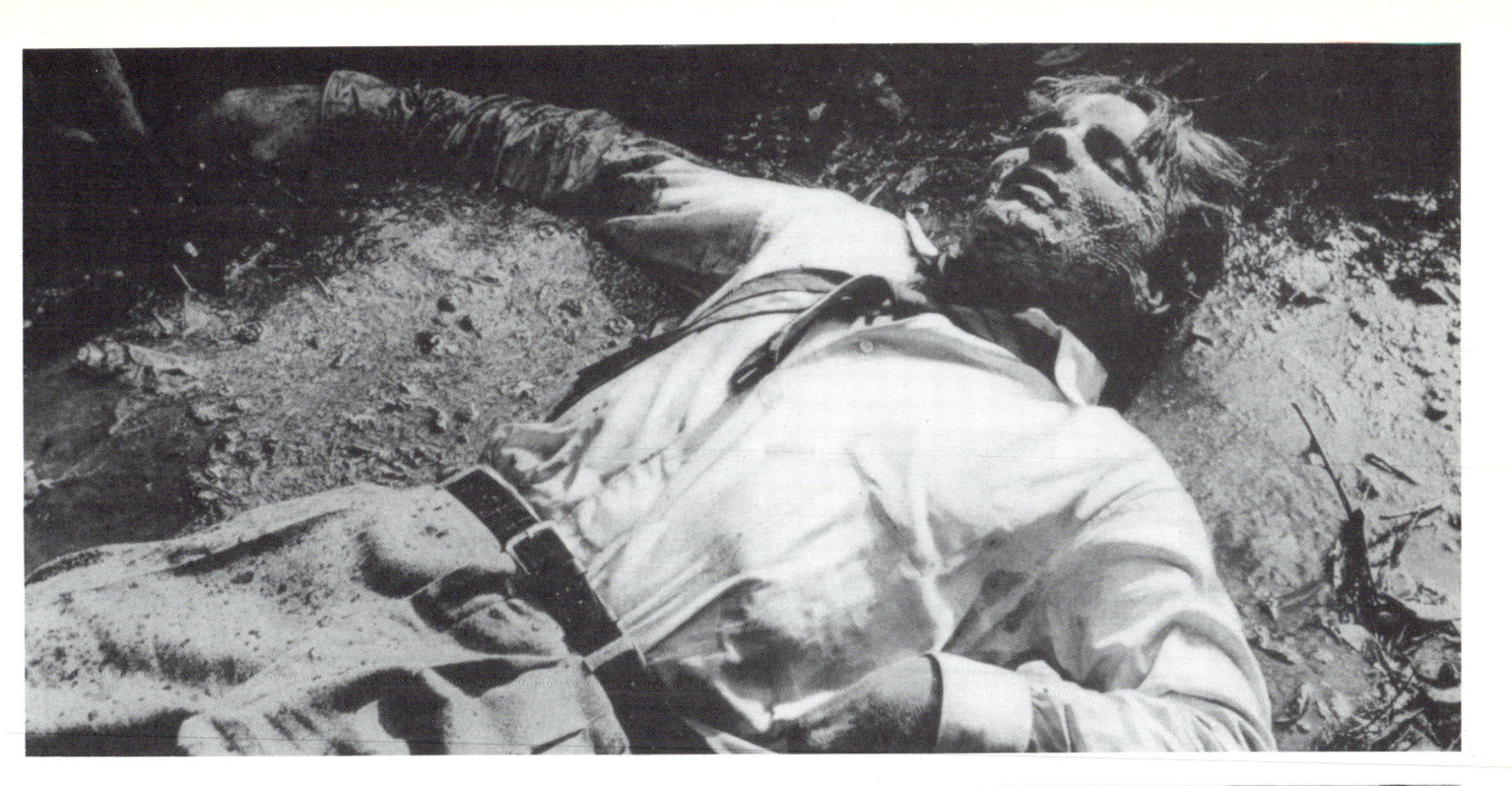

BRIDE OF THE MONSTER (1955) starred Bela Lugosi and Tor Johnson and was directed by Edward D. Wood, Jr. from a screenplay by Wood and Alex Gordon. In the film Lugosi plays Dr. Eric Vornoff, a mad scientist who harnesses atomic energy to create a breed of atomic monsters (one of which is played by Tor Johnson). The film was originally planned for Lugosi in 1953 under he title THE ATOMIC MONSTER, but lack of funding prevented the project to go into production until 1954. The film's title was then changed to THE MONSTER OF THE MARSHES, but eventually the film was released as THE BRIDE OF THE MONSTER.

BRIDE OF THE MONSTER was the last film to feature Bela Lugosi as a mad scientist and the actor's last speaking role. For his efforts, the actor was paid a mere $1,000.

Lon Chaney, who had not done much since ABBOTT AND COSTELLO MEET FRANKENSTEIN (1948), returned to the screen in THE INDESTRUCTIBLE MAN (1956). The film was a remake of Chaney's previous Universal classic MAN MADE MONSTER (1941). Chaney also starred in the obscure science fiction-horror programmer THE CYCLOPS (1956) in which he plays a pilot hired by actress Gloria Talbot to locate her lost husband, who turns out to be a radioactive, twenty-five foot tall monster!

THE WEREWOLF (1956) and THE VAMPIRE (1957) were both moderate attempts to bring the classic monsters of yesteryear into the atomic age. In THE WEREWOLF (1956), directed by Fred F. Sears, actor Steven Ritch plays an accident victim who is given a radioactive serum by two scientists as an experiment. The serum causes Ritch to transform into a murderous, talking werewolf. The film, produced by Sam Katzman, was a low budget attempt to cash in one the famous monsters of Universal and the atomic craze of the 1950's. The film did relatively well at the box office. THE VAMPIRE (1957), directed by Lew Landers on an even lower budget than THE WEREWOLF, starred John Beal as a scientist whose radioactive pills transform him into a murderous vampire whenever the moon is full.

Boris Karloff starred in Allied Artist's FRANKENSTEIN - 1970 (1958) as Baron Victor Von Frankenstein, a descendant of the original Dr. Henry Frankenstein. The low budget production was directed by Howard W. Koch and

138

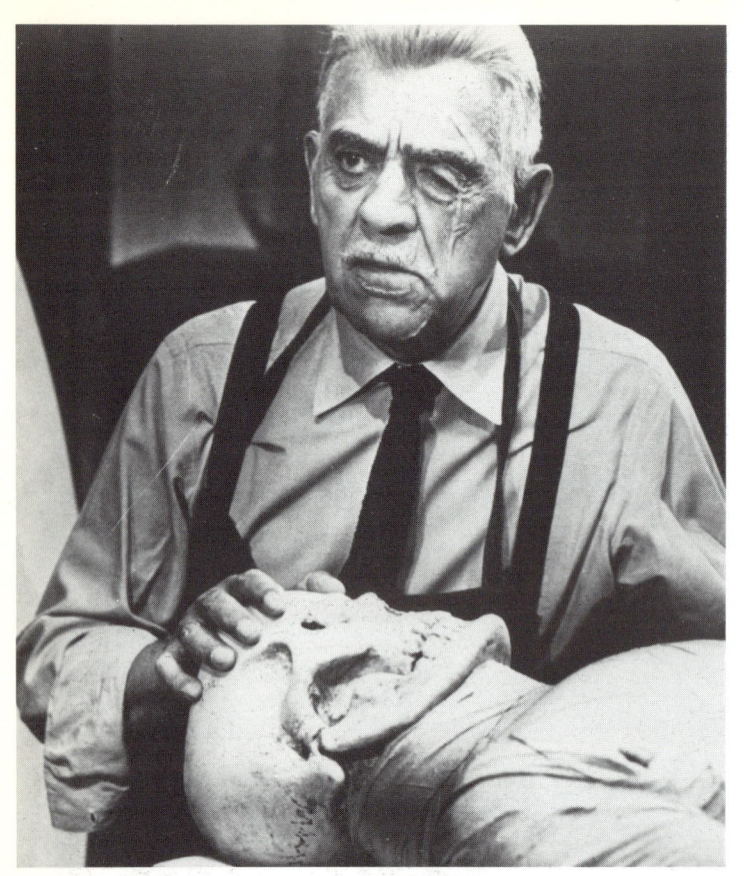

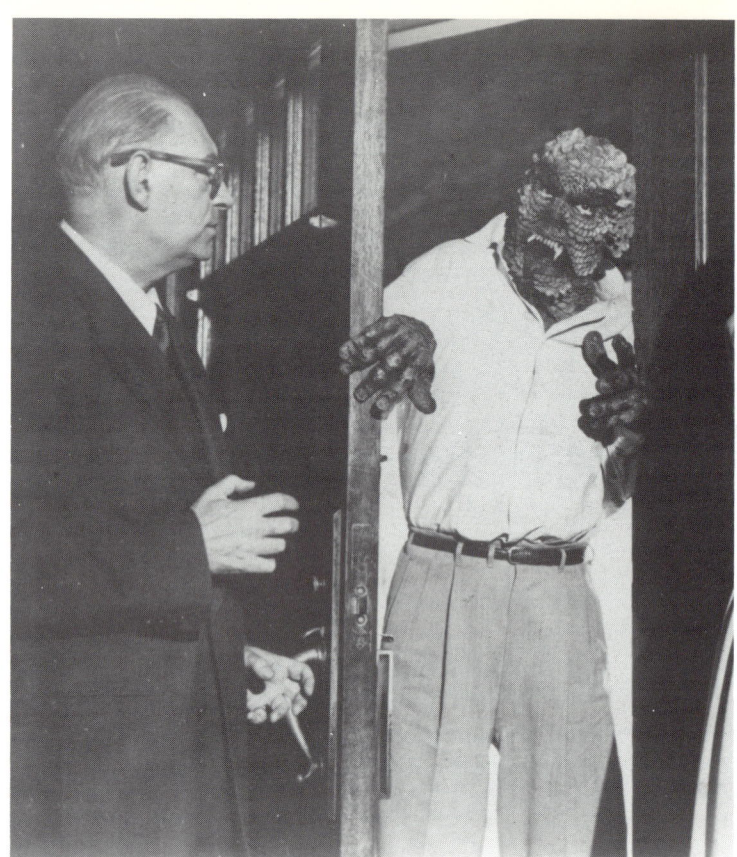

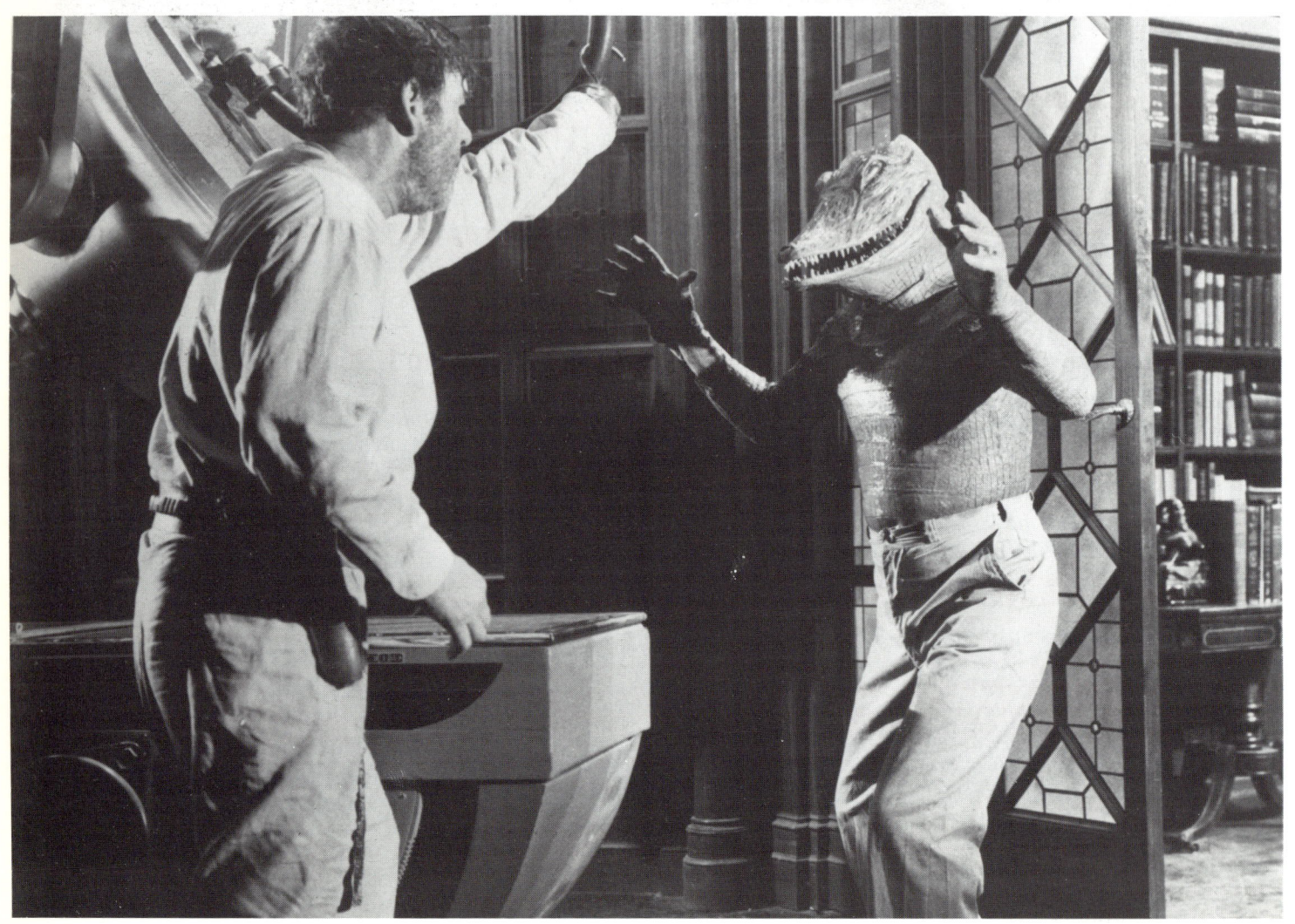

Opposite Top Left: Boris Karloff as Dr. Frankenstein in FRANKENSTEIN- 1970 (1958).
Opposite Top Right: Robert Clarke as THE HIDEOUS SUN DEMON (1959).
Opposite Bottom: Lon Chaney is attacked by one of the alligator people in THE ALLIGATOR PEOPLE (1959).
Above Left: A poster from THE BAT (1959).
Above Right: A poster from William Castle's HOUSE ON HAUNTED HILL (1958).

showed how Karloff revives the monster (played by Mike Lane) with an atomic reactor and some body parts from his friends. What are friends for? The film was the first to feature an older Karloff as the creator rather than the creation.

THE HIDEOUS SUN DEMON (1959), directed by Robert Clark for Pacific International, featured an atomic physicist named Dr. Gilbert McKenna who is exposed to a huge dose of radiation. The rays alter his genetic structure and the scientist transforms into the Hideous Sun Demon when exposed to the sun's rays. He attempts to stay inside to avoid the daylight, venturing outside during the night hours to seek a cure to his condition. The special effects of Thomas Cussarino and the above-average make-up effects make this film much more convincing and a league above most of the other atomic-related genre films.

Fox's THE ALLIGATOR PEOPLE (1959), directed by Roy Del Ruth, was intended to be a major horror - science fiction vehicle along the lines of the studio's biggest horror success THE FLY (1958). In fact, the film was produced to cash in on the "man into monster" sub-genre that was quickly becoming popular around that time. Unfortunately, THE ALLIGATOR PEOPLE is nothing like THE FLY. The film failed miserably at the box office, that is, in comparison to THE FLY. In the film, George Macready plays Paul Webber, who goes to a remote Bayou clinic run by a mad Dr. Sinclair, who has discovered a serum, extracted from alligators, that actually enables people to re-grow mutilated or damaged body parts in much the same way as alligators do. Paul arrives at the clinic with hopes of growing fresh skin to replace some very bad war burns on his face. But the scientist's experiments go wrong, and not only does Paul begin to take on the characteristics of an alligator, he begins to turn physically turn into an alligator. As the metamorphosis begins, Paul's skin becomes tough and rigid and even green. Eventually, his whole head becomes like that of an alligator's. His hands become claws. He becomes very strong and begins to crave raw meat! After killing the reached doctor, Paul commits suicide and drowns in a pool of quicksand.

THE ALLIGATOR PEOPLE could have been a much better film had it explored the main character's declining mentally to a degree more. The alligator effects are kind of fake, and the use of Lon Chaney in a supporting role as a one-armed drunk named Mannar discredits the film even further.

Finally, in Japan's H-MAN (1959), directed by Inoshiro Honda, a number of people are turned into radioactive blobs that kill other people. The entire Tokyo police department chase the H-men into the city sewers where they are destroyed with flame-throwers.

WILLIAM CASTLE: KING OF THE GIMMICK MONSTERS!

Producer and director William Castle, like Roger Corman and Herman Cohen, was a great contributor to the fantastic cinema of the 1950's and 1960's. Castle was born in 1914 in New York City and became an eccentric director of routine low budget horror films. He also had a knack for promoting his films. In fact, Castle came to be known in Hollywood as "The King of Gimmicks!" Most of the director's films included outrageous promotional gimmicks. For his film MACABRE (1958), Castle issued life insurance policies for $1,000 against death by fright. The imaginative promotional device worked miracles for the film at the box office. For his next film, THE HOUSE ON HAUNTED HILL (1958), Castle introduced "Emergo," in which skeletons whistled over the audience as they watched actor Vincent Price play a psychotic millionaire who murders his wife and her lover. The film was also a big money-maker at the box office, and Castle immediately featured Vincent Price in the follow-up film THE TINGLER (1959), his best gimmick movie ever. For this film, the director introduced his most audacious stunt, "Percepto!" This gimmick was an electrical device wired to key seats strategically located in certain theaters. Everytime the Tingler would appear, mild jolts of electricity would be administered to create a burst of terror throughout the audience. Another gimmick that was tied-into THE TINGLER was visual. Castle made a pause in the film in which actor Vincent Price warns the viewing audience that their own fright had created the Tingler and that it was loose somewhere in the theater (the Tingler was a creature that emerges from the human spine whenever a person is frightened to death. They bore a resemblance to the creatures shown in the science fiction thriller FIEND WITHOUT A FACE). In any event, the stunt worked miracles at the box office.

THE TINGLER was Castle's most successful project and his best shock film. The premise in which each of us have these parasites at the base of our spine that feed on our fears was quite original and worked well on film. Without all of the gimmicks, THE TINGLER was good enough to stand on its own concept.

The King of Gimmicks continued to produce horror films after the release of THE TINGLER. His other films were 13 GHOSTS (1960); HOMICIDAL (1961); MR. SARDONICUS (1961); THE OLD DARK HOUSE (1963); STRAIGHT JACKET (1964); and the masterpiece of horror and suspense known as ROSEMARY'S BABY (1968), which he produced not directed. The latter was by far his most superior film.

INTRODUCING THE NEW MONSTER: THE FLY!

One of the greatest monster movies to come out of the 1950's was THE FLY (1958). The unforgettable and disturbing film stars Al "David" Hedison as a scientist who invents an apparatus that can transport solid matter from one point of origin to another. The advent of teleporting was a brilliant and original concept for the 1950's, one that had not been explored to that date. However, the horror comes into play in this science fiction tale when Hedison comes to the risky decision to transport himself. Up until that point he had only experimented with transporting solid matter such as fruits and rodents, never humans. During the experiment wherein he uses himself as a guinea pig, a fly accidentally enters one of the teleporters and as a result of which, the transporter's electrical energy causes Hedison's molecules to merge with that

Above Left: A frightening moment from THE FLY (1958).
Above Right: Michael Landon as the werewolf claims another victim in I WAS A TEENAGE WEREWOLF (1957).
Right: A poster from MONSTER ON THE CAMPUS (1958).

of a fly. Thus, the incredible new monster known as the Fly comes into existence.

The Fly, a horrid combination of man and insect, was as complex a Hollywood monster to create in 1958 as was its modern-day imitation in the 1986 remake of the same title. The fly creature was impressive for its time and made quite an impact on moviegoers of that era as did the monster from THE CREATURE FROM THE BLACK LAGOON (1953) when that film was originally released. The surreal nightmare known as THE FLY was directed by Kurt Neumann for 20th Century Fox and featured Vincent Price in a supporting role.

THE FLY was a major success for Fox and the studio immediately launched a sequel with

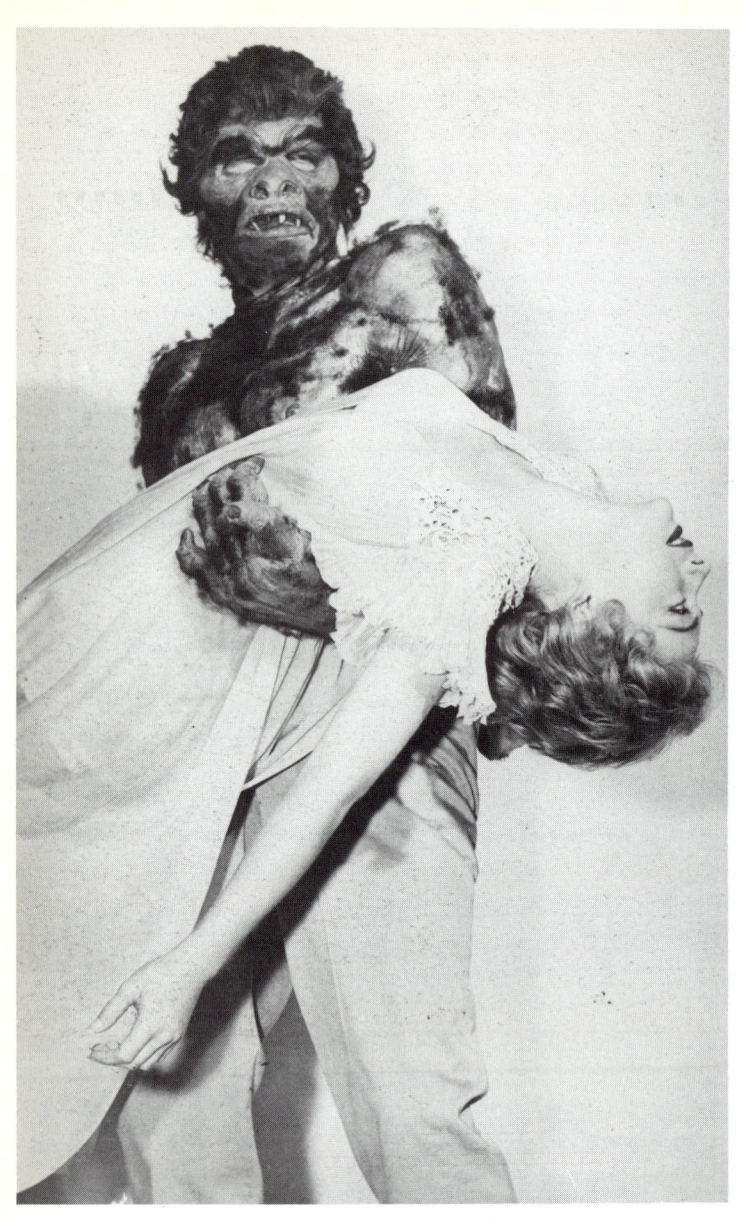

Vincent Price in the lead role. RETURN OF THE FLY (1959) followed the same basic premise developed in the original, but without most of the gloss and slick photography. Price, however, was quite competent as the scientist who falls into the same situation as Hedison's character in the original. The actor does a good job carrying the film through its slower moments.

CURSE OF THE FLY (1965) was the third and final film to feature the Fly, however, the film was not a legitimate sequel and was not produced by Fox. THE FLY (1958) was elaborately remade in 1986 with Jeff Goldblum as the scientist and with all the glossy special effects that Hollywood could muster-up; but somehow the translation of the story gets lost amidst all the special effects.

I WAS A TEENAGE MONSTER!

During the late 1950's, Hollywood suffered from a rash of horror films geared towards the young moviegoers- the teenagers. The most popular of these low budget vehicles were I WAS A TEENAGE WEREWOLF (1957) and I WAS A TEENAGE FRANKENSTEIN (1958).

I WAS A TEENAGE WEREWOLF was the most significant of all the teenage horror flicks. The premise used teenagers for what was an adult film because the majority of the horror film-loving audience were teenagers. The film starred a young Michael Landon as a very hostile juvenile delinquent who is used as a guinea pig by a mad scientist (Whit Bissel) in a series of bizarre experiments that cause the young man to transform into a savage, bloodthirsty werewolf. The film, directed by Gene Fowler, Jr. for American International Pictures, was very good, in a campy sort of way. For whatever it is worth, I WAS A TEENAGE WEREWOLF is definitely vintage horror despite its more commercial and trendy aspects.

I WAS A TEENAGE WEREWOLF inspired a vast number of other teenage horror films. BLOOD OF DRACULA (1957) and I WAS A TEENAGE FRANKENSTEIN (1958) were the first of these to be released, also from AIP. Both films were directed by Herbert Strock and released together on a double bill.

In BLOOD OF DRACULA, Sandra Harrison plays a neurotic Nancy Perkins, who has just enrolled into an all girls school. There she is coerced into wearing a centuries-old medallion that once belonged to a very powerful vampire (Dracula?) By a suspicious old chemistry

142

teacher. The amulet causes the teenager to transform into a bloodthirsty human vampire with long bushy eyebrows and two elongated fangs (created by make-up artist Philip Scheer).

BLOOD OF DRACULA was misleading in its title in that neither Dracula nor his blood is ever featured or mentioned. Strock's teenage version of the vampire lore, unlike his werewolf film, relied on the supernatural rather than scientific means.

In I WAS A TEENAGE FRANKENSTEIN, a descendant of Dr. Frankenstein creates a wretched-looking teenage monster by gathering parts from different dead bodies and sewing them together. Then, the scientist brings the creature to life with electricity. During the film's climax, the monster throws Frankenstein into his own crocodile pit once used to get rid of spare body parts. In a rage, the monster is destroyed by the very means that created him, electricity.

The teenage syndrome continued with TEENAGE MONSTERS (1957), directed by Jacques Marquette, in which a bunch of teenage

Opposite Left: University professor-turned monster from MONSTER ON THE CAMPUS (1958).
Opposite Right: A scene from WEREWOLF IN A GIRL'S DORMITORY (1959).
Above: A tense moment from WEREWOLF IN A GIRL'S DORMITORY (1959).

monsters run aimlessly amok. Then there were TEENAGE ZOMBIES (1958), TEENAGE CAVEMEN (1958), and TEENAGERS FROM OUTER SPACE (1959). Much more impressive, however, though not by far, was MONSTER ON CAMPUS (1958) directed by Jack Arnold. In this film, a university professor transforms into a menacing prehistoric creature whose only concern is to terrorize young teens. The monster is eventually shot down by police!

WEREWOLF IN A GIRL'S DORMITORY (1959) was actually an Italian-Austrian made film in which a chained werewolf escapes to prey upon the students of a corrective school for girls. The film was made strictly for shock by director Paolo Huesch for the Royal Film

THE LAUGHS ARE TWICE
AS MONSTER-OUS
AS EVER BEFORE!
BUD ABBOTT AND LOU COSTELLO
MEET
Dr. JEKYLL
AND Mr. HYDE
CO-STARRING
BORIS KARLOFF
ALL NEW!
ALL WILD!
ALL FUN!
with HELEN WESTCOTT · CRAIG STEVENS · REGINALD DENNY
Directed by CHARLES LAMONT · Screenplay by LEE LOEB and JOHN GRANT · Produced by HOWARD CHRISTIE · A UNIVERSAL-INTERNATIONAL PICTURE
Universal International

Opposite Page: A poster for the horror-comedy ABBOTT AND COSTELLO MEET DR. JEKYLL AND MR. HYDE (1953).
Above: Mr. Hyde (Eddie Parker) startles Helen Westcott in ABBOTT AND COSTELLO MEET DR. JEKYLL AND MR. HYDE from Universal - International.

Company.

FRANKENSTEIN'S DAUGHTER (1958), like I WAS A TEENAGE FRANKENSTEIN, tells how scientist Oliver Frank (actually Frankenstein) turns the young daughter of his assistant into a raving killer. The film, directed by Richard Cunha for Astor Pictures, suffers from a very low budget and severe technical problems, beginning with its horrid, unconvincing premise.

RETURN TO THE CLASSIC MONSTERS

Dracula, Frankenstein's monster, the Wolfman, the Mummy and the Invisible Man were among the most famous movie monsters during the 1930's and early 1940's, in addition to films about wax museums, gorillas at large and the walking dead. Somewhere among all the teenage monster movies and William Castle's gimmick horror films, Hollywood continued to produce monster movies faithful to but not as good as the early classics of the 1930's and 1940's. Even horror film legends Boris Karloff, Bela Lugosi, Lon Chaney, Jr., Vincent Price and John Carradine were called in to star in the third cycle of horror films.

The first was BRIDE OF THE GORILLA (1951), in which Lon Chaney was miscast as a police official who tries to unravel a series of murders by a gorilla-like monster.

Universal-International's ABBOTT AND COSTELLO MEET THE INVISIBLE MAN (1951), directed by Charles Lamont, was surprisingly consistent with Universal's original 1933 film THE INVISIBLE MAN with Claude Rains. The invisibility serum used in the Abbott and Costello film is actually the same serum Jack

145

Griffin (Rains) had discovered and has been inherited by Dr. Philip Gray (Gavin Muir), the New Invisible Man! As in the original film, Dr. Gray eventually begins to exhibit signs of insanity as a result of the serum and he also begins raving about ruling the world. The film also features the usual comic antics of Abbott and Costello, and as in both ABBOTT AND COSTELLO MEET FRANKENSTEIN (1948) and ABBOTT AND COSTELLO MEET THE KILLER: BORIS KARLOFF (1949), the comedy antics work well with the horror elements of the film.

Much more impressive was Universal's ABBOTT AND COSTELLO MEET DR. JEKYLL AND MR. HYDE (1953), also directed by Charles Lamont. In this film, Boris Karloff plays only Jekyll, while the monstrous Mr. Hyde (perhaps the most hideous movie Hyde ever) is portrayed by stunt-man Eddie Parker. Amazingly, Karloff's Jekyll was actually as fiendish as Parker's Hyde with very little duality in their personalities. The transformation scenes from Jekyll to Hyde were achieved by special effects artist Bud Westmore in the same manner as the transformation scenes of Universal and Lon Chaney's Wolfman.

Columbia Picture's THE SON OF DR. JEKYLL (1951) starred actor Louis Hayward as the illegitimate son of Dr. Jekyll in his Edward Hyde identity. Hayward's Hyde was a monstrous, sharp toothed werewolf-type beast; a true monster in the classic sense. Then there was Allied Artist's incredibly low budget film DAUGHTER OF DR. JEKYLL (1957), directed without style by Edgar G. Ulmer. In this film, Gloria Talbot is presumed to have inherited the werewolf tendencies of her father Mr. Hyde. The ridiculous premise, complete with several preposterous twists, just does not come off as good as it should have considering the fine cinematic credits of film director Ulmer, one of Hollywood's greatest directors.

Finally, there is HORRORS OF THE BLACK MUSEUM (1959), filmmaker Herman Cohen's answer to the Jekyll and Hyde theme. The color horror film was directed by Arthur Crabtree and featured actor Michael Gough as a lunatic journalist who transformed his assistant into a hideous murderer by injecting him with a serum formulated from Jekyll's own blood. The film offered a weak premise, but good a surprisingly good performance by Gough.

The Mummy also made a brief appearance during the 1950's in ABBOTT AND COSTELLO MEET THE MUMMY (1955) and THE PHARAOH'S CURSE (1956). In the Abbott and Costello film, directed by Charles Lamont, Klaris, the Prince of Evil, or mummy at large (played by stunt-man Eddie Parker), is brought back to life only to chase the infamous comedians at

Opposite Top Left: Francis Lederer as Count Dracula in the modest little horror film THE RETURN OF DRACULA (1958).
Opposite Right: Phyllis Kirk is awaken by the mysterious presence in HOUSE OF WAX (1953).
Above: Vincent Price as the demented curator of a wax museum in HOUSE OF WAX (1953).

large! The film degraded the traditional Kharis legend and the mummy make-up by Bud Westmore was ludicrous. The film marked the last such meetings for the comedians. THE PHARAOH'S CURSE, directed by Lee Sholem for United Artists was about the ghost of pharaoh Ra-Ha-Teb. In the film, the ghost possesses a man and gradually ages his body to that of a centuries-old mummy. It is actually the mummy's ghost that destroys those who have defied his tomb. Finally, there was the Mexican-made film THE MUMMY (1957), directed by Rafael Lopez Portillo, in which the Aztec mummy, a dull imitation of the American mummy from Universal, performs expected murders on those who have desecrated his tomb.

The legend of Count Dracula was far from idle and was also adapted to the screen during the 1950's. The first of the new wave of Dracula films was the Turkish made DRAKULA IN ISTANBUL (1953) directed by Mehmet Muhtar. In the film, Drakula is played by a grey and balding Atif Kaptan, baring fangs, cloak and penetrating eyes. The film follows the Bram Stoker novel relatively close as Drakula haunts a castle in the Turkish countryside. During the final moments of the film the vampire is staked and then beheaded.

THE RETURN OF DRACULA (1958) is an interesting variation to the Dracula legend. The film was one of the first of many unsuccessful attempts to remove the Count from his Gothic surroundings and transplant him into a more contemporary setting. Czechoslovakian actor Francis Lederer portrays the Count who assumes the identity of one of his enemy-turned-victim Bellac Gordal. Under his non de plume, Dracula travels to America as Bellac and terrorizes his dead nemesis's ancestors. THE RETURN OF DRACULA was quite a refreshing change from the old Bela Lugosi and John Carradine Dracula characterizations of the 1930's and 1940's and the film has held up rather well over the past thirty-some years. Unfortunately, the film seemed anemic next to Hammer's more vigorous and colorful HORROR OF DRACULA (1958).

NIGHT OF THE GHOULS (1956), directed by Edward D. Wood, Jr. on a very, very low budget, was a sequel of sorts to Wood's earlier release BRIDE OF THE MONSTER (1956) with Bela Lugosi and Tor Johnson. In the shoddy film, veteran western actor Kenne Duncan plays a phony swami named Dr. Acula who conjures the spirits of the dead which include appearances by Vampira and Tor Johnson, the latter as Lobo the vampire! The film was actually never released to theaters.

As for the werewolf legend, Lon Chaney, Jr. returned to the role of the Wolfman in the shoddy Mexican-made horror film LA CASA DEL TERROR (THE HOUSE OF TERROR) of 1959, released in America as FACE OF THE SCREAMING WEREWOLF in 1964. In the film, Chaney portrays an Egyptian mummy restored to life by a mad scientist. The revived mummy was a werewolf in an earlier life some centuries ago and is now fully restored to run rampant again. THE HOUSE OF TERROR was a feeble attempt to imitate the old Universal horror films. The film marked the first time the actor had played a werewolf since ABBOTT AND COSTELLO MEET FRANKENSTEIN (1948). The actor would never take on the role again.

Warner Brother's HOUSE OF WAX (1953) was a big budget remake of Lionel Atwill's classic 1932 horror film MYSTERY OF THE WAX MUSEUM. The remake starred still up-and-coming horror star Vincent Price in one of his better and more memorable roles.

Vincent Price, born May 27, 1911, would not become a major star of the horror cinema until the late 1950's and early 1960's. The actor was among the fourth generation of horror stars along with Hammer Studio's Christopher Lee and Peter Cushing, all of whom rose to fame about the same time. Price was the American horror star, while Lee and Cushing were British. HOUSE OF WAX was actually Price's first big horror film, even though he had been given the title role in THE INVISIBLE MAN RETURNS (1939).

The film was a full blown color spectacle and during its original release, HOUSE OF WAX was presented in amazing 3-D vision. In fact, it was the three dimensional gimmick photography that made the entire show during its initial release but when viewed today on either television or video the film actually looses nothing without the advent of the 3-D photography. Price's wonderful performance as the demented curator of a wax museum carries the entire film. Many snobbish aficionados have in the past spoken poorly about this horror film, classifying it as technically inferior, but I disagree. The film is totally entertaining from beginning to end and is perhaps one of the better genre films of the 1950's.

MURDERS IN THE RUE MORGUE (1954) and GORILLA AT LARGE (1954) were two more films made to cash in on the 3-D horror craze! Both films featured gorillas at large, the first of which starred Karl Malden reprising the role created by Bela Lugosi in MURDERS IN THE RUE MORGUE (1932), while GORILLA AT LARGE was nothing more than a rehashing of the old Bela Lugosi romp THE GORILLA (1939) now in 3-D and with new actors. Adverts for the film read " He's in the aisles! He's in the balconies! He's everywhere!" He, of course, refers to the gorilla!

BUCKET OF BLOOD (1959) was the feeble story about a mad sculptor who uses the murdered bodies of his victims to create his wax figures. The plot, obviously stolen from HOUSE OF WAX (1953), geared its setting towards the youth by setting the film among the world of beatniks. The film was produced and directed by Roger Corman.

Finally, THE HUNCHBACK OF NOTRE DAME (1956), directed by Jean Delannoy for Paris Film Productions, was another attempt at re-establishing the Gothic horror film. The colorful remake of the Chaney and Laughton classics featured Anthony Quinn as a less fearsome Quasimodo. If anything, the film is a tribute to the grandeur of both the 1923 and 1939 versions, and Quinn's characterization is ambitious to say the least.

THE RETURN OF TOURNEUR: MONSTER MAKER!

CURSE OF THE DEMON (1958), also known as NIGHT OF THE DEMON, was the last of the old-style horror films. The British-made film was directed by master filmmaker Jacques Tourneur and is considered by film historians and fans alike as a gem of a monster movie and an icon that symbolizes the death of the vintage monster movie.

CURSE OF THE DEMON was intelligently scripted by Charles Bennett, the supernatural elements

Above: Phylis Kirk races for her life from a demented killer in HOUSE OF WAX (1953).

of which are taken very seriously by Tourneur, thus they come off very frightening and believable. The director filmed most of the movie at night, the same technique that filmmaker Carl Dryer used while making his classic horror film VAMPYR (1932). The reason for filming at night was quite clear to both filmmakers. Darkness has also been associated with horror, weather it be vampires or demons. Tourneur, who was as much a master at creating mood as Alfred Hitchcock was at creating suspense, new how to develop a horror film. By using the darkness, stylish photography, shadows and suggestive dialogue, the director could create the most unspeakable of horrors. The director always believed that suggestive horror hit closer to home and was virtually more effective than physical horror.

In CURSE OF THE DEMON, however, the demon monster actually materializes during the film's climax, and in one of cinema's rarest occasions, the monster actually lives up to the audience's expectations.

CURSE OF THE DEMON stars actor Dana Andrews as a psychologist from America who inadvertently becomes involved with a British Satanic cult. Andrews is a non-believer whose eyes are quickly opened by the horrid reality of the supernatural. The cult is responsible for conjuring up the demon during the final moments of the film.

Showing the demon monster on screen was very uncharacteristic for Tourneur. In fact, in an interview published long after the release of the film, Tourneur admitted that he had no

HORROR!
MOST TERRIFYING STORY
THE SCREEN HAS
EVER TOLD!
DANA ANDREWS
CURSE
OF THE
DEMON
SCEPTICAL? Don't make
up your mind till you see this mas-
terpiece of the macabre!
PEGGY CUMMINS
NIALL MacGINNIS
CHARLES BENNETT and HAL E. CHESTER · Directed by JACQUES TOURNEUR
MONTAGUE R. JAMES · A HAL E. CHESTER PRODUCTION · A COLUMBIA PICTURE

Opposite Page: A highly graphic poster for the last vintage monster movie, CURSE OF THE DEMON (1958).
Above: The demon that materializes during the film's climax lives up to the viewer's expectations. From CURSE OF THE DEMON.

Above: A scene from the low budget sci-fi horror film PLAN 9 FROM OUTER SPACE (1959).
Left: Bela Lugosi in MY SON, THE VAMPIRE (1952).

intentions of actually showing the demon in the film. It was mostly producer Hal E. Chester who demanded he have a meaty horror film with a monster. Luckily, Tourneur delivered the monster with such great taste that its physical appearance did not hinder the film in any way.

CURSE OF THE DEMON was the last of the intelligent horror films from the vintage era of cinema. The film was leagues beyond such low-budget programmers as I WAS A TEENAGE WEREWOLF (1958) and THE BLOB (1959). Tourneur's CAT PEOPLE (1942), I WALKED WITH

A ZOMBIE (1943) and CURSE OF THE DEMON are all fine examples of literate, intelligent horror films that do not give into cheap, unexplainable and exploitable thrills just for the sake of creating interest by way of shocks. The Tourneur films are monuments and CURSE OF THE DEMON was a fitting way to say good-by to the vintage monsters of yesteryear!

FAREWELL TO THE MASTERS OF THE VINTAGE MONSTER MOVIES!

The closing of the 1950's marked the end of an era, and with the closing of that era diminished some of the cinema's greatest talents. Although many of the vintage monster movie stars that were still alive like Boris Karloff and Lon Chaney continued to star in horror films throughout the 1960's.

For poor Bela Lugosi, who had only reached stardom once in his entire career with his memorable performance as the infamous vampire Count Dracula in Universal's DRACULA (1931), the 1950's held nothing but horrible roles in low-budget, poverty-row films like MY SON THE VAMPIRE (1952) and THE BRIDE OF THE MONSTER (1955). After THE BRIDE OF THE MONSTER (1955), which was the final film in which the actor spoke, Lugosi wrapped up his career with United Artists's THE BLACK SLEEP (1956) and Reynolds Pictures' PLAN 9 FROM OUTER SPACE (1959). In THE BLACK SLEEP, Lugosi played Casmir, a mute monstrosity created by brain surgeon Basil Rathbone. The star studded cast also featured genre legends Akim Tamiroff, John Carradine, Tor Johnson, and Lon Chaney, Jr.

Bela Lugosi's final film was PLAN 9 FROM OUTER SPACE. The film was not a fitting end to a long-lasting movie career that stretched over four decades, but the role of a Dracula-looking corpse risen from the dead by a group of aliens with plans of invading Earth was all the actor could secure for himself. Lugosi was paid a mere $350 for his five minute performance. The actor died during production of the low budget effort and was replaced by a half-wit look-alike for the remainder of the film. The film, written and directed by Edward Wood, Jr., was originally announced as GRAVE-ROBBERS FROM OUTER SPACE.

Bela Lugosi died of a heart attack on August 16, 1956. The actor who created a sensation as Count Dracula in DRACULA (1931) never lived to see his career as one of Hollywood's greatest horror film legends immortalized as it is today by film historians, horror movie fans, and admirers of classic cinema. The actor was buried dressed with the cloak he wore in DRACULA.

No other actor has ever been associated with the horror film than screen legend Boris Karloff. Raised from bit roles to stardom by the accident of his casting as the immortal Frankenstein Monster in James Whale's FRANKENSTEIN (1931), Karloff dominated the horror movie for forty years as mad scientists, monsters and madmen. He is most remembered for his characterization as the sympathetic Frankenstein Monster, the role originally intended for Bela Lugosi, in FRANKENSTEIN , THE BRIDE OF FRANKENSTEIN (1935) and SON OF FRANKENSTEIN (1939). In addition to that legendary performance, the actor also created THE MUMMY (1932), THE GHOUL (1932), THE BODY SNATCHER (1945) and a host of mad scientists in films like THE MAN WHO LIVED AGAIN (1936), THE DEVIL COMMANDS (1941) and HOUSE OF FRANKENSTEIN (1944). Like Lugosi, Karloff has had his share of memorable parts in such vintage horror masterpieces as THE OLD DARK HOUSE (1932), THE BLACK CAT (1934), ISLE OF THE DEAD (1945), and BEDLAM (1946).

Besides portraying the screen's most diabolical Dr. Jekyll (not Mr. Hyde) in ABBOTT AND COSTELLO MEET DR. JEKYLL AND MR. HYDE (1953) and Dr. Frankenstein in FRANKENSTEIN 1970 (1958), the actor also starred in THE BLACK CASTLE (1952) from Universal in which he played a physician who helps a man capture a murderer in a castle.

Karloff's last horror films during the 1950's VOODOO ISLAND (1957) and THE HAUNTED STRANGLER (1958), the first of which is a vapid genre film in which the actor plays a man hired to look into voodooism on an island. THE HAUNTED STRANGLER (1958) featured the actor as a criminologist who turns out to be a murderer.

The 1960's was good to Karloff. The actor starred in such very good films as CORRIDORS OF BLOOD (1963), THE RAVEN (1963), THE TERROR (1963), THE COMEDY OF TERRORS (1964), BLACK SABBATH (1964) and DIE MONSTER, DIE (1964). The actor continued to star in horror films up until 1969, and even until 1971 his films were still being released: CURSE OF THE CRIMSON ALTAR (1969-1970) and CAULDRON OF BLOOD (1971). The actor died from respiratory ailment on February 2, 1969.

Like Lon Chaney, Sr. and Bela Lugosi, Boris Karloff left behind a legacy of fantastic movie characterizations. Karloff is truly the king of the vintage monster movies because of his many fine accomplishments.

Despite his arrogance and alcohol abuse during the 1940's, Lon Chaney, Jr. survived the decade of the 1940's to star in numerous science fiction and monster movies during the 1950's. 1960's and 1970's. The actor is undoubtedly most remembered for his Wolfman characterizations in THE WOLFMAN (1941), FRANKENSTEIN MEETS THE WOLFMAN (1943), HOUSE OF FRANKENSTEIN (1944), HOUSE OF DRACULA (1945) and ABBOTT AND COSTELLO MEET FRANKENSTEIN (1948).

The 1950's was not good for Chaney. The actor was featured in BRIDE OF THE GORILLA (1951), THE BLACK CASTLE (1952), MANFISH (1956) and THE BLACK SLEEP (1956), the latter of which featured the actor as another of Basil Rathbone's mute victims. The actor starred in several genre films during the 1960's and 1970's, the last of which was DRACULA VS. FRANKENSTEIN (1972), a low budget fiasco that features Chaney as a mute and murderous henchman. Not a fitting way to end a career.

Lon Chaney, Jr., the man who gave us the original Wolfman, died on July 12, 1973. He was the star of the second cycle of vintage monster movies launched by Universal during the 1940's. His contributions to the genre are immense and equally important as those of Boris Karloff, Bela Lugosi and his own father, Lon Chaney, Sr.

John Carradine, a fine actor in his own right, continued to star in numerous horror and science fiction films during the 1950's, 1960's and 1970's. Carradine's credits in fantasy films are too extensive to list here, but his career spans from 1930 to 1988. The actor's final horror films include THE HOWLING (1980), THE MONSTER CLUB (1980), HOUSE OF LONG SHADOWS (1982), MONSTER IN THE CLOSET (1983), ICE PIRATES (1983), EVILS OF THE NIGHT (1985), and BURIED ALIVE (1990).

Carradine, who began his career with small bit roles in classic horror films such as THE INVISIBLE MAN (1933), THE BLACK CAT (1934) and THE BRIDE OF FRANKENSTEIN (1935), was a major contributor to the genre of horror films, primarily the vintage monster movies of the 1940's as the memorable Count Dracula. John Carradine died November 27, 1988.

Actor Vincent Price is one of the few surviving actors from the vintage years of horror movies, and is today considered one of the legends from that era. The actor, who made his first horror film with Boris Karloff in TOWER OF LONDON (1939) and who went on to play the new Invisible Man in THE INVISIBLE MAN RETURNS (1939) and in ABBOTT AND COSTELLO MEET FRANKENSTEIN (1948), is mostly remembered for his many memorable characterizations of madmen. His best films are HOUSE OF WAX (1953), THE FLY (1958), RETURN OF THE FLY (1959), THE HOUSE OF USHER (1960), THE PIT AND THE PENDULUM (1961), THE RAVEN (1964), in which the actor teamed up with Boris Karloff and Peter Lorre, MASQUE OF THE RED DEATH (1964) and THE ABOMINABLE DR. PHIBES (1971). The actor was recently featured as a kind, eccentric scientist in the horror spoof EDWARD SCISSORHANDS (1991), and he continues to keep himself associated with the horror and fantasy film even today. His influence on the genre is immense and lasting to even this date.

As for all the other fine actors, actresses, directors, writers, producers, special effects artist and make-up technicians such as Peter Lorre, George Zucco, Lionel Atwill, Claude Rains, Basil Rathbone, Evelyn Ankers, Dwight Frye, Anne Gwynne, Rondo Hatton, Fay Wray, Charles Laughton, Otto Kruger, J. Carroll Naish, Glenn Strange, Edward Van Sloan, Colin Clive, Tor Johnson, David Manners, Ernest Thesiger, Lon Chaney, Sr., Conrad Veidt, Max Schreck, Tod Browning, James Whale, Michael Curtiz, F.W. Murnau, Jack Arnold, Fritz Lang, Erle C. Kenton, Edgar G. Ulmer, Robert Wiene, Ernest B. Schoedsack, George Waggner, Karl Freund, John P. Fulton, Jack Pierce, Ray Harryhausen, Willis O'Brien, Marcel Delgado and Curt and Robert Siodmak - my hat goes off to you! Thanks for all the wonderful memories that have filled my childhood and my life with such great moments; moments that will never be forgotten. The vintage monster movie is unlike any other genre in cinematic history. May its memory and enjoyment live eternally in the pages of this book and in the years to come on video and television.

THE END?

Opposite: Poster for THE BLACK SLEEP (1956), the last outing to star all the stars of the vintage monster movie.

155

FILMOGRAPHY

The following is a partial list of vintage monster movies that appear in this book and their cast and credits.

ABBOTT AND COSTELLO MEET DR. JEKYLL AND MR. HYDE

USA 1953; Universal; Director: Charles Lamont; Written by Sidney Fields and later rewritten by Grant Garrett from the novel by Robert Louis Stevenson and the characters created by Universal; Make-up & SPFX: Bud Westmore.

Cast: Bud Abbott, Lou Costello, Boris Karloff, Helen Westcott, Craig Stevens.

ABBOTT AND COSTELLO MEET FRANKENSTEIN

USA 1948; Universal; Director: Charles T. Barton; Producer: Robert Arthur; Written by Robert Lees, Frederic I. Rinaldo & John Grant; Music: Frank Skinner; Photography: Charles Van Enger; Make-up: Bud Westmore.

Cast: Bud Abbott, Lou Costello, Lon Chaney, Bela Lugosi, Glenn Strange, Lenore Aubert, Jane Randolph, Vincent Price.

ABBOTT AND COSTELLO MEET THE INVISIBLE MAN

USA 1951; Universal; Director: Charles Lamont; Written by Frederic I. Rinaldo & John Grant; Photography: Charles Van Enger; SPFX: John P. Fulton.

Cast: Bud Abbott, Lou Costello, Gavin Muir, Arthur Franz, John Day, Sheldon Leonard.

ABBOTT AND COSTELLO MEET THE KILLER: BORIS KARLOFF

USA 1949; Universal; Dircetor: Charles Barton; Producer: Robert Arthur; Written by Robert Lees & Frederic Rinaldo.

Cast: Boris Karloff, Bud Abbott, Lou Costello.

ABBOTT AND COSTELLO MEET THE MUMMY

USA 1955; Universal; Director: Charles Lamont; Producer: Robert Arthur Written by Robert Lees & Frederic Rinaldo; Make-up: Jack Pierce.

Cast: Bud Abbott, Lou Costello, Eddie Parker, Richard Deacon, Marie Windsor.

THE APEMAN

USA 1943; Monogram; Director: William Beaudine; Producer: Sam Katzman & Jack Dietz; Written by Barney Sarecky; Photography: David Milton..

Cast: Bela Lugosi, Wallace Ford, Louise Currie, Henry Hall, Ralph Littlrfield, Emil Van Horn.

BEAUTY AND THE BEAST

France 1946; Written & Directed By Jean Cocteau from his play and the fairy tale; Producer: Andre Paulve; Music: Georges Auric; Photography: Henri Alekan.

Cast: Jean Marais, Josette Day, V Thorn.

BELA LUGOSI MEETS A BROOKLYN GORILLA

USA 1952; Jack Broder Productions; Director: William Beaudine; Producer: Jack Broder; Written by Tim Ryan.

Cast: Duke Mitchell, Sammy Petrillo, Bela Lugosi, Muriel Landers, Charlita, Ray Corrigan.

THE BLACK CAT

USA 1934; Universal; Director: Edgar G. Ulmer; Written by Edgar G. Ulmer & Peter Ruric from the short story by Edgar Allan Poe; Photography: John Mescall.

Cast: Boris Karloff, Bela Lugosi, David Manners, Jacqueline Wells, Lucille Lund, Egon Brecher, John Carradine.

THE BLACK CAT

USA 1941; Universal; Director: Albert S. Rogell; Written by Robert Lees, Fred Rinaldo, Eric Taylor & Robert Neville from the story by Edgar Allan Poe; Photography: Stanley Cortez.

Cast: Basil Rathbone, Hugh Herbert, Broderick Crawford, Bela Lugosi, Gale Sondergaard, Anne Gwynne, Alan Ladd.

BLACK FRIDAY

USA 1940; Universal; Director: Arthur Lubin; Written by Curt Siodmak & Eric Taylor.

Cast: Bela Lugosi, Boris Karloff, Anne Gwynne, Stanley Ridges, Anne Nagel, Edmund MacDonald.

THE BLACK ROOM

USA 1935; Columbia; Director: Roy William Neill; Written by Arthur Strawn & Henry Myers from an original story by Arthur Strawn; Photography: Al Siegler.

Cast: Boris Karloff, Marian Marsh, Robert Allen, Thurston Hall, Katherine DeMille, Edward Van Sloan.

THE BLACK SLEEP

USA 1956; United Artists; Director: Reginald Le Borg; Written by John C. Higgins; Make-up: Volpe & Gordon Bau.

Cast: Basil Rathbone, Akim Tamiroff, Lon Chaney, Jr., Bela Lugosi, John Carradine, Tor Johnson, Patricia Blake, Phyllis Stanley, Herbert Rudley.

BLOOD OF DRACULA

USA 1957; American International Pictures; Director: Herbert L. Strock; Producer: Harman Cohen; Written by Ralph Thornton; Make-up: Philip Scheer.

Cast: Sandra Harrison, Louise Lewis.

THE BODY SNATCHER

USA 1945; RKO Radio; Director: Robert Wise; Producer: Val Lewton; Written by Phillip MacDonald & Carlos Keith from the short story by Robert Louis Stevenson; Photography: Robert de Grasse.

Cast: Boris Karloff, Bela Lugosi, Henry Daniell, Edith Atwater, Russel Wade, Rita Clarke, Mary Gordon, Bill Williams.

BOWERY AT MIDNIGHT

USA 1942; Monogram; Director: Wallace Fox; Producer: Sam Katzman & Jack Dietz; Written by Gerald Schnitzer.

Cast: Bela Lugosi, John Archer, Wanda McKay, Tom Neal, Dave O'Brien.

THE BRIDE OF FRANKENSTEIN

USA 1935; Universal; Director: James Whale; Written by William Hurlbut & John L. Balderston; Music: Franz Waxman; Photography: Hohn Mescall; Make-up: Jack Pierce.

Cast: Boris Karloff, Colin Clive, Valerie Hobson, Ernest Thesiger, Elsa Lanchester, Dwight Frye.

BRIDE OF THE MONSTER

USA 1955; Rolling M Productions; Director: Edward D. Wood, Jr.; Written by Edward Wood, Jr. & Alex Gordon from the original story by Alex Gordon.

Cast: Bela Lugosi, Tor Johnson, Tony McCoy, Loretta King, Harvey Dunn, Bud Osborne.

THE CABINET OF DR. CALIGARI

Germany 1919; Delca-Bioscop; Director: Robert Wiene; Writen by Carl Mayer, Hans Janowitz & Fritz Lang (uncredited); SPFX: Walter Reimann, Hermann Warm & Walter Rohrig.

Cast: Werner Krauss, Conrad Veidt, Lil Dagover

CAT PEOPLE

USA 1943; RKO; Director: Jacques Tourneur; Producer: Val Lewton; Written by Dewitt Bodeen; Music: Roy Webb; Photography: Nicholas Musuraca.

Cast: Simone Simon, Kent Smith, Tom Conway.

CHANDU THE MAGICIAN

USA 1932; 20th Century Fox; Directors: William Cameron Menzies & Marcel Varnel; Written by Philip Klein & Barry Connors from the Radio Serial by R.R. Morgan, Harry Earnshaw & Vera Oldham.

Cast: Bela Lugosi, Edmund Lowe, Irene Ware, Herbert Mundin, Henry B. Walthall.

THE CORPSE VANISHES

USA 1942; Monogram; Director: Wallace Fox; Producer: Sam Katzman & Jack Dietz; Written by Harvey Gates, Sam Robbins & Gerald Schnitzer.

Cast: Bela Lugosi, Luana Walters, Tristram Coffin, Elizabeth Russell, Angele Rossitto.

CREATURE FROM THE BLACK LAGOON

USA 1954; Universal; Director: Jack Arnold; Producer: William Alland; Written by Harry Essex & Arthur Ross; Photography: William E. Snyder & Charles S. Welbourne; Make-up: Bud Westmore & Jack Kevan.

Cast: Richard Carlson, Julie Adams, Ricou Browning, Whit Bissell.

THE CREATURE WALKS AMONG US

USA 1956; Universal; Director: John Sherwood; Producer: Richard Allen; Written by Harry Essex; Make-up: Bud Westmore.

Cast: Jeff Morrow, Rex Reason, Leigh Snowdon, Ricou Browning, Don Megowan, Gregg Palmer.

CURSE OF THE DEMON

UK 1958; Sabre-Columbia; Director: Jacques Tourneur; Producer: Hal E. Chester; Written by Charles Bennett & Hal E. Chester from the novel Casting The Runes by M.R. James; Music: Clifton Parker; Photography: Ted Scaife; SPFX: Wally Veevers & S.D. Onions.

Cast: Dana Andrews, Peggy Cummins, Niall MacGinnis.

DARK EYES OF LONDON

British 1939; Pathe Films; Director: Walter Summers; Written by Patrick Kirwin, Walter Summers & John Argyle from a novel by Edgar Wallace.

Cast: Bela Lugosi, Hugh Williams, Greta Gynt, Edmond Ryan, Wilfred Walter, Alexander Field, Arthur E. Owen.

DAUGHTER OF DR. JEKYLL

USA 1957, Allied Artists; Director: Edward G. Ulmer.

Cast: John Agar, Gloria Talbot, Arthur Shields.

DER JANUSKOPF

Germany 1920; Lipow Film; Director: F.W. Murnau.

Cast: Conrad Veidt, Margarete Schlegel, Bela Lugosi.

THE DEVIL COMMANDS

USA 1941; Columbia; Director: Edward Dmytryk; Producer: Wallace MacDonald; Written by Robert D. Andrews & Milton Gunzburg from the novel by William Sloane; Photography: Allen Siegler.

Cast: Boris Karloff, Amanda Duff, Richard Fiske, Ann Revere, Ralph Penney, Kenneth McDonald.

THE DEVIL BAT

USA 1941; Producers Releasing Corp.; Director: Jean Yarbrough; Producer: J. Arthur Rank; Written by John Thomas Neville from the story by George Bricker;

Cast: Bela Lugosi, Suzanne Kaaren, Dave O;Brien.

THE DEVIL DOLL

USA 1936; MGM; Director: Tod Browning; Producer: E J. Mannix; Written by Tod Browning, Guy Endore, Garrett Fort, Erich Von Stroheim from the novel Burn, Witch, Burn by Abraham Merritt; Photography: Leonard Smith.

Cast: Lionel Barrymore, Maureen O'Sullivan, Frank Lawton, Henry B. Walthall, Rafaela Ottiano.

DR. CYCLOPS

USA 1939-1940; RKO; Director:

Ernest B. Schoedsack; Producer: Merian C. Cooper; Written by Tom Kilpatrick; Music: Ernest Toch; SPFX & Photography: Farcoit Edouart & W. Wallace Kelley.

Cast: Albert Dekker, Janice Logan, Thomas Coley, Victor Killian, Charles Halton.

DR. JEKYLL AND MR. HYDE

USA 1912; Thanhouser; Director: Lucius Henderson; Producer: Thanhouser, From the novel by Robert Louis Stevenson.

Cast: James Cruze, Marguerite Snow, Harry Benham.

DR. JEKYLL AND MR. HYDE

USA 1913; Independent Moving Picture Co.; Written & Directed by Herbert Brenon from the novel by Robert Louis Stevenson; Producer: Carl Laemmle.

Cast: King Baggot, Jane Gail, Matt Snyder, Howard Crampton.

DR. JEKYLL AND MR. HYDE

USA 1920; Paramount; Director: John S. Robertson; Producer: Adolph Zukor; Written by Clara S. Beranger from the novel *The Strange Case of Dr. Jekyll and Mr. Hyde* by Robert Louis Stevenson; Photography: Roy Overbaugh.

Cast: John Barrymore, Brandon Hurst, Matha Mansfield, Charles Lane.

DR. JEKYLL AND MR. HYDE

USA 1932; Paramount; Director: Rouben Mamoulian; Written by Samuel Hoffenstein & Percy Heath from the novel by Robert Louis Stevenson; Photography: Karl Struss; Make-up & SPFX: Wally Westmore.

Cast: Fredric March, Miriam Hopkins, Rose Hobart.

DR. JEKYLL AND MR. HYDE

USA 1941; MGM; Producer - Director: Victor Fleming; Written by John Lee Machin from the novel by Robert Louis Stevenson; Music: Franz Waxman; Photography: Joseph Ruttenberg; Make-up: Jack Dawn.

Cast: Spencer Tracy, Ingrid Bergman, Lana Turner, Donald Crisp.

DOCTOR X

USA 1930; Color; First National-Warner; Director: Michael Cutiz; Written by Robert Tasker & Earl Baldwin from the play by Howard Comstock and Allen Miller; Photography: Richard Tower;

Cast: Lionel Atwill, Fay Wray, Lee Tracy, Preston Foster

DRACULA

USA 1931; Universal; Director: Tod Browning; Producer: Carl Laemmle, Jr.; Written by Garrett Fort & Dudley Murphy from the novel by Bram Stoker and the play by Hamilton Deane and John L. Balderston; Photography: Karl Freund; Make-up & SPFX: Jack Pierce.

Cast: Bela Lugosi, Helen Chandler, David Manners, Edward Van Sloan, Dwight Frye.

DRACULA

USA 1931; Universal (Spanish Version); Written & Directed by: George Melford from the screenplay by Garret Fort & Dudley Murphey and the novel by Bram Stoker; Producer: Carl Laemmele.

Cast: Carlos Villarias, Lupita Tober, Barry Norton, Alvarez Rubio, Carmen Guerro.

DRACULA'S DAUGHTER

USA 1936; Universal; Director: Lambert Hillyer; Producer: Carl Laemmle, Jr.; Written by Garrett Fort from the novel *Dracula's Guest* by Bram Stoker; Photography: George Robinson; Make-up: Jack Pierce.

Cast: Gloria Holden, Nan Grey, Edward Van Sloan, Irving Pichel, Otto Kruger, Billy Bevan.

DRAkULA IN ISTANBUL

Turkish 1953; And Film; Director: Mehmet Muhtar; Producer: Turgut Demirag; Written by Umit Deniz from the novel *Dracula* by Bram Stoker and the novel *Kasigli Voyvoda* by Ali Riga Seifi.

Cast: Atif Kaptan, Annie Ball.

FAUST

Germany 1926; UFA; Director: F.W. Murnau; Written by Hans Kyser; Photography: Carl Hoffmann.

Cast: Emil Jannings, Gosta Ekman, Wilhelm Dieterle.

THE FLY

USA 1958; 20th Century Fox; Producer-Director: Kurt Neumann; Written by James Clavell from the short story by George Langelaan; Music: Paul Sawtell; Photography: Karl Struss; SPFX: L.B. Abbott.

Cast: Vincent Price, Al (David) Hedison, Patricia Owens.

FRANKENSTEIN

USA 1910; Edison Film Co.; Written & Directed by J. Searle Dawley from the novel by Mary Wolfsonctraft Shelley; Producer: Thomas Edison; Make-up: Charles Ogle.

Cast: Charles Ogle, Agustus Phillips, Mary Fuller.

FRANKENSTEIN

USA 1931; Universal; Director: James Whale; Producer: Carl Laemmle, Jr.; Written by Robert Florey, Garrett Fort, Francis Edward Faragoh, Tom Reed & John L. Balderston from the novel by Mary W. Shelley; Photography: Arthur Edeson; Make-up and SPFX: Jack Pierce.

Cast: Colin Clive, Mae Clarke, Edward Van Sloan, Dwight Frye & Boris Karloff.

FRANKENSTEIN MEETS THE WOLFMAN

USA 1943; Universal; Director: Roy William Neill; Producer: George Waggner; Written by Curt Siodmak from his original story; Music: Hans J. Salter; Photography: George Robinson; SPFX: John P. Fulton; Make-up: Jack Pierce.

Cast: Ilona Massey, Patric Knowles, Lon Chaney Lionel Atwill, Bela Lugosi, Maria Ouspenskaya, Dwight Frye.

FRANKENSTEIN'S DAUGHTER

USA 1958; Astor Pictures; Director: Richard Cunha; Make-up: Harry Thomas.

Cast: John Ashley, Donald Murphy, Susan Knight, Sally Todd.

GHOST OF FRANKENSTEIN

USA 1941; Universal; Director: Erle C. Kenton; Producer: George Waggner; Written by W. Scott Darling from a story by Eric Taylor; Music: Hans J. Salter; Photography: Milton Krasner & Woody Bredell; Make-up: Jack Pierce.

Cast: Sir Cedric Hardwicke, Ralph Bellamy, Lionel Atwill, Bela Lugosi, Evelyn Ankers, Lon Chaney, Dwight Frye.

GHOSTS ON THE LOOSE

USA 1943; Monogram; Director: William Beaudine; Producer: Sam Katzman & Jack Dietz; Written by Kenneth Higgins.

Cast: Bela Lugosi, Leo Grocey, Huntz Hall, Bobby Jordan, ava Gardner, Rick Vallin, Minerva Urecal, David Grocey, Wheeler Oakman, Frank Moran.

THE GHOUL

British 1933; Gaumont; Director: T. Hayes Hunter; Written by Rupert Downing from the play by Dr. Frank King & Leonard Hines; Photography: Gunther Krampf.

Cast: Boris Karloff, Dorothy Hyson, Sir Cedric Hardwicke, Ernest Thesiger, Ralph Richardson.

THE GOLEM

Germany 1914; Bioscop; Director: Paul Wegener; Written by Wegener and Henrik Galeen from the novel by Gustav Meyrink; Photography: Guido Seeber.

Cast: Paul Wegener; Lyda Salmonova, Henrik Galeen, Carl Ebert.

THE GOLEM

Germany 1920; UFA; Directors: Paul Wegener & Carl Boese; Written by Wegener & Henrik Galeen from the novel by Gustav Meyrink; Photography: Karl Freund.

Cast: Paul Wegener, Lyda Salmonova, Hans Strum, Lothar Muthel, Albert Steinruck.

THE GORILLA

USA 1939; 20th Century Fox; Director: Alan Dwan; Producer: Darryl F. Zanuck; Written by Rian James & Sid Silvers from the play by Ralph Spence; Make-up: Perc Westmore.

Cast: Anita Louise, Patsy Kelly, Lionel Atwill, Bela n Lugosi, Edward Norris & The Ritz Brothers.

THE HANDS OR ORLAC

Austria 1924; Pan-Film; Director: Robert Wiene; Written by Ludwig Nertz; Photography: Gunther Krampf & Hans Androschin.

Cast: Conrad Veidt, Alexandra Sorina, Fritz Strassny, Paul Askonas.

HOUSE OF FRANKENSTEIN

USA 1944; Universal; Director: Erle C. Kenton; Producer: Paul Malvern; Written by Edward T. Lowe from an original story by Curt Siodmak; Music: Hans J. Salter; Photography: George Robinson; SPFX: John P. Fulton; Make-up: Jack Pierce.

Cast: Boris Karloff, Lon Chaney, John Carradine, Anne Gwynne, Peter Coe, Lionel Atwill, George Zucco, Elena Verdugo, J. Carrol Naish, Sig Rumann, Glenn Strange.

HOUSE OF DRACULA

USA 1945; Universal; Director: Erle C. Kenton; Producer: Paul Malvern; Written by Edward T. Lowe; Music: Edgar Fairchild; Photography: George Robinson; SPFX: John P. Fulton; Make-up: Jack Pierce.

Cast: Lon Chaney, John Carradine, Martha O'Driscoll, Lionel Atwill, Onslow Stevens, Glenn Strange, Jane Adams.

THE INVISIBLE AGENT

USA 1942; Universal; Director: Edwin L. Martin; Written by Curt Siodmak suggested by the novel by H.G. Wells; SPFX: John P. Fulton.

Cast: John Hall, Sir Cedric Hardwicke, Peter Lorre, Ilona Massey, Albert Basserman.

THE INVISIBLE GHOST

USA 1941; Monogram; Director: Joseph L. Lewis; Producer: Sam Katzman; Written by Al & Helen Martin.

Cast: Bela Lugosi, Polly Ann Young, John McGuire, Clarence Muse, Terry Walker.

THE INVISIBLE MAN

USA 1933; Universal; Director: James Whale; Producer: Carl Laemmle, Jr.; Written by R.C. Sherriff from the novel by H.G. Wells; Music: W. Franke Harling; Photography: Arthur Edeson; SPFX: John P. Fulton & John Mescall.

Cast: Claude Rains, Gloria Stuart, Henry Travers, William Harrigan, Una O'Connor.

THE INVISIBLE MAN RETURNS

USA 1939; Universal; Director: Joe May; Written by Joe May & Curt Siodmak from the characters created by H.G. Wells; SPFX: John P. Fulton; Make-up: Jack Pierce.

Cast: Vincent Price, Nan Grey, Sir Cedric Hardwicke.

THE INVISIBLE MAN'S REVENGE

USA 1944; Universal; Director: Ford Bebe; Written by Bertram Millhauser suggested rom the novel b H.G. Wells; SPFX: John P. Fulton.

Cast: John Hall, Leland Hodgson, Gale Sondergaard, Alan Curtis, John Carradine, Evelyn Ankers.

THE INVISIBLE RAY

USA 1936; Universal; Director: Lambert Hillyer; Written by John Colton from the story by Howard Higgin & Douglas Hodges; PHOTOGRAPHY: George Robinson: SPFX: John P. Fulton.

Cast: Boris Karloff, Bela Lugosi, Frances Drake, Frank Lawton.

THE INVISIBLE WOMAN

USA 1940; Universal; Director: A. Edward Sutherland; Written by Joe May and Curt Siodmak; SPFX: John P. Fulton & Ken Stickfaden; Make-up: Jack Pierce.

Cast: Virginia Bruce, Charles Lane, John Howard, Oscar Homolka.

ISLAND OF LOST SOULS

USA 1932; Paramount; Director: Erle C. Kenton; Written by Waldemar Young & Philip Wylie from the novel *The Island of Dr. Moreau* by H. G. Wells; Photography: Karl Struss; Make-up & SPFX: Wally Westmore.

Cast: Charles Laughton, Richard Arlen, Leila Hyams, Bela Lugosi.

ISLE OF THE DEAD

USA 1945; RKO Radio; Director: Mark Robson; Producer: Val Lewton; Written by Ardel Wray & Josef Mischel; Music: Leigh Harline; Photography: Jack Mackenzie.

Cast: Boris Karloff, Ellen Drew, Marc Cramer, Katherine Emery.

I WALKED WITH A ZOMBIE

USA 1943; RKO Radio; Director: Jacques Tourneur; Producer: Val Lewton; Written by Curt Siodmak & Ardel Wray from a story by Inez Wallace; Music: Roy Webb & Roy Hunt.

Cast: Frances Dee, Tom Conway, James Ellison, Sir Lancelot, Darby Jones.

I WAS A TEENAGE FRANKENSTEIN

USA 1958; American International Pictures; Director: Herbert L. Strock; Producer: Herman Cohen; Written by Ralph Thornton; Make-up: Robert Harris.

Cast: Whit Bissell, Gary Conway, Phyllis Coates, Robert Burton.

I WAS A TEENAGE WEREWOLF

USA 1957; American International Pictures; Director: Gene Fowler; Producer: Herman Cohen; Written by Ralph Thornton; Make-up: Philip Scheer.

Cast: Michael Landon, Whit Bissell.

KING KONG

USA 1933; RKO Radio; Director: Ernest B. Schoedsack & Merian C. Cooper; Producer: David O'Selznick; Written by James Creelman & Ruth Rose from a story by Mirian C. Cooper and Edgar Wallace; Music: Max Steiner; Photography: Edward Linden, Verne Walker & J.O. Taylor; SPFX: Willis O'Brien, E.B. Gibson & Marcel Delgado.

Cast: Fay Wray, Robert Armstrong, Bruce Cabot & King Kong!

LA CASA DEL TERROR (THE HOUSE OF TERROR)

Mexican 1959; Clasa Mohme & Azteca; Written & Directed by Gilberto Martinez Solares; Photography: Jaun Solares; Make-up: Roberto Salvador.

Cast: Lon Chaney, Jr., Tin Tan.

THE LADY AND THE MONSTER

USA 1944, Republic; Pproducer & Director: George Sherman; Written by Dane Lussier & Frederick Kohner from the novel *Donovan's Brain* by Curt Siodmak; Music: Walter Scharf; Photography: John Alton; SPFX: Theodore Lydecker.

Cast: Erich Von Stroheim, Vera Hruba Ralston, Richard Arlen, Sidney Blackmer, Mary Nash, Helen Vinson.

LIFE WITHOUT SOUL

USA 1915; Ocean; Director: Joseph W. Smiley; Producer: George DeCarlton; Written by Jesse J. Goldburg from the novel by Mary Wolfstonecraft Shelley.

Cast: Percy Darrell Standing, William A. Cohill, Jack Hopkins, Lucy Cotton.

LONDON AFTER MIDNIGHT

USA 1927; MGM; Director: Tod Browning; Written by Waldemar Young from an original story by Tod Browning; Photography: Merritt Gerstad; Make-up: Lon Chaney.

Cast: Lon Chaney, Marceline Day, Henry B. Walthall, Percy Williams, Conrad Nagel, Polly Moran.

THE LOST WORLD

USA 1925; First National-Warner; Director: Harry O. Hoyt; Producer: Earl Hudson; Written by Marion Fairfax from the novel by Arthur Conan Doyle; Photography: Arthur Edeson; SPFX: Willis O'Brien & Marcel Delgado.

Cast: Bessie Love, Lloyd Hughes, Lewis Stone, Wallace Beery, Arthur Hoyt.

MAD LOVE

USA 1935; MGM; Director: Karl Freund; Producer: John W. Considine, Jr.; Written by Guy Endore, P.J. Wolfson & John L. Balderston from the novel *The Hands Of Orlac* by Maurice Renard; Music: Dimitri Tiomkin; Photography: Chester Lyons & Gregg Toland.

Cast: Peter Lorre, Frances Drake, Colin Clive, Edward Brophy.

THE MAD MONSTER

USA 1942; Producers Releasing Corp.; Written & Directed by Sam Newfield; Producer: Sigmund Neufeld; Make-up: Harry Ross.

Cast: George Zucco, Glenn Strange.

THE MAGICIAN

USA 1926; MGM; Producer & Director: Rex Ingram; Written by Rex Ingram from the novel by Somerset Maugham; Photography: John F. Seitz.

Cast: Alice Terry, Paul Wegener, Ivan Petrovich, Gladys Hamer, Firmin Gemier, Henry Wilson.

MAN MADE MONSTER

USA 1941; Universal; Director: George Waggner; Written by Joseph West from an original story by Sid Schwartz, H.J. Essex & Len Golos; Photography: Eldwood Bredell; SPFX: John P. Fulton.

Cast: Lon Chaney, Lionel Atwill, Anne Nagel, Frank Albertson, Samuel S. Hinds, William B. Davidson.

THE MAN WHO CHANGED HIS MIND

British 1936; Gaumont; Director: Robert Stevenson; Written by Sidney Gilliat & John L. Balderston from a story by L. duGarde Peach; Photography: Jack Cox.

Cast: Boris Karloff, Anna Lee, John Loder, Frank Cellier, Lyn Harding, Cecil Parker, Donald Calthrop.

THE MAN WHO LAUGHS

USA 1928; Universal; Director: Paul Leni; Producer: Carl Laemmle; Written by Grubb Alexander & Charles Whittaker from the novel by Victor Hugo; Photography: Gilbert Warrenton.

Cast: Conrad Veidt, Mary Philbin, Olga Baclanova, Josephine Crowell, George Siegmann, Brandon Hurst, Edgar Norton.

MARK OF THE VAMPIRE

USA 1935; MGM; Producer & Director: Tod Browning; Written by Guy Endore & Bernard Schubert from an original story by Tod Browning; Photography: James Wong Howe.

Cast: Lionel Barrymore, Elizabeth Allan., Bela Lugosi, Lionel Atwill, Jean Hersholt, Henry Wadsworth, Donald Meek, Holmes Herbert, Carol Borland.

THE MASK OF FU MANCHU

USA 1932; MGM; Director: Charles Brabin & Charles Vidor; Producer: Irvin Thalberg (uncredited); Written by Irene Kuhn, Edgar Allen Woolf & John Willard from the novel by Sax Rohmer; Photography: Tony Gaudio.

Cast: Boris Karloff, Lewis Stone, Karen Morley, Myrna Loy.

METROPOLIS

Germany 1926; UFA; Director: Fritz Lang; Producer: Erich Pommer; Written by Thea Von Harbou from her novel; Photography: Karl Freund & Gunther Rittau; SPFX: Eugen Shuftan.

Cast: Alfred Abel, Gustav Frolich, Brigitte Helm, Rudolf Klein-Rogge.

THE MUMMY

USA 1932; Universal; Director: Karl Freund; Producer: Carl Laemmle, Jr. & Stanley Bergerman; Written by John L. Balderston from a story by Nina Wilcox Putnam & Richard Schayer; Photography: Charles Stumar; SPFX: John P. Fulton; Make-up: Jack Pierce.

Cast: Boris Karloff, Zita Johann, David Manners, Edward Van Sloan, Bramwell Fletcher, Noble Johnson, Arthur Byron, Henry Victor.

THE MUMMY'S CURSE

USA 1945; Universal; Director: Leslie Goodwins; Written by Bernard Schubert, Dwight V. Babcock & Leon Abrams; Make-up: Jack Pierce.

Cast: Lon Chaney, Dennis Moore, Peter Coe, Martin Kosleck, Virginia Christine, Kay Harding

THE MUMMY'S GHOST

USA 1944; Universal; Director: Reginald Le Borg; Written by Griffin Jay; Make-up: Jack Pierce.

Cast: Lon Chaney, George Zucco, John Carradine, Ramsay Ames, Robert Lowery.

THE MUMMY'S HAND

USA 1940; Universal; Director: Christy Cabanne; Written by Griffin Jay based on the character created by John L. Balderston's screenplay; Make-up: Jack Pierce.

Cast: Tom Tyler, Dick Foran, Wallace Ford, George Zucco, Peggy Moran, Cecil Kellaway, Eduardo Cianelli.

THE MUMMY'S TOMB

USA 1942; Universal; Director: Harold Young; Written by Griffin Jay; Make-up: Jack Pierce.

Cast: Lon Chaney, Jr.; Dick Foran, Wallace Ford, John Hubbard, Elyse Knox, Turhan Bey.

MURDER BY THE CLOCK

USA 1931; Paramount; Directed by Edward Sloman; Written by Henry Myers from an original story by Rufus King & Charles Beahan; Photography: Karl Struss.

Cast: William Boyd, Lilyan Tashman, Irving Pichel.

MURDERS IN THE RUE MORGUE

USA 1932; Universal; Director: Robert Florey; Producer: Carl Laemmle, Jr.; Written by Tom Reed & Dale Van Every from the story by Edgar Allan Poe.

Cast: Bela Lugosi, Sidney Fox, Leon Waycoff, Brandon Hurst, Noble Johnson, Arlene Francis.

MURDERS IN THE ZOO

USA 1933; Paramount; Director: Edward Sutherland; Written by Philip Wylie & Seton Miller; Photography: Ernest Haller.

Cast: Lionel Atwill, Randolph Scott, Charlie Ruggles, Gail Patrick, John Lodge, Kathleen Burke.

MY SON THE VAMPIRE

USA 1952; Renown Pictures; Director: John Gilling; Producer: George Minter; Written by Val Valentine.

Cast: Bela Lugosi, Arthur Lucan, Dora Bryan, Richard Wattis.

MYSTERY OF THE WAX MUSEUM

USA 1933; Warner; Director: Michael Curtiz; Written by Don Mullaly & Carl Erickson from a

158

story by Charles Beldon; Photography: Ray Ranahan.

Cast: Lionel Atwill, Fay Wray, Glenda Farrell, Frank McHugh, Arthur Edmund Carewe, Holmes Herbert.

NIGHT OF THE GHOULS

USA Made 1958 - never released; Produced, Written & Directed by Edward Wood, Jr.; Co-producer: J. Edward Reynolds; SPFX: Tommy Kemp.

Cast: Tor Johnson, Vampira,

NOSFERATU

Germany 1922; Prana Films; Director: F.W. Murnau; Written by Henrik Galeen from the novel *Dracula* by Bram Stoker; Photography: Fritz Arno Wagner & Gunther Krampf.

Cast: Max Schreck, Alexander Granach, Greta Schroder, Ruth Landshoff.

THE OLD DARK HOUSE

USA 1932; Universal; Director: James Whale; Producer: Carl Laemmle, Jr.; Written by Benn W. Levy & R.C. Sheriff from the novel *Benighted* by J.B. Priestley; Photography: Arthur Edeson.

Cast: Melvyn Douglas, Charles Laughton; Raymond Massey, Ernest Thesiger, Boris Karloff, Gloria Stuart, Lillian Bond, Eva Moore, John Dudgeon, Brember Wells.

THE PHANTOM CREEPS

USA 1939; Universal; Director: Ford Bebe & Saul Goodkind; Written by George Plympton, Basil Dickey & Mildred Barish from the story by Willis Cooper.

Cast: Bela Lugosi, Robert Kent, Regis Toomey, Edward Van Sloan, Dorothy Arnold, Charles King.

PHANTOM OF THE OPERA

USA 1925; Universal; Director: Rupert Julian (Additional scenes directed by Edward Sedgwick; Producer: Carl Laemmle; Written by Raymond Shrock & Elliott J. Clawson from the novel by Gaston Leroux; Photography: Virgil Miller; Make-up: Lon Chaney, Sr.

Cast: Lon Chaney, Mary Philbin, Norman Kerry, Arthur Edmund Carewe, Gibson Gowland.

PHANTOM OF THE OPERA

USA 1943; Universal; Director: Arthur Lubin; Producer: George Waggner; Written by Eric Taylor and Samuel Hoffman from an adaptation by John Jacoby based on the Gaston Leroux novel.

Cast: Nelson Eddy, Susana Foster, Claude Rains, Edgar Barrier, J. Edward Bromberg, Hume Cronyn.

PLAN 9 FROM OUTER SPACE

USA 1959; Reynolds Pictures; Director: Edward Wood, Jr.; Producer: J. Edward Reynolds; Written by Edward Wood, Jr.; SPFX: Tommy Kemp.

Cast: Bela Lugosi, Tor Johnson, Vampira, Gregory Walcott, Mona McKinnon.

THE RAVEN

USA 1935; Universal; Director: Louis Fridlander; Producer: Carl Laemmle; Written by David Boehm from the poem by Edgar Allan Poe; Make-up: Jack Pierce; Photography: Artur Edeson.

Cast: Boris Karloff, Bela Lugosi, Irene Ware, Lester Matthews, Samuel Hinds, Arthur Hoyt.

THE RETURN OF CHANDU

USA 1934; Principal; Director: Ray Taylor; Written by Barry Barringer from the Radio Serial by Harry M. Earnshaw, R.R. Morgan & Vera Oldham.

Cast: Bela Lugosi, Maria Alba, Clara Kimbell, Dean Benton.

THE RETURN OF DRACULA

USA 1958; United Artists; Director: Paul Landres; Producers: Arthur Gardner & Jules Levy.

Cast: Francis Lederer, Virginia Vincent, Ivan Young, Norma Eberhardt, Gage Clark.

RETURN OF THE APEMAN

USA 1944; Monogram; Director: Phil Rosen; Producer: Sam Katzman; Written by Robert Charles.

Cast: Bela Lugosi, John Carradine, Frank Moran, Judith Gibson, Michael Ames.

RETURN OF THE VAMPIRE

USA 1944; Columbia; Director: Lew Landers (a.k.a. Louis Friedlander); Producer: Sam White; Written by Griffin Jay from the original idea by Kurt Neumann; Make-up: Clay Campbell.

Cast: Bela Lugosi, Frieda Inescort, Nina Foch, Matt Willis, Roland Varno, Miles Mander.

REVENGE OF THE CREATURE

USA 1955; Universal; Director: Jack Arnold; Producer: William Alland; Written by Martin Berkeley from the story by Alland; Music: Herman Stein; Photography: Charles S. Welbourne; SPFX & make-up: Bud Westmore.

Cast: John Agar, Lori Nelson, John Bromfield.

SCARED TO DEATH

USA 1947; Screen Guild; Director: Christy Cabanne; Producer: Robert Lippert; Written by W. J. Abbott.

Cast: Bela Lugosi, Douglas Fowley, Joyce Compton, George Zucco, Angelo Rossitto.

THE SON OF DR. JEKYLL

USA 1951; Columbia; Director: Seymour Friedman; Written by Edward Huebsch suggested from the novel by Robert Louis Stevenson. Make-up: Clay Campbell.

Cast: Louis Hayward, Alexander Knox, Lester Matthews, Jody Lawrence.

SON OF DRACULA

USA 1943; Universal; Director: Robert Siomak; Producer: George Waggner; Written by Eric Taylor from an original story by Curt Siodmak; SPFX: John P. Fulton; Make-up: Jack Pierce.

Cast: Lon Chaney, Jr., Louise Albritton, J. Edward Bromberg.

SON OF FRANKENSTEIN

USA 1939; Universal; Producer & Director: Rowland V. Lee; Written by Willis Cooper; Music: Frank Skinner; Photography: George Robinson; SPFX: John P. Fulton; Make-up: Jack Pierce.

Cast: Basil Rathbone, Boris Karloff, Bela Lugosi, Lionel Atwill, Josephine Hutchinson, Edgar Norton, Gustav von Seyffertitz, Dwight Frye.

SON OF KONG

USA 1933; RKO Radio; Director: Ernest B. Schoedsack; Producer: Merian C. Cooper; Written by Ruth Rose; Photography: Eddie Linden, Vernon Walker, J.O. Taylor; SPFX: Willis O' Brien & Marcel Delgado.

Cast: Robert Armstrong, Helen Mack, Frank Reicher, John Marston & Son Of Kong!

SPOOKS RUN WILD

USA 1941; Monogram; Director: Phil Rosen; Producer: Sam Katzman; Written by Carl Foreman & Charles Marion.

Cast: Bela Lugosi, Leo Grocey, Huntz Hall, Bobby Jordan, David Grocey, Sammy Morrison, Angelo Rossitto, Joe Kirk.

STRANGLER IN THE SWAMP

USA 1945; Producers Releasing Corp; Director : Frank Wisbar; Written by Frank Wisbar from his original story; Photography: James S. Brown.

Cast: Rosemary LaPlanche, Robert Barrat, Blake Edwards, Charles Middleton.

THE STUDENT OF PRAGUE

Germany 1926; Sokal; Written & Directed by Henrik Galeen from the screen treatment by Hans Heinz Ewers & Edgar Allen Poe's *William Wilson*; Photography: Gunther Krampf;

Cast: Conrad Veidt, Agnes Esterhazy, Werner Krauss.

THE TINGLER

USA 1959; Columbia; Produced & Directed by Wiliam Castle; Written by Robb White; Music: Von Dexter; Photography: Wilfrid M. Cline.

Cast: Vincent Price, Judith Evelyn, Philip Coolidge, Darryl Hickman.

THE UNDYING MONSTER

USA 1942; 20th Century Fox; Director: John Brahm; Producer: Bryan Foy; Written by Like Hayward & Michael Jacoby from the novel by Jessie Douglas Kerruish.

Cast: John Howard, Heather Angel, Bramwell Fletcher (Voice only).

THE UNINVITED

USA 1944; Paramount; Director: Lewis Allen; Producer: Charles Brackett; Written by Dodie Smith & Frank Partos from the novel by Dorothy Macardle; Music: Victor Young; Photography: Charles Lang.

Cast: Ray Milland, Ruth Hussey, Donald Crisp, Gail Russell.

THE VAMPIRE

USA 1957; United Artists; Director: Paul Landres; Producers: Jules Levy & Arthur Gardner.

Cast: John Beal, Colleen Grey.

VAMPYR

France-Germany 1931-1932; Tobis-Klang; Director: Carl Dryer; Producers: Carl Dryer, Baron Nicolas de Gunzburg; Written by Carl Dryer & Christian Jul from the novel *Carmilla* by Sheridan Le Fanu; Music: Wolfgang Zeller; Photography: Rudolph Mate & Louis Nee.

Cast: Julian West, Sybille Schmitz, Henriette Gerard, Jan Hieronimko.

VOODOO MAN

USA 1944; Monogram; Director: William Beaudine; Producer: Sam Katzman & Jack Dietz; Written by Robert Charles.

Cast: Bela Lugosi, John Carradine, George Zucco, Michael Ames, Wanda McKay, Ellen Hall, Henry Hall.

THE WALKING DEAD

USA 1936; Warner; Director: Michael Curtiz; Written by Ewart Adamson, Peter Milne, Robert Adams & Lillie Hayward from an original story by Ewart Adamson & Joseph Fields; Photography: Hal Mohr.

Cast: Boris Karloff, Edmund Gwen, Ricardo Cortez, Marguerite Churchill, Warren Hull, Barton MacLane.

WEREWOLF OF LONDON

USA 1935; Universal; Director: Stuart Walker; Producer: Stanley Bergerman; Written by John Colton & Harvey Gates from a story by Robert Harris; Photography: Charles Stumar; SPFX: John P. Fulton; Make-up: Jack Pierce.

Cast: Henry Hull, Valerie Hobson, Werner Oland.

WHITE ZOMBIE

USA 1932; United Artists; Director: Victor Halperin; Producer: Edward Halperin; Written by Garnett Weston from the Magic Island by William Seabrook; Music: Abe Meyer; Photography: Arthur Martinelli; SPFX & make-up: Jack Pierce.

Cast: Bela Lugosi, Madge Bellamy, Jospeh Cawthorn, Robert Frazer.

THE WIZARD

USA 1927; Fox; Director: Richard Rosson; Screenplay: Harry O. Hoyt and Andrew Bennison based on the story Balaoo by Gaston Leroux; Photography: Frank Good.

Cast: Gustav von Seyffertitz, Edmund Lowe, Leila Hyams, Barry Norton, George Kotsonaros.

THE WOLFMAN

USA 1941; Universal; Director: George Waggner; Written by Curt Siodmak & Gordon Kahn; Music: Charles Previn; Photography: Joseph Valentine; Make-up: Jack Pierce; SPFX: John P. Fulton.

Cast: Lon Chaney, Jr., Claude Rains, Ralph Bellamy, Evelyn Ankers, Bela Lugosi., Maria Ouspenskaya.

FILM INDEX

Abbott & Costello Meet Dr. Jekyll & Mr. Hyde 57,145,146,153
Abbott & Costello Meet Frankenstein 31,99,100,101,129,137,146
Abbott & Costello Meet The Invisible Man 145,146
Abbott & Costello Meet The Killer: Boris Karloff 146
Abbott & Costello Meet The Mummy 146
Alligator People, The 138,139,140
Ape, The 118
Ape Man, The 114
Atomic Kid, The 136
Bargain With The Devil, A 25
Bat, The 30
Bat, The (1959) 139
Bat Whispers, The 30
Beast With Five Fingers, The 108
Beauty & The Beast 115,116
Bedlam 112,113
Before I Hang 62,103
Bells, The 34
Black Cat, The (1934) 37,43,44, 58,68,69
Black Cat, The (1941) 106,107
Black Friday 102,103
Black Room, The 58,59
Black Sleep, The 153,154,155
Blind Bargain, A 20
Blood of Dracula 142, 143
Body Snatcher,The 110-113
Boogie Man Will Get You, The 62, 103
Bowery At Midnight 105
Bride of Frankenstein 11,18,28, 33,35,36,37,38,51,54,62,70,81,90,153
Bride of The Gorilla 145
Bride of The Monster 134,135, 137,148 153
Brute Man, The 116
Bucket of Blood 148
Cabinet of Dr. Caligari, The 8,12,13,25
Captive Wild Woman 92
Cat & The Canary, The (1927) 24,25,26,30
Cat & The Canary, The (1939) 49,50
Cat Creeps, The 30,49,50,65
Cat People 112
Chandu The Magician 54
Climax, The 124
Corpse Vanishes, The 105,118
Creature From The Black Lagoon 131,132,133, 134,135,136,141
Creature Walks Among Us 132, 133,135
Creature With The Atom Brain, The 136,137
Cry of The Werewolf 96,108, 110
Curse of The Cat People 112

Curse of The Demon 148,149,150,151,152,153
Curse Of The Fly 142
Cyclops, The 137
Dark Eyes of London 58,59,81, 105
Daughter of Dr. Jekyll 146
Dead Men Walk 118,119
Dead of Night 106,108
Devil Bat,The 102,103,118,120
Devil Bat's Daughter 103
Devil Commands,The 62,96, 101,103
Devil Doll, The 60,61
Dinosaur & The Missing Link, The 19
Doctor X 39,41,47
Dr. Cyclops 60,61
Dr. Jekyll & Mr. Hyde (1908) 11
Dr. Jekyll & Mr. Hyde (1910) 11
Dr. Jekyll & Mr. Hyde (1912) 11,12
Dr. Jekyll & Mr. Hyde (1920) 12,13,20
Dr. Jekyll & Mr. Hyde (1932) 35,56,57,62
Dr. Jekyll & Mr. Hyde (1941) 104,105
Dr. Renaukt's Secret 15,105
Dracula (1931) 29,30,31,32,33,34,38,41,42,44,62,66,75,78,79,90,132,153
Dracula's Daughter 32,33, 66,74,90
Duality of Man, The 11
Drakula In Istanbul 147
Face Of Marble 106, 120
Faust 25,26
Fly, The 139, 140,141,142
Flying Serpeant, The 103,120
Frankenstein (1910) 9,30
Frankenstein (1931) 10,18,25, 30-35,38,41,42,50,62,67,71,76,83,90,132,153
Frankenstein Meets The Wolfman 93-95
Frankenstein -1970 137-139
Frankenstein's Daughter 145
Ghost Breakers, The 50,86,87, 89,90
Ghost of Frankenstein, The 10, 84,95,108
Ghost of Slumber Mountain 19
Ghost Ship 112
Ghoul, The 46,47,60,153
Golem, Der (1914) 10
Golem, Der (1916) 10
Golem (1920) 10,11,25
Golem & The Dancing Girl 10
Gorilla, The (1927) 24
Gorilla, The (1939) 41,50,148
Gorilla At Large 148
H-Man, The 140
Hands of Orlac (1924) 13,24,25
Haunted Strangler, The 153
Hideous Sun Demon 138,139
Horror Island 106
Horrors of The Black Museum 146
Hound of The Baskervilles 41

House of Dracula 90,97-100, 123,
House of Frankenstein 90,96, 97,125,126
House on A Haunted Hill 139, 140
House of Horrors 116
House of Wax 146-149
Hunchback of Notre Dame, The (1923) 9,19,20,22,30
Hunchback of Notre Dame, The (1939) 62,91
Hunchback of Notre Dame, The (1959) 148
I Walked With A Zombie 96, 110,111, 112
I Was A Teenage Frankenstein 142,143,145
I Was A Teenage Werewolf 113,141,142
Indestructible Man 136,137
Invisible Agent, The 92
Invisible Ghost, The 118
Invisible Man, The 51,62,63, 65,76,90,92
Invisible Man Returns, The 51, 80,91,148
Invisible Man's Revenge, The 92
Invisible Ray, The 57,58,76
Invisible Woman, The 91,92
Island of Lost Souls 52,54
Isle of The Dead 111-113
Januskopf, Der 12,18,30
Jungle Captive 92,116
Jungle Woman 92
King Kong 48,49,61,72,73,118
King of The Zombies 118,121
Lady & The Monster, The 106
Leopard Man, The 112
Life Without Soul 9,30
London After Midnight 22-25, 31
Lost World, The 16-19
M 55
Macabre 140
Mad Doctor of Market Street, The 104
Mad Genius, The 34
Mad Ghoul, The 120,121
Mad Love 57,58
Mad Monster, The 113,118
Magician, The 14,15
Man In Half Moon Street 106
Man Made Monster 33,86,90, 103,122
Man They Could Not Hang, The 61,63
Man Who Laughs, The 24,25, 26,30,58
Man Who Lived Again, The 63
Man With Nine Lives 62,101
Mark of The Vampire 22,31, 32, 41,74,79,82
Mask of Fu Manchu, The 54
Metropolis 15,18,25
Mighty Joe Young 116,118
Miracle Man, The 20
Missing Link, The 14

Monster, The (1925) 22
Monster & The Girl, The 104
Monster Maker, The 106
Monster of Frankensetin 9
Monster of Piedras Blancas 133,135
Monster on Campus 141-143
Most Dangerous Game, The 55
Mummy, The (1932) 33,45-47, 62,67,74,83,89,153
Mummy, The (Mexican) 147
Mumy's Curse, The 89
Mummy's Ghost 89,124,127
Mummy's Hand 88,89,125
Mummy's Tomb 89,90,122
Murder By The Clock 44
Murders In The Rue Morgue 31,32,42-44,69,148
Murders In The Zoo 41
My Son, The Vampire 152
Mystery of The Wax Museum 39-41,47,148
Night of The Ghouls 148
Nosferatu 18,25,30
Old Dark House, The 43,49, 50,65,80
Pearl of Death 116
Phantom of The Opera (1925) 15,20-22,24,30,41
Phantom of The Opera (1943) 90,91,93,126,128
Phantom Creeps, The 60
Pharoah's Curse, The 146,147
Plan 9 From Outer Space 152, 153
Raven, The 43,44,58,62,69
Return of Chandu, The 43,55
Return of Dr. X, The 39
Return of Dracula 146-148
Return of The Ape Man 114-116
Return of The Fly, The 142
Return of The Terror 30
Return of The Vampire 96, 108,109
Revenge of The Creature 133,134
Revenge of The Zombies 119
Scared To Death 119,120
7 Footprints To Satan 25,26,29
Seventh Victim, The 112
She Creature, The 135
She-Wolf of London 108,110
Siegfried 19
Son of Dr. Jekyll 146
Son of Dracula 88,90,124,129
Son of Frankenstein 37-39,41, 70,86,98,153
Son of Kong 48,49
Spider Woman, The 116
Spider Woman Strikes Back, The 116
Spooks Run Wild 118
Strangler of The Swamp 120
Strange Case of Dr. Rx, 103,104
Student of Prague, The 25
Teenage Cavemen 143
Teenage Monsters 143

Teenage Zombies 143
Teenagers From Outer Space 143
Terror, The 29,30
Thirteen Ghosts 140
Thirteenth Chair, The 24,30
Tingler, The 140
Tower of London 59,62,154
Undying Monster, The 113,114
Unholy Night, The 34
Unholy Three, The (1925) 22
Unholy Three, The (1930) 22
Uninvited, The 106,107
Valley of The Zombies 106
Vampire, The 137
Vampire Bat, The 40,41
Vampyr 31,106
Voodoo Island 153
Voodoo Man 119
Walking Dead, The 46,47
Waxworks 24
Werewolf, The (1956) 136,137
Werewolf In A Girl's Dormitory 142,143
Werewolf of London 53,62,76
White Zombie 44,64,75,83
Wizard, The 14,15,105
Wolfman, The 51,54,84,86, 89-91, 113,123,126,154
You'll Find Out 103